P9-DBL-469

DIVINING THE FUTURE

DIVINING
THE FUTURE

SALLY MORNINGSTAR

BARNES & NOBLE
NEW YORK

This edition published by
Barnes & Noble Publishing, Inc.,
by arrangement with Anness Publishing Limited

2006 Barnes & Noble Books

M 10 9 8 7 6 5 4 3 2 1

ISBN 0-7607-7999-6

© Anness Publishing Limited 2000, 2006

All rights reserved. No part of this publication may
be reproduced, stored in a retrieval system, or
transmitted in any way or by any means, electronic,
mechanical, photocopying, recording or otherwise,
without the prior written permission of the
copyright holder.

Publisher: Joanna Lorenz
Project editor: Emma Gray
Authors: Sally Morningstar, Richard Craze,
Staci Mendoza, David Bourne,
William Adcock, Rosalind Powell,
Laura Watts, Andy Baggott
Designer: Juliet Brown, Axis Design
Photographers: Don Last and John Freeman
Production Manager: Steve Lang
Illustrators: Anna Koska, Giovanna Pierce
and Garry Walton
Editorial reader: Hayley Kerr

Previously published as *How to Tell the Future*

The author and publishers have made every effort
to ensure that all instructions contained within this
book are accurate and safe, and cannot accept
liability for any resulting injury, damage or loss to
persons or property, however it may arise.

Printed in China

contents

preface

The wise ones of old were the healers and herbalists, the oracles and medicine men, the witch doctors and diviners. They were most often born with the seed of knowing, choosing to be chosen by the magical world, and often going through intense personal experiences before their gifts were revealed to them. The wise ones became ever wiser by being of service to others, and by sharing their gifts with sensitivity and compassion. They were mostly simple people, living simple lives. What made many of them different was their discovery that ancient wisdom lay within the self.

The way of ancient wisdom is the way of truth, of revealing the secrets locked within the self. To this end, every civilization has had ways of communicating with this inner world, utilizing the powers of the mind, the psyche, and the spirit, and frequently calling upon the wise ones of their tribe to help to guide them to their own inner teacher.

The first section of this book offers a grounding in the physical reality of divination, helping you to understand how the magic of the moon influences your moods, your dreams, and your relationships. It shows you how your birth date on an astrological chart, or the lines on the palm of your hand, can act like maps to guide you through your strengths and weaknesses and so assist in developing your understanding of who you are. As you change, so do the lines on your hand. They are not fixed, and show that the future is yours in the making. You can

influence the course of your life and change your destiny, if you act consciously from a place of inner knowing.

Having grasped the basics of your personality, you can use the second part of the book to aid in developing your inner world through shamanic practices, working with dreams and meditation. To be a true shaman is to walk between worlds, having no fear of death or darkness, understanding this to be the other side of life and light. The shaman works with energy, with natural forces as well as nature herself. Acting as an intermediary, the shaman will seek the help of "good spirits" (or vital energies) and will negotiate with "bad spirits" (or dense energies) to return a sick person to health or to help someone acting out of character back to their happier self. The shaman is the spiritual warrior, who faces life's challenges with courage and daring.

Shamanic practices help to develop a deeper relationship with all life, including your own inner world. There is nothing to fear, because at the heart of you is a beautiful being of light.

influences

destinies   spiritual

divination

Your journey will be taking you only through the darkness of your own ignorance to the wise one that waits within. Dreams hold the key to understanding the world of subconscious fears, hopes and ideals. They can also reveal areas of your life that require your attention, asking you to heal unresolved issues. Out of the darkest recesses of your being, your dreams can reveal far more than you ever imagined, if you are prepared to spend the time reaching an understanding of their message.

One way to achieve such an understanding is to develop a deeper relationship with patterns and symbols, as outlined in the section on mandalas. To meditate upon geometric shapes, patterns or symbols can be a very powerful experience of an unspoken language. From this source, you can begin to find your own patterns, and also create new ones that reflect who you would like to be as you journey through life.

On your journey, you may well find questions rising out of some confusion or doubt. The third section of this book offers you three ways to find answers to those questions, using the Tarot, the I Ching and the Runes. The visual images of the Tarot can help to connect you to your intuition, allowing your personal story to unfold before you, and helping you to find the threads that bind your situation together. This gives your inner teacher the opportunity to speak to you and will help you to understand the language that is beyond words.

The I Ching originated in China over 4,000 years ago. The sage (or wise one) would use coins to divine the rising and falling of positive or negative influences – the yin and yang (or two sides) of the universe. By asking a question of the I Ching, you can build an understanding of those things that are good for your personal growth as well as those things that are limiting your progress.

The Runes are an ancient magical tool of northern Europe. Their name means "secret" and each one carries a message which can be used in meditation, for guidance or for personal protection. Runes can help you to find your personal gifts and powers, and can also help you to strengthen your resolve as you travel your spiritual path.

Walking the wheel of life with an open heart and a willingness to learn will bring a richness into your world that is beyond anything you will have experienced before. The ways of ancient wisdom are available to anyone who steps out to claim them. You can choose to be chosen – all you have to do is take the first step.

Sally Morningstar

knowledge

centring

wholeness

ancient wisdom

Like a great over-arching roof, the sky seemed to ancient observers to encompass and enclose everything on earth. Beneath its giant canopy hung the sun, the moon and the stars, watching over the world as they moved across the sky. From the earliest times, human communities have learnt to watch the movements of these great heavenly bodies and to chart their regular paths, coming to understand something of their power and influence over the earth. Over many centuries of careful measurement and recording, a huge body of wisdom has been built up to give an insight into the cyclical nature of the universe and our place within it.

moon magic

moon magic

The moon is mysterious. She is known by many names and is worshipped by many cultures throughout the world, both ancient and modern. Our great Mother Moon inspires wonder when we see her silver light shining upon the shadows of the night. Both men and women are intimately linked to her changing faces of crescent, full, waning and dark, as she progresses through her lunar cycle. When she pulls and tugs at the waters of the earth, creating high and low tides, she also pulls at the water within our bodies, affecting our moods, sleep patterns, health, and women's "moontime" cycles. It is well documented that the full moon has powerful effects upon human mental and emotional stability.

Because the moon is within the gravitational field of the earth, her interaction with us affects weather patterns around the world. Rainfall, tropical storms, hurricanes and earthquakes have all been associated with lunar influence and acitvity. The moon is intimately linked to our world and we are deeply affected by her, as is the planet we inhabit.

By discovering some of her magical mysteries, you can get to know her better and come to understand the complex nature of her rhythms and cycles. The moon is the personification of female wisdom, the wisdom of intuitive knowledge and deep instincts. She cannot be tamed by rational thought; she is a free spirit.

lunar wisdom

Though the moon is the close companion of the earth, she retains many mysteries, and her origin is still unknown. She is, however, thought to be about 4,600 million years old, the same age as the earth. Her power was recognized in ancient cultures. She was depicted as both the giver and the taker of life, and many legends surrounding the creation concerned the complementary powers of the sun and the moon.

Facts

The moon measures 3476km/2160 miles across and her gravity is one-sixth that of the earth. The craters on the moon, which measure up to 240km/150 miles across, may be the result of impacts from comets and asteroids over millions of years, or may stem from volcanic activity within the moon itself. Humans first landed on the moon in 1969, but with hardly any atmosphere and no water, it is not possible for the moon to sustain life as we know it.

This limestone relief depicts Nanna, the Assyrian moon god, crowned with a crescent moon.

Because of the moon's elliptical orbit, she can be anything between 356,398km/221,466 miles and 406,698km/252,722 miles away from earth. This orbit pattern also means that we only ever get to see one side of her. Surface temperatures range from -233°C/-387°F at night to 127°C/260°F at midday, as the light of the sun is reflected back from the moon's surface to earth. A moon–sun conjunction creates the image of the crescent, or new, moon and a full moon occurs when the sun and moon are in alignment with each other. The moon is slowly pulling away from the earth's gravitational influence, by 3cm/1½ in annually, so the length of our daily cycle is actually increasing by a miniscule amount each year.

Legends

Because of her ever-changing and yet regenerative cycle, the moon was seen as immortal and as the place to which souls departed at death. She could bring gentle rain, but could also raise storms and ruin crops, so she was considered unpredictable and potentially destructive. Moon goddesses were endowed with both destructive and creative powers. The Mayans' moon deity was called Ixchel, and was feared as the bringer of floods and storms. Her skirt was decorated with bones, and her crown was a serpent. Despite this she was also a protector of women in childbirth.

In Sumerian mythology, the principal moon deity, Sin, was male. He was associated with the new moon and was responsible for the fertility of the land, for food production and the protection of herds, especially cattle. The re-enactment of the sacred marriage between the male (waxing) and female (waning) aspects of the lunar cycle was undertaken between the king of Ur, embodying the god Sin, and the goddess in the person of a priestess. By performing this ceremony, they were enacting the continuance and co-operation of the two opposites.

In Native American mythology, the spider, who has universal links with the moon, was the weaver of the web of creation, producing the physical world, and then supporting and nurturing life on earth. The snail, because of its moisture trail and its seeming ability to vanish and reappear, is also linked to the moon. It was thought that the snail could travel into the underworld and re-emerge unharmed. The Mexican moon god, Tecciztecatl, was depicted in the shell of a snail.

Mirrors figure prominently in moon lore, because of their reflective qualities, and have long been used for divination. In 19th-century Britain it was common for girls to use a mirror and the full moon to find out when they would be married. Two and a half thousand years earlier, it is said that Pythagoras was taught mirror divination by the wise woman of Thessaly.

Some believe that the moon and the earth were once a single planet, others that the moon was drawn into the earth's force field at some point. Yet another hypothesis is that the two planets were formed together out of the same space dust and cosmic gases. The actual origin of the moon remains a mystery.

moon worship

Many ancient civilizations venerated the moon because they witnessed her regenerative powers, saw how she influenced the growth of crops, how she matched the average female menstrual cycle, and how she affected weather. Even her dark time was seen to hold secrets about death and the veil that separates spirit from matter. She seemed to hold the key to deep and profound wisdom about the rhythms and cycles of existence.

Goddesses

Because it was important to differentiate between the phases of the moon, different goddesses represented them. The Greeks, for example, worshipped Artemis as the new moon, Selene as the full moon and Hecate as the waning moon. In Rome, Artemis became Diana. The cult of Isis, the Egyptian "Good Mother", spread through Greece and Rome and was eventually absorbed by the cult of the Virgin Mary, also a lady of the moon.

So strong was the compulsion to honour the moon goddess and keep her favour, that sacrifices and orgiastic rites were regularly performed to appease her. All phases of the moon held secrets about the circle of life. By worshipping the appropriate goddess, humankind could try to tame her influence on such issues as pregnancy, agriculture or divination.

The dual powers of creation were represented by Isis and Osiris.

Angels

As the Great Mother, the moon has considerable influence over her "children" – angels. The angel associated with the moon is Gabriel, the healer. He is the Angel of the Annunciation, who visited the Virgin Mary (a lady of the moon). He is sometimes depicted carrying white lilies, the flowers of the Virgin, and is intimately linked with healing and with alleviating suffering on earth.

On the lunar wheel Gabriel stands in the west, in the position of the waning moon. This direction is represented by the water element. Stand facing west during a waning moon (especially if it is in a water sign) to say prayers for healing. You should also face west if you are making a water offering, which can be anything that is taken from the waters, such as watercress, a river stone, seaweed or a shell.

An Angel Healing

Perform this ceremony just after a full moon to seek healing for someone who is sick. Camphor, eucalyptus and sandalwood are all linked to the healing qualities of the moon. Write down the name of the person requiring healing, and their ailment, fold the paper twice and hold it while you say: "Angel Gabriel I ask for your help. Please bring your healing touch to [name]. By divine will, remove [this condition] from [name], for the highest good of all." End by giving thanks and blowing out the candles.

You will need

- 2 light blue candles
- white lilies
- water offering
- aromatherapy burner
- clear quartz crystal
- 9 drops of eucalyptus, sandalwood or camphor oil
- 9 white nightlights
- matches
- pen with silver ink
- natural paper
- heatproof container

1 Arrange candles, flowers, water offering and burner. Place the crystal in the water.

2 Place the nightlights in a circle around the other ingredients and light them.

3 Write your message and, holding it in your hand, ask Gabriel for his help.

4 Burn the paper in the candle flame, visualizing the ailment being carried away.

moon signs

In astrology, the position of the sun at birth represents your outer personality, whereas the position of the moon indicates your inner world of feelings and emotions. To discover the position of the moon at your birth, you will need to consult an astrologer for a natal chart. Once this has been established, you can refer to the information in the relevant section below.

When the moon is transiting Aries, there will be an increase in fiery energy, leading to the potential for confrontations.

Moon in Aries

Aries moon people tend to be impulsive and hasty, and often make quick (and sometimes rash) decisions. Their impulsiveness can make them impatient, and increase the probability of accidents. They have agile minds and are natural leaders, but need to guard against being bossy, arrogant, or dismissive of others.

Aries moons crave independence and can feel very trapped by possessive or jealous behaviour. They do not understand the depths of emotions or feel particularly comfortable with them. As this is a fire moon, their feelings are very self-orientated.

They are forward thinkers, inspired by new opportunities, wanting to carve their own path through life. People with their moon in Aries will be innovators in business, but because of their "go it alone" attitude, Aries moons can sometimes be insensitive and thoughtless. They will often regret things that they have said or done through lack of sensitivity and will then try to make up for it.

Stones:
diamond, bloodstone
Flower:
wild rose
Animal:
ram

Moon in Taurus

People with their moon in Taurus are easy-going and generally fun to be with. They appreciate fine art, music and the creative arts as well as good food and entertaining. These people are sensualists, with a love of beautiful things. They can, however, have a tendency to get stuck in ritual and routine. They dislike change and will not be pushed into anything. Above all, they are practical and down-to-earth.

Taurus moons are careful with money. Being materialistic, they like to buy good quality products and will work hard to be able to afford them. This moon's message is that life is for enjoying, but they must guard against becoming addicted to rich and unhealthy foods.

Taurus moons can feel very threatened by challenges to family life, and will do anything to maintain security. Their possessiveness can sometimes be stifling for others.

Stones:
emerald
Flower:
rose
Animal:
bull

When the moon is passing through Taurus, be careful with your possessions. Take care of personal finances and practical matters.

When the moon is transiting Gemini it is an important time to make sure that everything is based on fact, not to get carried away, and to guard against being too flippant about responsibilities. Be aware that stress will be an issue during this time, with an increase in the possibility of nervous tension and exhaustion.

Moon in Gemini

People with their moon in Gemini are mentally agile, flitting from one idea to another with ease. They have many projects on the go and need to learn to complete what they begin. Gemini moons can be gossips and chatterboxes, because of their love of the spoken word (and the sound of their own voices). The greatest challenges for Gemini moons are an appreciation of silence and consolidation of actions.

Stones:
agate
Flower:
lavender
Animal:
monkey

Boredom sets in quickly because their minds are constantly thinking up better ideas or solutions to problems. Their quickwittedness and versatility is therefore a strength as well as a potential weakness. Because of their tendency to move on quickly (unless the conversation is fascinating), they often miss opportunities to learn from, or understand, others.

Gemini moons find emotional people difficult to be around, and often have difficulty expressing their own feelings. They are drawn to the lighter side of life, where chatting and social interaction prevail. As long as they have stimulating outlets for their inspirations and sociability, they will be happy and content.

Gemini parents like to stimulate the minds of their children, providing them with opportunities for exploration. They find it difficult to remain constant but are fun to be with and will spend hours at play with their family.

Moon in Cancer

The moon is exalted in Cancer. This means that she is in her best placement here. The moon governs this zodiacal sign and so will be a powerful influence. Cancer moon people are highly sensitive and crave emotional security. They need to be accepted for who they are, so can become extremely defensive when challenged. They are sensitive to atmospheres and are very intuitive. Their feelings are often correct, but they need to guard against presuming they are correct all the time, falling into the negative trap of feeling wronged, hurt or rejected.

Cancer moon people are the carers of the zodiac, taking on the sick and the weak. This gives them the opportunity to excel in what they do best, but this caring should not be allowed to spill over into obsessional behaviour. They must learn to let others make their own mistakes and try not to rescue everyone they perceive is in need. They can be possessive and clingy, often retreating from areas of conflict instead of discussing them. They have a tendency towards self pity and sometimes have a moody and unpredictable side. They often expect the worst.

Cancer moon women can suffer more than most from pre-menstrual tension.

Stones:
moonstone
Flower:
waterlily
Animal:
crab

Cancer moon people make caring and supportive parents. When the moon is transiting Cancer, it is a good time to spend with the family, or helping others. Try to avoid depressing situations.

Moon in Leo

People with their moon in Leo are naturally gregarious and love being the centre of attention. They know little fear and will have a go at most things, believing that everything is attainable. They may tend to be bossy and self-centred, but this

Stones:
ruby
Flower:
sunflower
Animal:
lion

is a double-edged tendency, because they can also be great motivators to others who lack their level of confidence. They need to ensure that they find ways to balance their extrovert side with steadying activities that slow them down a little.

Above all, Leo moons need to be recognized and appreciated. Like the lioness, Leo moon people are proud and able. They love romance, and may often have a string of admirers who adore them. It is important to learn humility when your moon is in Leo and to sprinkle this over a naturally flamboyant lifestyle.

Caution is not the strongest characteristic when the moon is placed here. Think before you act, and plan before you begin, otherwise several very creative ideas may get lost in a whirl of self-aggrandizement. Leo moons are sociable and enjoy mixing with others. As parents, they see their children as extensions of their own egos, and so will push them to succeed. This pressure can drive a child away early from the home, if levels of control or domination are just too overwhelming.

When the moon is transiting Leo, you need to guard against being self-centred, over-opinionated or pushy.

When the moon is transiting Virgo, issues surrounding health and exercise will arise. This is a good time to begin a new fitness plan.

Moon in Virgo

Moon in Virgo people are discriminating, exacting and extremely clean and tidy. They are tactful and diplomatic, so make excellent peacemakers and negotiators.

Virgo moon people tend to be nervous and highly strung, lacking a basic confidence. Their way with words can sometimes be wonderful, and writers often have their moon in this sign. They need to guard against being too critical or judgemental: their high standards and expectations can make others feel inadequate or uncomfortable. They excel in most things they attempt, because they are methodical in their approach. Their attention to detail means that their homes are spotless, their offices organized, and all plans are made with care, leaving little room for error. This strictness can be limiting sometimes, and learning a level of flexibility and fluidity can, therefore, be highly beneficial.

Virgo moons are steady and reliable partners, good at handling and investing money. They approach parenting as they do everything else – with orderly correctness – and everything is taken care of in a practical way. However, paranoia about mess can cause friction in the family and Virgo moon parents need to learn to loosen up and allow their children the freedom to get dirty once in a while.

Stones:
jade
Flower:
buttercup
Animal:
cat

Moon in Libra

Moon in Libra people love beauty and harmony. They are naturally charming and likeable, and are able to see an argument from many different points of view. This makes them excellent lawyers, diplomats, or politicians. Ultimately,

Stones:
opal
Flower:
violet
Animal:
hare

however, the final decision-making is quite distasteful to them.

They are understanding and sensitive to the thoughts and feelings of others, which means that they can often be used as a shoulder to cry on. But other people would be wise to understand that the Libra moon's sensitivity can also be withdrawn if it is taken for granted or seen as a weakness.

Being naturally creative, their homes are artistically decorated and put together, even if little money is available. This artistic streak can also extend into their working lives, with a job in the performing or visual arts, such as theatre, painting, dance or music.

They fall in love easily and enjoy their relationships, having a need to relate to other people. They must, however, avoid escapism and learn to face up to their own faults. Disharmony in the home can lead quite quickly to ill health, producing headaches and physical tension.

Libra parents want to share their cultured interests with their children, but they need to allow their offspring to develop their own identity, follow their own particular talents and allow their creativity to shine however they choose.

Moon in Libra people create lovely homes with relaxing environments. When the moon is passing through Libra it is a good time to focus upon harmony within relationships.

When the moon is passing through Scorpio, destructive attitudes are possible. This is not the time to talk about sensitive issues.

Moon in Scorpio

People with their moon in Scorpio will be intensely secretive and difficult to fathom, and any hurts will be stored away for a long, long time. The light-hearted side of life often escapes them, and they are sometimes much too serious.

Stones:
topaz
Flower:
chrysanthemum
Animal:
eagle

This can lead to addictive patterns of behaviour. Scorpio moons need to learn how to channel their feelings into such things as self-healing, team games, and a healthy routine. They can, however, utilize their intuitive skills in medicine, research, healing and detective work, and they are happiest when left to get on with a task quietly.

In relationships, they have a lot to give, if they will let go enough to give it. They should not bear grudges or carry hurt feelings for too long, but learn how to forgive and move on.

Scorpio moon parents are fiercely protective of their offspring, sometimes bordering on possessiveness and jealousy, and do not welcome advice. They need to understand that children need a diversity of relationships in order to develop a well-rounded sociability. Any over-protectiveness is extremely supportive when necessary, but stifling when it is not.

When the moon is passing through Sagittarius, things may not go according to plan. It is a time to be adaptable.

Moon in Sagittarius

Sagittarius moon people are gregarious, funny, witty and tactless. Often speaking without thinking, these people need to learn how to be sociable without putting their foot in it. They are highly independent and individualistic, not worrying too much about what others think of them, since they hold quite a high opinion of their own abilities anyway.

They are very able, but a lack of sensitivity can sometimes mean that they tread on other people as they climb or travel to the top. They rise to a challenge, but need to guard against carelessness, including carelessness with money. Gambling is a strong temptation. Sagittarius moons can be reckless and would benefit from learning to pay attention to detail.

They have a naturally carefree attitude, which sometimes borders upon restlessness if their intellect is not sufficiently stimulated. Their work needs to be challenging, so that they can rise to the task. This moon placement can bring great wisdom, if the carefree attitude is tempered with sensibility.

They make good partners and are probably among the best parents in the zodiac. However, if things start to go wrong in a relationship you will not see Sagittarians for dust. They will have left already, looking for a more optimistic landscape. Generally happy people, they find it hard to stay where they feel uncomfortable.

Stones:
sapphire
Flower:
carnation
Animal:
horse

Moon in Capricorn

People with their moon in Capricorn will be hard-working, perhaps even workaholics. They have an almost fanatical dedication to making money and becoming successful, often at the expense of personal relationships. This placement is not an easy one, and lunar Capricorns often have to make sacrifices, which can lead them to become martyrs, with a tendency to moan about their lot. Capricorn moons can suffer with allergies and skin complaints, and benefit from being spontaneous, especially when the limitations of martyrdom are affecting their health.

Women with their moon in Capricorn often put their feelings aside and settle with a partner who will provide them with material security. Men, on the other hand, will often connect with a woman who can further their career. This is not a sign that is willing to take risks. Emotions do not figure strongly with Capricorn moons, and there can be a tendency to aloofness and detachment. This is sometimes balanced with a warm and funny sense of humour which rises spontaneously and can help to balance the rather superior, rigid exterior so often presented to the world.

Stones:
onyx
Flower:
pansy
Animal:
goat

When the moon is passing through Capricorn, it is a good time to work on your finances, and attend to any practical matters. Capricorn men and women set great store by financial security.

Moon in Aquarius

People with the moon in Aquarius can be highly original thinkers and extremely creative, often following a career in the performing or creative arts. They are interesting and unusual, and have many fascinated friends. However,

Stones:
jet
Flower:
snowdrop
Animal:
swallow

Aquarius moons must guard against careless talk or flippant actions at times when life is too dull or humdrum for them. They need to find a balance between innovative ideas and practical actions, and to avoid getting carried away with the next brilliant brainwave before it proves to be workable. They are outspoken and inventive. As lovers of freedom, they are often drawn to improving society in some way. Their need for independence runs deep, and Aquarius moons hate to be tied down. They frequently present mysterious and magnetic qualities that draw the unusual to them. They can be secretive and difficult to fathom because of this rather enigmatic predisposition.

Aquarius moons are unpredictable, never quite reacting as expected, and sometimes causing confusion as a result. They need to ensure that they stay well grounded in material matters and in business concerns. Nervous tension can affect their health adversely, especially the eyes and lower body.

Moon in Aquarius parents are double-sided. They give strong moral support to their children, but also expect them to become independent at a young age.

When the moon is passing through Aquarius, there will be an increase in creative and metaphysical ideas, with the opportunity to perform charitable acts. This is a good time to have a party.

When the moon is passing through Pisces, guard against emotional outbursts or negative and depressive tendencies.

Moon in Pisces

Stones:
amethyst
Flower:
mosses
Animal:
fish

People with their moon in Pisces are extremely sensitive, and often psychic, with a natural intuitive ability. They are kind, compassionate and understanding. There is also a creative streak in lunar Pisceans, and once they have gained confidence in their abilities, they have the potential to be extremely successful. They see life as far more than material, and give a great deal to those in need.

However, they can also be dishonest, out of a fear of conflict. Piscean moons can tend to put things off, making all kinds of excuses, but with the right kind of encouragement, they have the ability to make a great contribution to society.

Being romantic by nature, they require strong and positive partners, who will understand the Piscean sensitivity and vulnerability, and who will give back as much as they contribute to any partnership. It is easy to abuse the goodwill of Piscean moons, or to misunderstand their deep emotional nature.

Piscean parents are kind and sensitive to their children's needs, but sometimes lean on them for support.

the lunar year

Ancient civilizations calculated their festivals according to the lunar cycles of the year. Our present Gregorian calendar is calculated according to the position of the earth in relation to the sun – measuring the length of a solar day – rather than by the far less predictable monthly cycle of the moon. Although it is more complicated, many cultures, such as the Hebrews and Muslims, still have the means to calculate time by the moon.

Lunar Festivals

A lunar year is calculated by months rather than days, each incorporating the new, full, waning and dark aspects of the moon. For Buddhists, who use a lunar calendar, full and new moons are very important times, because they believe that Buddha was born, achieved enlightenment and died during the period of the full moon. Several of our solar festivals were originally lunar festivals, hence their appearance in the lunar wheel of the year. Easter still coincides with a particular full moon. The Celtic celebrations of Imbolc (celebrated on 1 February) and Beltane (1 May) were also dedicated to the moon.

Some days are dedicated to moon goddesses. One of Diana's festivals is called the Ides of May, and falls at the time of the May full moon. At this time, women would clean and tidy grottos, streams and water holes, and then wash the water over themselves as an act of cleansing and to encour-

The Celts often lit ceremonial fires when the moon rose on the evening before the day of a festival.

age personal fertility. Diana is also venerated at the Harvest moon. Hecate, a moon goddess of the dark aspect, has her annual festival day on 13 August. This is the time when ancient peoples would call for her blessing on fair weather for a safe harvest.

The moon is honoured in many cultures. Zhong Qiu Jie is an autumnal lunar festival held by the Chinese, when offerings are made and celebrations abound to honour a bountiful harvest. The lunar cycle is celebrated by pagans in the form of "full moon esbats". These ceremonies involve celebrating the full moon and sharing a feast, after any requests or dedications have been made, to signify the great abundance of the mother aspect of the moon and her ripeness at the full phase, being the most powerfully fertile. In many ancient cultures, torches were lit to direct the rays of the moon down to the earth, to ensure her continued influence upon crops, childbirth, and fair weather.

Lunar Festivals of the Year

30 November eve	Festival of Hecate: weather	1 May	Beltane/May Day: fertility, warmth and light
20/21 December eve	Winter Solstice – Celtic festival of the stars: light and life	9 May	Festival of Artemis
31 January eve	Imbolc: rejuvenation, fertility	26–31 May	Diana's Ides of May: fertility, abundance
7 February	Festival of Selene	21 June eve	Festival of Ceridwen
12 February	Festival of Diana	13 August eve	Festival of Hecate: torchlit procession; weather and thanksgiving
15 March	Festival of Cybele		
20 March	Festival of Isis	September full moon eve	Festival of Candles/Harvest moon: crop yield
20 March eve	Festival of Eostre (Easter): fertility	31 October eve	Festival of Hecate: remembrance of ancestors
31 March	Festival of all Lunar Goddesses		

lunar phases
Traditionally, the moon has four phases: new, full, waning and dark. In ancient civilizations, the moon was considered to have three faces: the crescent, the full and the waning/dark. These three faces were embodied in the maiden, mother and crone of the Triple Goddess. Ancient tribal ceremonies, although led by the chief, were always presided over by women, who were considered the potentizers of the moon's energy.

The New Moon
Associated with Artemis, the new moon heralds the beginning of a new cycle, and is the time in magic when new opportunities can be called for. On the magic circle, the new moon is placed in the east – the place of the moonrise and the place of a rising dawn. This slender beauty is seen as young and vulnerable, filled with the potential of a full moon yet to come, but as yet unrealized. The new moon is the maiden, the innocent, the conception, and this is a good time to work on health and personal growth, and to put plans into action for the month ahead. The new moon time lasts for approximately three days of the first quarter.

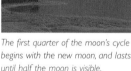

The first quarter of the moon's cycle begins with the new moon, and lasts until half the moon is visible.

The first quarter is a time of expansion, development and growth, and can still be used for the same purposes as the new moon, as long as you have completed your groundwork.

The Full Moon
The full moon is the moon at her fullest and ripest. Represented by Isis, Selene, and Diana, amongst others, she is the embodiment of fertility, abundance and illumination. She is the moon at her most powerfully feminine and so is the fruit-bearer, the one who can encourage any seeds to grow. The full moon can be called upon to give fertility in the fields as well as fertility of the body, and safe journeys across water. The most potent time for full moon magic occurs in the three days prior to a full moon and at the actual time of the full moon. This is called the second quarter.

In full moon ceremonies, the high priestess draws down the energies of a full moon into herself, embodying the great mystery of the feminine, by adopting the pentagram position within a sacred circle she has cast. Having drawn down the energies, she can be filled and refreshed, so that she can complete the next cycle of events in her life and the life of her community.

The full moon is also well known as the time of moon madness, or "lunacy" (from *luna*, "the moon"). The powerful energy of a full moon can trigger such things as epilepsy, as well as increasing the potential for accidents. People vulnerable to the influence of the full moon will feel more emotionally or mentally shaky at this time. In the female reproductive cycle, the full moon is the time of ovulation.

The Waning/Dark Moon
The waning and dark moon is ruled by Hecate, Cybele and Ceridwen. The waning moon, the third quarter, is when things can be released and insights gained. This is the power time for healings. After this period, the moon enters the rising power time of the fourth quarter. This is a necessary part of the circle of Luna, when things can retreat into themselves and rest before the pull of the new moon draws everything out again.

The dark moon is the time of black magic, especially during the winter months, when the light is low. However, it is the most potent time for gaining understanding, and should ideally be spent in contemplation and medi-tation, seeking the spiritual guidance of Isis or of Sophia, holy lady of wisdom. The dark moon is not the time for action unless it is of a banishing nature, and this is best done during the waning moon, the first to fourth day after the full moon, and not on the nights of true darkness, unless you know what you are doing.

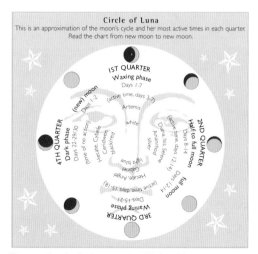

Circle of Luna
This is an approximation of the moon's cycle and her most active times in each quarter. Read the chart from new moon to new moon.

The exact length of a lunar month is 29 days, 12 hours, 44 minutes and 28 seconds.

the influence of the moon

Before the advent of calendars, the king (or "moonman") was responsible for watching the moon's cycle and informing the tribal members when the new moon arrived, so that activities associated with the crescent could begin. Ancient people were well aware of the profound influence the moon had on their lives, influencing the weather and the tides and reflecting the natural cycles of fertility.

The Moon and Women

As the protector and guardian of women, the moon has long been associated with the female reproductive cycle. Many ancient civilizations performed fertility rituals and celebrated the moon at annual festivals dedicated to the goddess, to seek her help and favour with conception.

The female menstrual cycle mirrors the cycle of the moon in duration. The Latin word *mens* meaning both mind and moon is the basis for our word menstruation. Women, the bearers of life, were seen by ancient civilizations as children of the moon goddess. Women can be very powerful, if their deep intuition is blended with spiritual wisdom. The full cycle of Luna must be travelled if wisdom is to be found. This can be achieved easily with meditation and devotion to the heart.

Within the heart of all women is the cycle of love. A woman generally finds it easy to nourish and care for others, to devote her life to beauty and harmony, and to speak from feeling rather than intellect. This reflects her "brightmoon" phase. Then there is the part of a woman that is jealous, possessive, scheming, vengeful, malicious, pre-menstrual – her "darkmoon" phase.

Like women, the moon has cycles. Both of them possess the ability to generate the right conditions for life.

During their menstruation, women find that they are extremely sensitive and highly perceptive. Many ancient civilizations considered them too powerful when they were on their "moontime" and it was common for women to remove themselves from the tribe. Though this is not a practice that is observed in modern societies, it may still be a good idea to set time aside to go within and use each "moontime" as a time to let go of the past cycle, and to allow the flow to cleanse and take away any problems or difficulties, thus making way for the new.

Once wisdom spills into her heart, a woman passes the highest initiation and the lunar cycle takes on its greater perspective. No longer dictated to by emotions, but rather by insight and discrimination, no longer attached, but rhythmical, no longer selfish or jealous but unconditionally compassionate, the wise woman has an extraordinary power.

The Moon and Numerology

In numerology the moon is associated with the number two, a highly feminine number, although in magic she is assigned the number nine. Any years or months that add up to the number two will come under the influence of the moon. Moon years are romantic, creative, unpredictable, deep and intuitive, with a need to bring harmony and stability. However, if the negative aspects of the moon prevail during a number two year, there will be a tendency for depression, cruelty, and possessiveness.

To discover if you are in a moon year, take the four figures and add them together. (For example, the year 2090 becomes 2 + 9 = 11; 1 + 1 = 2.)

If we look at the turn of the millennium, the year 1999, when broken down into a single number, becomes the number one (1 + 9 + 9 + 9 = 28; 2 + 8 = 10; 1 + 0 = 1). The number one represents the sun.

The year 2000, however, adds up to the number two. Thus, being a lunar year, it heralded an important time to get in touch with inner feelings and emotions, to be with the family, to enhance productivity, and to promote the good of the whole. As the wheel of time turned from sun to moon, so the less predictable but fruitful moon held sway into the new millennium.

A single halo around a full moon means mild breezes are due.

1	2	3	4	5	6	7	8	9
A	B	C	D	E	F	G	H	I
J	K	L	M	N	O	P	Q	R
S	T	U	V	W	X	Y	Z	

To discover if you are a moon person, take the letters of your chosen name and translate them into numbers using this chart. If they add up to two you will feel a strong affinity with the moon.

Moon people (those whose name or date of birth adds up to the number two) are dedicated parents, have a need for security and emotional reassurance, and have close links with nature and water, in a positive or negative way. Darker aspects of this personality include jealousy, manipulation, deception and vindictiveness. "Two" people need to guard against being two-faced.

Turning Names into Numbers

Using either your full name, your first name or a name that you have chosen for yourself, translate the letters into numbers to discover your affinity with the moon. "Sarah", for example, becomes 2 (1 + 1 + 9 + 1 + 8 = 20; 2 + 0 = 2). Sarahs will therefore feel a strong connection with the attributes of the moon. If you want to work out if you are a moon child, add up the numbers of your full birth date (for example, 2.4.1967 becomes 11 = 1 + 1 = 2).

The Moon and the Weather

The moon has a profound effect upon the earth's climate and atmosphere. She also affects the electromagnetic field that surrounds the earth, creating changes in atmospheric pressure that bring variations in the weather. Research into the moon's effect upon the earth's magnetic field has shown that the full moon increases the incidents of meteorites falling to earth, and also affects the amount of ozone in the atmosphere.

The earth's magnetic field changes enough, during the monthly cycle of the moon, to affect not only the weather but our health as well, since human beings are sensitive to magnetism. The old wives' tale of feeling things in one's bones can act as a good predictor of rain. Our rheumatic aches and pains can be a valid interpretation of increased dampness in the air.

The moon is known to influence rainfall, to raise storms, tidal flows, earthquakes, hurricanes and volcanic eruptions. Increases in these events have all been recorded just after a full moon. This aspect of the moon's power has psychological effects too. It has been found that mental instability increases dramatically during very unsettled or stormy weather. In severe drought, tribal people would make an offering of precious water to the moon, or milk a cow and offer the fluid in her honour. Clay balls were often flung at the full moon to encourage rain (clay being excellent at retaining water).

The Blue Moon

The old saying "once in a blue moon" refers to a time when two moons occur in the same calendar month, a rather rare occurrence. During the 20th century, for example, there were only 40 blue moons.

A blue moon appears about every two and a half years, usually during a month that has 31 days in it, because there is simply a greater time period in which it can happen. It signifies a special time, a doubling of the moon's powers during the month that she appears. Considered unlucky by some, the blue moon is, in fact, a magical moon, when long-term objectives can be set. So, a blue moon can be used to sow seeds for your future, giving them time to germinate and grow until the next blue moon rises. But you should be careful if you intend to weave magic during a blue moon. Be very clear about what you ask for, because this moon will be potent, doubling your intent.

People born during a blue moon have great potential, but may have difficulty bringing their gifts into action. Their strengths are also their weaknesses, and blue moon people have to learn how to harness their powers to benefit themselves and others.

A blue moon increases the lunar influence on the weather, with a high probability that rainfall, storms and exceptional tides will be more prevalent than usual during that month.

A different type of blue moon occurs when there are certain dust particles in the atmosphere making the moon appear blue.

Because of the power she brings to those born during this time, the blue moon's magic needs to be understood. Those born under a blue moon may have a tendency to moodiness, volatility and emotionalism, as well as the gentler attributes of compassion, caring, sensitivity and natural intuition.

harnessing the moon

harnessing the moon

An appreciation of the rhythms and cycles of the moon can give you new insight into its influence on the world, yourself and those around you, and consequently enhance your understanding of their behaviour. But you can also use this knowledge in more positive ways, grasping the subtle power of the moon to bring benefits into many aspects of your life. The moon's energy is powerful and mysterious, but is always there for you if you are able to tune into its gentle rhythms.

Since it has such a strong influence over the natural patterns of climate and growth you can exploit that strength in your own garden, by planting, sowing and harvesting during the most auspicious lunar phases. There are four phases to be considered. The moon is increasing in influence between the new and full phases (brightmoon) and decreasing in influence between the waning and dark phases (darkmoon).

For your rituals and ceremonies connected with the moon, remember that the moon, like the planets, has particular plants with which she is associated. Flowers of the moon include aquatic plants like water lilies, lotus and watercress, as well as jasmine and poppies. All flowers that are white or that blossom at night come under the regulation of the moon. Arrange a vase of moon flowers on the night of the full or new moon. The willow tree is known as the moon's wishing tree: calling for favour by tying white, silver or light blue ribbons to her branches on lunar festival days can help to draw attention to a wish.

Another moon tree is sandalwood. Associated with protection, purification and healing, bark chippings are used in ceremonies requiring these qualities. It has a beautifully calming and a very soothing smell.

Using plants and flowers of special lunar significance will heighten your sense of connection with the moon. Lunar talismans, used with sensitivity to the moon's cycles, can also help your perception to unfold. The tarot, which includes a depiction of the moon as the Wheel of Fortune, can act as a focus of attention, making a very powerful means of connecting with the intuitive forces of the moon.

Certain crystals have a sympathetic resonance with the cool, subtle energies of the moon. These crystals can help to align your vibrations to hers, so inducing lucid dreaming, clairvoyant awakening, deep and accurate perceptions and better emotional understanding.

All these things can put you in closer touch with the magical mystery of the moon, helping you to foster your intuitive wisdom and balance the rhythm of your life.

lunar gardening

Because the moon has such a strong influence over crop yields, for hundreds of years farmers, agriculturists and gardeners have all used their traditional knowledge of the lunar phases when planting, tending and harvesting crops. This is done by observing the correct phase of the moon for a particular activity, and also by adhering to the sign of the zodiac through which it is passing.

The Cycle

As a general rule, the moon's first and second quarter are the most auspicious times for planting and tending cereal crops, leafy crops and annual plants and flowers. The third quarter is good for root crops and bulbs, trees, shrubs and rhubarb. The fourth quarter is the best time for garden maintenance: for weeding, cultivation and the removal of pests, especially when the moon is in Aries, Gemini, Leo, or Aquarius.

Start a compost heap during the darkmoon time, or harvest and dry herbs and everlasting flowers, especially if the moon is in a fire sign. A water moon is the best time to irrigate fields and gardens.

Each zodiac sign is most auspicious for a particular range of activities in the garden. You will need to consult a lunar calendar to find out when each one falls. However, if to begin with you find it a little too complicated to check the appropriate signs for your gardening tasks, you can simply follow the moon's phases of waxing and waning to reap some of the beneficial effects.

Lunar gardening doesn't mean gardening by night, but rather by the moon's phases through the month.

New Moon

Seeds of plants that flower above the ground should be sown at the new moon. This is the time for farmers to sow cereals such as barley, and for the garden to be planted with asparagus, broccoli, sprouts, cabbage, melons, cauliflower, celery, courgettes, cress, horse-radish, kohlrabi, leeks, peas, peppers, parsley, spinach, squash and tomatoes. This is also the time for fertilizing, feeding and cultivating anything that you wish to flourish and grow.

Full Moon

Around the full moon is the time to plant watery or fleshy plants like marrows and cucumbers. The moon is at her most influential at this time over the water element. This is also a good time for harvesting leaves, stems, or seeds of herbs for drying, especially when the moon is transiting a fire sign. Pick your herbs on a dry day, so that the parts to be harvested will not rot when stored. The best time to harvest is just before midday. String the stems together and hang upside down in an airy but dry atmosphere, until ready for use.

Elemental Gardening Table

Gardening by the moon's phases is very simple once you have mastered the basic principles. Just ensure that you are within the correct moon phase for your gardening task, and that the moon is passing through an appropriate sign. For this, you will need a lunar almanac. Refer to this chart to discover which zodiacal sign is most appropriate for each activity.

AIR	FIRE	WATER	EARTH
Gemini (barren, dry)	**Aries (barren, dry)**	**Cancer (fertile, moist)**	**Taurus (fertile, moist)**
Weeding, clearing, pest control	Weeding, clearing, garden maintenance	Best time for planting, sowing and cultivating	Plant root crops and leafy vegetables
Libra (moist)	**Leo (barren, dry)**	**Scorpio (very fruitful and moist)**	**Virgo (barren, moist)**
Plant fruit trees, fleshy vegetables, root vegetables	Bonfires, ground clearance, weeding	Planting, sowing and general cultivation, especially vines	Cultivation, weeding and pest control
Aquarius (barren, dry)	**Sagittarius (barren, dry)**	**Pisces (fertile, moist)**	**Capricorn (productive, dry)**
Garden maintenance, weeding and pest control	Plant onions, garden maintenance	Excellent for planting, especially root crops	Good for root vegetables

Plant sweetcorn during the new moon to encourage crisp, fleshy kernels of corn.

Farmers should concentrate on cereal crops during the brightmoon phase.

Harvesting your vegetables should be done during a waning or dark moon.

Radishes, carrots and other roots should be planted during a waning moon.

Waning and Dark Moon

The waning moon is the time in the moon's cycle for root vegetables, peas and beans, and garlic. Anything undertaken during this time will benefit underground development or retard growth. This is therefore an excellent time to mow the grass, when its return growth will be slowed, or to plough and turn the soil. Gather and harvest crops during the waning moon, especially in late summer, the traditional harvest time. This is an excellent time to prune trees, roses and shrubs, and to water the garden. Making jams and pickles should also be done during a waning moon, for best results. Establish a compost heap, preferably when the moon is in Scorpio, to increase the fertility of the whole garden.

Crops that are particularly well suited to planting during the waning moon are endive, carrots, garlic, onions, potatoes, radishes, beetroot and strawberries.

All flowering bulbs, biennials, and perennials should be planted during this time, especially when the moon is in a water sign. Saplings also benefit from being planted during the waning moon, when she is in Cancer, Scorpio, Pisces or Virgo.

The principles of lunar gardening take a while to adjust to, but after a while, you will begin to find that your flowers bloom more brightly, your crops grow more succulent and flavoursome and your trees have stronger roots. In fact, your whole garden will benefit from this ancient way of gardening.

A Water Garden Offering to the Moon

The moon goddess Diana's festival days fall upon the May and September full moons each year. At one of these times, you may like to perform a simple water ceremony in your garden or beside a local waterfall, well, stream, lake or river, or possibly on the seashore. The form of this offering is inspired by the ancient art of well-dressing, still practised in some places, when communities "dress" their local source of water with a plaque decorated with symbols, flowers, corn, rice, stones and twigs, placing it by the water as a way of giving thanks.

Perform the ceremony two days before the full moon. As you place your plaque next to the water, you may like to say a prayer to the moon, asking for her blessing and protection for the year to come. Use your own words, as they come.

You will need

- potter's clay
- rolling pin
- knife
- wood, cut to shape
- stick or skewer
- petals, leaves, twigs, shells, flowers, corn, rice, and pebbles

1 Roll out the clay. Use the wooden template and knife to cut the shape from the clay.

2 Press the clay down firmly on to the wood, then mark out your design on the surface.

3 Fill in the design, pushing petals, leaves and other elements into the soft clay.

tarot and the moon

Tarot cards are believed to have originated in Egypt although, like most inherited systems of divination, we cannot be certain of this. In medieval times, the moon was depicted as Fortuna, the Wheel of Fortune in the tarot deck. This card depicts the ups and downs of life, the cycles that represent life's changing fortunes. Like the Wheel of Fortune, the moon is ever-changing, and reminds us that life ebbs and flows.

Reading the Moon Card

The moon card in the tarot deck is numbered 18 (1 + 8). This gives the number nine, which is the magical number of the moon. Nine signifies the completion of a cycle and so signifies a new beginning. Drawing this card tells you that intuition and perception will be your greatest allies in the days to come. Trust your feelings, and take a little time before making decisions of a life-changing nature.

This is a card of feelings and emotions, of all aspects of the feminine, and so may represent an emotional or psychic understanding or change, especially if time is spent in contemplation of the moon's present message.

Number eighteen is the moon card in the tarot deck.

It also conveys a warning that emotionalism and negative reactions that are not tempered with any higher wisdom can lead you into emotional confusion. This card signifies that you are completing one cycle and not yet beginning another – so can raise fears, doubts, and upsets. Don't get carried away with fantasies; stay practical and well grounded in reality, and trust that as every door closes, so another opens.

Take the moon card from the deck and hold it so that the picture is touching your third eye (in the centre of your forehead). Close your eyes and melt into the card, noting symbols, images and feelings that arise.

A Lunar Tarot Card

One way to deepen your connection with the moon is to make your own lunar card. Make up a design of your own that represents the moon for you, just allowing the ideas to form. Make the card just before the new moon, to ensure that your intuition and perception increase as the new moon grows.

You will need

- scissors
- white card
- ruler
- silver pen
- paints or crayons
- paint brush
- glue
- selection of the following: silver glitter, blue and/or silver sequins stars and moon sequin shapes
- pictures of moon animals, birds, trees, crystals, moon flowers, water
- white feathers (dove or duck)
- blue ribbons
- silver tape
- 2 blue or silver candles

1 Cut out a piece of card measuring 9 x 13cm/3½ x 5in and draw your chosen design on it. You can make the card bigger if you feel confident to do so.

2 Paint your design or glue on your chosen collage materials. Let your mind be led by imagination and creativity as you make up your design.

3 If you do not feel confident about drawing a design, cut out pictures of moon animals, trees or flowers, water or crystals and glue them on the card instead. When it is complete, place the card on your altar or special area. Light two blue or silver candles. Meditate upon the images for three nights. Make a note of any unusual dreams you have.

talismans

A talisman can be any small object invested with magical or protective powers, such as a crystal or silver charm. Its potency can be heightened by inscribing it with your sigil, a sign of your name traced on the "kamea", or magic square. In magic, the moon is associated with the number nine. The kamea of the moon adds up to the number nine in all directions and can be used in magic to connect with the powers and gifts the moon provides.

Attracting and Releasing Talismans

When you are making a lunar talisman it is important to observe the correct timing: from the new moon to the full moon is the time for drawing things to you, and from the full moon to the beginning of the dark moon is the time for releasing things. For example, if you are seeking new beginnings or fertility, use the new moon, and if you are asking for healing, use the waning time. The new to full phase is for growth and attraction. The waning to dark phase is for decrease and removal.

Place an attracting talisman in the light of the moon with a moonstone or white circular stone on top, until your wish is granted. Take a releasing talisman to a river or seashore on the first night after a full moon and place it in the water to be taken away. Watch it leave, and then turn away. Do not look back.

To make your talisman you will first need to work out the sigil of your name. Convert your name into numerals using the numerology chart. For example, "Isabel" becomes the numbers 911253. Trace the shape those numbers make on the kamea. Begin with a small circle, then draw a line connecting the numerals until you have a sigil, or pattern. Isabel would begin by joining nine to one, then one to two and so on. End the sigil with a line.

The sigil of Isabel makes this pattern on the kamea.

The Kamea of the Moon

A lunar kamea can be used to balance the emotions, to call for fertility, and to enhance perceptions and psychic abilities, as well as for journeys at night or over water.

37	78	29	70	21	62	13	54	5
6	38	79	30	71	22	63	14	46
47	7	39	80	31	72	23	55	15
16	48	8	40	81	32	64	24	56
57	17	48	9	41	73	33	65	25
26	58	18	50	1	42	74	34	66
67	27	59	10	51	2	43	75	35
36	68	19	60	11	52	3	44	76
77	28	69	20	61	12	53	4	45

A Lunar Talisman

Use the sigil of your name to make an attracting talisman on which you can write a wish, and then leave it in the moonlight until your wish is granted.

You will need

- 2 silver or white candles
- matches
- silver pen
- ruler
- 23cm/9in square of natural paper

1 Light two silver or white candles, invoking the aid of the moon as you do so with these words: *"Hail to you Levanah. I light these candles in your honour and ask for your assistance this night."*

2 Draw a 5cm/2in square in the top left-hand corner of a square sheet of natural paper. Copy the sigil of your name (do not include any numbers from the kamea with it) into the square using a silver pen.

3 Write your wish (this might be for a safe journey, for example) in the remaining space on the paper. Fold the four corners of the paper into the centre to make a diamond shape, then repeat the folds twice more.

4 Leave your talisman on a windowsill or somewhere in the light of the moon, to draw her favour to your wish. Place a moonstone, or some other circular white stone to represent the moon, on top of the folded talisman.

lunar crystals, colours and circles

The moon has been associated with particular sacred stones for thousands of years. Traditionally, white, clear or watery bright stones are associated with the waxing and full moon and black or dark stones with the waning and dark aspects when insights can be gained and wisdom can be sought. They will help to align your vibrations with those of the moon.

Bright Moontime Crystals

You can take your crystals to lakes or the seashore during a full moon and cleanse them there in the water.

Celestite, in its blue or white varieties, links you to your spirit guides, to light your way in the dreamtime.

Azurite, known as the stone of Heaven, can help you attune your mind to the psychic world.

Pearls are symbolic of the moon because they come from the sea and represent purity, clarity and grace.

Aquamarine makes an ideal dream crystal, tuning you into the rhythms of the sea and into the depths of your own spirit.

Circular white stones or pebbles of any kind can be used to represent the full moon, or to increase your connections with her.

Clear quartz looks like frozen water, and has a strong affinity with the moon. It can be used in healing or invoking ceremonies.

Moonstone can be used to balance the hormonal cycle, calm any unsettled emotions, and will help induce lucid dreaming.

Dark Moontime Crystals

Holy flint is normal flint but with a natural hole in it. It can protect the wearer from night terrors, fears and from negative thought forms.

Jet, a deeply black mineral, is symbolic of the dark moon. It clears a heavy head, and can help in the lifting of depression or gloominess.

Black stones can be found by the riverside or on beach walks. Carry them with you whenever you are feeling confused or disorientated.

Citrine is actually a crystal of the sun. It has been included here as a preventer of nightmares, to enable you to get a good night's sleep.

Casting a Brightmoon Circle

This ceremony can be performed every month to honour the moon, as the protector and guardian of women. When women cast the circle it will refresh and rejuvenate them for the month to come. For a man it will have a symbolic rather than biological significance as he follows his own rhythms and cycles from the female within. The ceremony can be done indoors or outdoors, during the two days leading up to a full moon.

As you light the candles, say: "Magna Dei, light of the night, I light these candles to guide your moonrays here. I ask you to come and bless this circle." Once you are standing in the circle, say the lunar invocation: "Hail to thee Sophia, holy spirit of the wisemoon. I call upon you to enter and fill me with your light. Protect me and guide me on the moonway. Teach me your wisdom and truth as I seek your clarity and guidance."

Imagine yourself drawing down the powers of the moon into yourself. Allow yourself to be refreshed and re-filled with the feminine virtues of wisdom, beauty and grace. Let the moon bless your feelings and perceptions until you feel energized and content. Bring your arms down to your sides. Close your circle by saying "Thank you". Blow out your candles and dispose of organic ingredients outside.

You will need

- 13 circular stones, river stones or moon crystals
- salt
- aromatherapy burner
- matches
- jasmine essential oil
- 9 candles

1 Turning clockwise, lay down 12 of your chosen stones (these can be all different sizes) in a circle around you, beginning in the south. Place the last stone in the centre.

2 Sprinkle each of the stones around the circle with a little salt. Light the aromatherapy burner and put in three drops of jasmine essential oil.

3 Place eight candles around the circle and one by the centre stone. As you light the candles, say the invocation to Mother Moon.

4 Facing south, stand with your arms outstretched above your head and your feet quite wide apart. Reach towards the sky.

Lunar Colours

The moon has colours that are traditionally associated with her. Use and wear them when you are performing ceremonies, or simply to maintain your connection with the moon's phases.

White, associated with purity and innocence, represents the new moon. White and milky stones are also associated with the new moon. Burn white candles when working during this phase – for example, to call for new opportunities. Silver has the most favourable lunar associations, because of its coolness and fluidity. Silver jewellery, especially when worn during the new to full moon phase, can enhance all the magical qualities of the moon.

Light blue is a very healing colour. It can soothe, calm and cool heated emotions, illness, or burns and stings. Once appropriate medical attention has been administered, visualize a light blue colour bathing a specific area, or the whole person, and you will notice a marked reduction in the symptoms.

Black is the colour of the darkmoon, when the inner world can speak most clearly. It is associated with Hecate, goddess of death and the underworld. Black is a silent, inward colour, so can be worn as protection or when seeking insight. It is a colour of power and identity. Burn white candles during the darkmoon phase, and meditate in black clothes or cloaked in a black cloth.

If you feel drawn to setting up an altar to the full moon, you may like to use a light blue cloth, silver candles, sandalwood incense and wild water meadow or riverside flowers.

astrology

astrology astrology

As long ago as 30,000 BC early humans were charting the passage of the stars across the night sky. We know this from finds of bone fragments that have definite star cycles marked on them. But it was the Chaldeans from Assyria who first recorded that the stars ran in a fixed way but that planets wandered. They could see that these wanderers – the Moon, Venus, Mercury, Mars, Jupiter and Saturn – passed in front of fixed star positions, which they called constellations, and that the affairs and events of humans seemed to be linked with the passage of these planets. As each planet moved into and through the backdrop of a particular constellation, similar events seemed to occur. For instance, when Mars was visible humans seemed more ready to go to battle – hence Mars was called the god of war. Venus, on the other hand, seemed to promote peace and harmony, and was called the goddess of love. Thus was formed the basis of astrology around the seventh century BC.

Gradually, the movements of the stars and planets were observed over longer periods of time, and the more subtle relationships between their positions on the horizons and human nature were verified, and astrology came to be part of everyday life. It became clear that the power of foresight or divination could be used to advantage to improve and predict relationships between subjects and rulers, countries and kingdoms. Astrology was to stay, for all time.

the sun signs

Your sun sign dominates everything else. It is the outer you, the part you show to others, and it is difficult to hide. Your sun sign is the one you read about in daily horoscopes in newspapers and magazines, and these analyses are based on 12 possible birth periods. You may share characteristics of the sign next to yours if you were born within a few days of the next or previous sign – this is known as being on the cusp.

Aries 22 March–20 April ♈

The Aries character is one of adventure and enterprise. If you are a typical Aries you will know no fear. You have extremely high energy levels, love your freedom and hate having any sort of discipline imposed on you. You can be quick-tempered and impulsive. You may well be impatient – you want everything now. You are, however, enthusiastic and generous and very quick-thinking in emergencies.

Taurus 21 April–21 May ♉

The Taurus character is one of reliability, strength and patience. If you are a typical Taurus you will have limitless energy to see through any project you start. You are stubborn and relentless but have a broad back to cope with life's adversities. You are a lover of good food and wines and work hard for luxury. You have a very strong moral code and stick to strict high principles in everything you do.

Gemini 22 May–22 June ♊

The Gemini character is entertaining, lively and a good communicator. A typical Gemini is quick-witted, highly intelligent and extremely versatile – there is nothing a true Gemini won't try to turn their hand to. You have strong opinions but may change them. You can be extremely amusing and talkative and have a great flair for languages and ideas. Gemini is known as the Two Stars – Castor and Pollux (or Hercules and Apollo) represent its communicating aspect – you always need (and have) someone to talk to.

Cancer 23 June–23 July ♋

The Cancer character is caring and protective. A typical Cancer will feel things deeply and care a great deal about loved ones. You can be over-emotional and too sensitive sometimes but you are sympathetic and kind. You have very strong intuition and imagination. You have strong parenting instincts and depths of feelings which others can only guess at. Cancer is represented in the constellations as the Crab – you need desperately to be by water but you also need the land to give you your reality.

Leo 24 July–23 August ♌

The Leo character is dominant and powerful, and won't shun the limelight. You are creative, enthusiastic and energetic. You can be too dramatic but you have talents, charm and personality. You are a great organizer and love being surrounded by people and action. The Sun is represented by the lion killed by Hercules and the lion's mane is Leo's distinguishing feature – your hair is important to you.

Virgo 24 August–23 September ♍

The Virgo character has taste and refinement; a typical Virgo won't put up with anything second-best. You are tidy and organized and expect as much of others. You have strict rules and could be seen as fussy or critical. You are meticulous, work hard and delight in constant activity. Virgo was the daughter of Jupiter and the goddess Themis, and became the goddess of justice.

Libra 24 September–23 October ♎

The Libra character is calm and rational. A typical Libra will be charming, loved and respected. You like an easy-going life and are idealistic and romantic. You may be seen as frivolous because you back away from confrontation and unpleasantness but you are refined and elegant and don't need confusion around you. Libra is represented by the Scales – you see balance in everything and weigh all decisions carefully. You understand give and take and are prepared to compromise – sometimes too readily.

Scorpio 24 October–22 November ♏

The Scorpio character is one of indulgence and excess, passion and emotions. If you are a typical Scorpio you will feel things intensely and be driven by a strong sense of purpose. You are discerning and imaginative. Whatever you dedicate yourself to you will do wholeheartedly and completely. You have great endurance and strength and are a powerful person. Scorpio is represented by the scorpion who rose from the earth to attack Orion. You have a hard outer shell but are warm and soft inside – however, you are the one with the sting in your tail.

Sagittarius 23 November–22 December ♐

The Sagittarius character is one of freedom, loving travel and a search for knowledge and depth in all things. If you are a typical Sagittarius you simply love to know. You keep an open mind and are adaptable and friendly. You are wise and clever with sound judgement and a responsible nature. You value your freedom highly and do not like discipline, rules or routine. You are a seeker after truth and knowledge above all things. Sagittarius is represented by the centaur Cheiron: half-man, half-horse, to symbolize your love of travelling, with a drawn bow to symbolize your ability to cut straight to the truth.

Capricorn 23 December–19 January ♑

The Capricorn character may be seen as very serious but in reality you are determined and relentless. If you are a typical Capricorn you place great emphasis on hard work, fulfilling your obligations and improving. You don't like to stand still and be bored. You are a determined seeker after understanding and power. You are ambitious and persevering. You have a tremendous sense of humour and fun but don't allow it to show except when you are with very close friends. The world sees you as steady and reliable. Capricorn is symbolized by Pan, the goat, a seducer of nymphs and a knower of secret things.

Aquarius 20 January–19 February ♒

The Aquarius character is one of independence and friendliness. There is nothing you wouldn't do for others. If you are a typical Aquarius you will be modern in your outlook. You follow your ruling planet closely – you collect nothing and get rid of everything. You prune everything in your life – friendships, ideals, dreams and goals – closely and carefully. You are interested in ideas not possessions. You are an intellectual, and are inventive and resourceful. You are a loyal idealist, kind and a champion of the underdog. Aquarius is symbolized by the upturned water jug – a constant stream of ideas and inspiration.

Pisces 20 February–21 March ♓

The Pisces character is one of change and intuition. If you are a typical Pisces you change your feelings many times during a day and you feel everything intensely. You are kind and receptive and genuinely care about others. Like any water – changing from ice to water, from water to steam, and back to water – the true Pisces character cannot be grasped, for it is unworldly and nebulous. Pisces is symbolized by Venus and Cupid, who changed themselves into fish to escape the amorous advances of the giant Typhon.

Sun Sign Qualities

Each of the 12 sun signs has a masculine or feminine quality, as well as an element – fire, water, earth or air – which governs it. Each sign also has a general quality: it is either cardinal (that is, it initiates things), mutable (it sees things through) or fixed (it completes things). Each sign has a ruling planet which gives it its strengths and qualities.

Aries is the first sign of the zodiac and its ruling planet is Mars, the god of war. Aries is a cardinal masculine fire sign. Keywords for Aries are urgent and assertive.

Taurus is the second sign of the zodiac and its ruling planet is Venus, goddess of love. Taurus is a fixed feminine earth sign. Keywords for Taurus are determined and honourable.

Gemini is the third sign of the zodiac and its ruling planet is Mercury, the messenger. Gemini is a mutable masculine air sign. Keywords for Gemini are versatile and expressive.

Cancer is the fourth sign of the zodiac and its ruling planet is the Moon, goddess of the emotions. Cancer is a cardinal feminine water sign. Keywords for Cancer are intuitive and emotional.

Leo is the fifth sign of the zodiac and its ruling planet is the Sun, king of the universe. Leo is a fixed masculine fire sign. Keywords for Leo are powerful and dramatic.

Virgo is the sixth sign of the zodiac and its ruling planet is Mercury, the messenger. Virgo is a mutable feminine earth sign. Keywords for Virgo are discriminating and analytical.

Libra is the seventh sign of the zodiac and its ruling planet is Venus, goddess of love. Libra is a cardinal masculine air sign. Keywords for Libra are harmony and diplomacy.

Scorpio is the eighth sign of the zodiac and its ruling planet is Pluto, planet of regeneration and change. Scorpio is a fixed feminine water sign. Keywords for Scorpio are passion and power.

Sagittarius is the ninth sign of the zodiac and its ruling planet is Jupiter, planet of wisdom and vision. Sagittarius is a mutable masculine fire sign. Keywords for Sagittarius are freedom and optimism.

Capricorn is the tenth sign of the zodiac and its ruling planet is Saturn, planet of practicality and lessons to be learnt. Capricorn is a cardinal feminine earth sign. Keywords for Capricorn are duty and discipline.

Aquarius is the eleventh sign of the zodiac and its ruling planet is Uranus, planet of elimination. Aquarius is a fixed masculine air sign. Keywords for Aquarius are independence and compassion.

Pisces is the twelfth and last sign of the zodiac and is ruled by the planet Neptune, watery god of the depths. Pisces is a mutable feminine water sign. Keywords for Pisces are nebulous and receptive.

the houses

The sky is divided into twelve sectors, each known as a house. The houses are not heavenly bodies or star systems but they neatly cover every area of human development. The house in which a planet or a constellation lies is important as it gives a clue to the area that will be influenced. The planet shows how something will manifest, the constellation gives the manner of its manifestation and the house indicates what it will affect.

The 12th house represents what we fear and cannot know: unconscious impulses, seclusion, sleep and death.

First House: Birth
The first house represents your basic personality, physical health, the way you reveal yourself to others around you and your physical appearance.

Second House: Possessions
The second house represents what you own. It is bound up with wealth, material possessions and personal belongings. It also represents feeling.

Third House: the Mind
The third house is to do with how you think about the world, communicate ideas and how you express yourself.

Fourth House: the Home
The fourth house is about where you live: your roots, your ancestry, your parents and family.

Fifth House: Creativity
This is the house of pleasure, leisure and socializing.

Sixth House: Work
The house of employment, business, career opportunities and working relationships.

Seventh House: the Heart
The seventh is the house of relationships and love affairs, marriage and long-term partnerships.

Eighth House: Sharing
The eighth is the house of attitudes, whether on sex, money or ideas. It is where you reveal your generosity – or lack thereof.

Ninth House: the Intellect
The ninth house represents how you learn: your education and upbringing but also your study as an adult in later life.

Tenth House: Personal Ambitions
This is the house of your aspirations: your dreams and goals, longings and drives.

11th House: Friendship
The 11th house is to do with how you entertain your friends and social acquaintances, and with the way you indulge your personal pleasures.

12th House: Escapism
The 12th is the house of seclusion and loneliness, death and the unconscious. It represents what you fear.

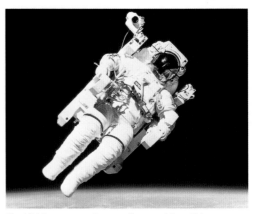

The 10th house covers the area of your worldly ambitions, aspirations and drive to success in your life.

the planets

Although strictly speaking the sun is not a planet but a star, it is still included as a planet in charts for astrological purposes. In terms of the zodiac, everything revolves around the earth, which lies at the very centre of your chart. As the exploration of space progresses and we begin to travel to other planets, it may be that astrologers will need to draw up new charts, with earth as one of the planets and perhaps Mars or Venus in the centre.

The Sun
This is the most important of the planets. It governs character and determines power and vitality, life and growth.

The Moon
For insights into your emotional side, the moon is the place to look. It is mysterious and dark, deep and secret. It is the planet of the imagination.

Mercury
The planet of communication is Mercury the messenger. It governs the way in which you express yourself and communicate with others. It is also the planet that rules the area of mental powers.

Venus
The planet of love is Venus. It is also the planet of beauty and the appreciation of fine things. It is refined and harmonious.

Mars
Mars is the planet of war, conflict and disagreements. It represents aggression and force, power and dynamic movement. It is also the planet of sex.

Saturn is the planet of practicality and lessons to be learnt. It is the ruler of the sun sign Capricorn.

Jupiter
The planet of Jupiter is luck and kindness. It governs pleasure and recreation. Jupiter is a planet of philosophy and expansion.

Saturn
This is the planet of lessons. It tells you what it is that you need to learn in order to progress or move on. It is the planet of duty and responsibility, security and discipline.

Uranus
This planet represents what you need to eliminate from your life, and what you need to avoid repeating. It is the planet of change and sudden unexpected events.

Neptune
The planet of religion and spirituality is Neptune. It is here you would look for your intuition and imagination. Neptune represents the realm of idealism and sensitivity.

Pluto
The planet of the 12th House: Pluto – the unconscious. It governs the way you think and feel about death, and the dark secret things you fear most.

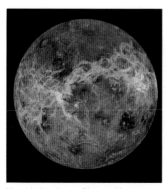

Venus is the planet of love and beauty, personified by the goddess of love. It rules the feminine sign Taurus and Libra.

Neptune is the planet of spirituality, personified by the ruler of the sea. It rules the water sign Pisces.

Mars is the fiery planet of conflict, personified by the god of war. It rules the masculine fire sign Aries.

using astrology

Once the foundations of astrology had been laid, a way was devised to represent the heavens on paper so the positions of all the planets, stars, constellations and houses could be plotted. A circular representation was used with the earth in the centre surrounded by the heavens. The sun was regarded as a planet – although supremely important – and was depicted as revolving around the earth with the rest of the planets.

The Zodiac

The circular chart of the heavens was called a zodiac – which, in old French and Greek, means circle of animal signs – as an animal was chosen to represent each constellation of stars. Originally a zodiac was drawn up only to forecast the outcome of major events and catastrophes, such as a forthcoming war, a flood or a plague. Gradually, as events seemed to be linked to a country's ruler, a zodiac chart would be drawn up for the king of the people. This was taken very seriously in China where the succession was determined astrologically: as each child was born to the ruling emperor, a court astrologer would see whether the auspices were right for them to become the heir to the throne. The notion of a personal chart gradually spread from the ruler to his subjects.

In this celestial chart, the constellations are shown as animals circling the earth.

Your Personal Chart

As a visual reference to your life the zodiac chart is both mathematically intricate and beautifully simple. It shows the exact moment in the history of the universe at which you entered it, and thus begins your own personal history. Your chart could only be identical to someone else's if they were born at the same moment as you and in exactly the same place.

The zodiac still shows the earth at the centre and has the 12 constellations, the 12 houses and the planets surrounding it. The additional planets Uranus, Neptune and Pluto were included as they were discovered, and are known as the fixed planets as they move so slowly that they influence a whole generation.

The position of the planets in relation to one another on your birth chart is known as the aspect. Aspects are major or minor depending on their angle relative to one another. This angle determines how they affect you.

How Astrology Works

Astrology is based on the expected turn of events. Around 9,000 years of observations have shown that when planets are in certain positions, some things are much more likely to occur. However, nothing is set in stone, and nothing will guarantee that events will turn out in a particular way, but the probabilities are based on the observations of countless millions of people. The only test of astrology is to try it for yourself and see how accurate it is for you.

Astrology cannot foretell the future, but it can illuminate the basic building blocks of your personality, character and potential, for you to make what you will of them. The gravitational and electromagnetic effects of the moon are well known, so what effect may the pull of the planets, the electromagnetic influences of the stars and solar activity have on us? We know the sun can influence radio reception on earth in quite dramatic ways and, despite our sophistication, we are very sensitive creatures. There may be a more scientific basis to astrology than we have yet been able to discover.

Finding your Sign

Each sign is represented by an animal or mythical character which symbolizes its inherent nature. Your sun sign shows which constellation was behind the sun at your birth. While this cannot give as much information as an entire chart, it can help you to understand yourself in astrological terms. To have a chart prepared for you, you will need to visit an astrologer or find a computer programme that will do it for you.

Sun Sign Dates

Aries: 22 March – 20 April
Taurus: 21 April – 21 May
Gemini: 22 May – 22 June
Cancer: 23 June – 23 July
Leo: 24 July – 23 August
Virgo: 24 August – 23 September
Libra: 24 September – 23 October
Scorpio: 24 October – 22 November
Sagittarius: 23 November – 22 December
Capricorn: 23 December – 19 January
Aquarius: 20 January – 19 February
Pisces: 20 February – 21 March

astrology and you

An astrological chart will show how you are likely to react in love or business, how your basic personality might appear to those around you – and those things that you like to keep secret. And of course this applies equally to other people close to you. What better way can there be to know how your lover or business might respond to a situation than to look at their astrological chart?

Personality

Your character is revealed by your sun sign and is the fundamental you. Your personality, however, is how you come across to other people and is revealed by your ascendant or rising sign: the constellation on the eastern horizon at the time of your birth. For instance, Aries is a dynamic sign with leadership qualities and a forthright approach to life, but an ascendant in Cancer might make those qualities somewhat muted and kinder. On the other hand, an Aries with a Scorpio ascendant would lead in a much more rigid and authoritarian manner. An Aries with a Sagittarius ascendant might be happier leading only very small groups.

The typical Aries character is fearless and adventurous.

There are 12 signs and 12 ascendants, giving 144 possible combinations. You may find it is simply not enough to say "I am a Taurean" or "I am a Capricorn". It becomes increasingly necessary to add to that definition, and say "I'm a Taurean with Virgo rising" or "I'm Capricorn with Pisces rising".

Character

Your sun sign is the real you, but it is modified by your rising sign, and by the position of the moon and the mid-heaven in your chart. This gives four distinct parts to your character and 20,736 possible combinations, without looking at other factors in your chart such as the position of the planets, houses or aspects. Astrologers are usually pretty good at "guessing" your sun sign: actually they aren't guessing at all but reading the clues you yourself present to them.

Relationships

The moon governs your emotional side whereas the sun rules your outer personality. Your moon is the secret, loving part of you that you keep hidden except in a trusting and loving relationship. You need to check in which constellation and which house it appears. Next to the sun, the moon sign is the most important part of your chart and not only shows your emotional side but also your relationships with your family, your parents and your children, as well as your dreams, goals and aspirations.

The moon rules Cancer, which is the sign of home, security and protection. The nearer to Cancer the moon appears in your chart, the closer you will be to these qualities. Compare your moon with your lover's to see how compatible you are. If your two moons are in opposition you can expect clashes, whereas if they are in conjunction (next to each other) then you will be helpful and loving to each other.

Career

Your mid-heaven, at the top of your chart, tells you which constellation was directly overhead when you were born and points to career possibilities. If your mid-heaven falls in Aries, you will be dynamic at work, a leader and in charge. A Taurean mid-heaven would ideally be suited to farming or horticulture. Gemini points to a career as an entrepreneur or sales person. Cancer indicates work in a caring profession such as counselling or therapy. Leo would indicate someone in the public eye, such as an actor or politician. Virgo would be happiest working in research, planning or computer programming. Libra would be ideally suited to design work. Scorpio is best suited to anything secret, such as spying, research or crime writing. Sagittarius is the traveller of the career world. Capricorn is best at anything that requires an organized, methodical approach. Aquarius is best involved with new ideas – science, analysis, and inventing. Pisces is the problem-solver of the zodiac, best in advertising, charity work or astrology.

Geminis have strong opinions, and are good communicators.

compatibility chart

This chart is designed to show which signs are compatible in love, but don't dismiss incompatible signs altogether – you may be suited in other ways. While a romantic pairing looks inauspicious, a different kind of relationship might be successful. For instance, Aries people can never seem to fall in love with Taureans, but they certainly can go into business with them and are likely to do very well indeed.

	Aries ♈	Taurus ♉	Gemini ♊	Cancer ♋	Leo ♌	Virgo ♍	Libra ♎	Scorpio ♏	Sagittarius ♐	Capricorn ♑	Aquarius ♒	Pisces ♓
Aries ♈	✓	✓✓	✓	✓✓	✓✓✓	✓✓	XXX	XX	✓✓✓	XX	✓✓	✓✓
Taurus ♉	✓✓	✓	XX	✓✓	XX	✓✓✓	XX	XXX	✓	✓✓✓	XX	✓
Gemini ♊	✓	XX	✓	✓✓	✓✓	XX	✓✓✓	✓	XXX	XX	✓✓✓	✓✓
Cancer ♋	✓✓	✓✓	✓✓	✓	XX	✓✓	XX	✓✓	XX	XXX	✓✓	✓✓✓
Leo ♌	✓✓✓	XX	✓✓	XX	XX	✓✓	✓	XX	✓✓✓	✓	XXX	✓✓
Virgo ♍	✓✓	✓✓✓	XX	✓✓	✓✓	✓	XX	✓✓	XX	✓✓✓	✓	XXX
Libra ♎	XXX	XX	✓✓✓	XX	✓	XX	✓	✓✓	XX	✓✓	✓✓✓	✓
Scorpio ♏	XX	XXX	✓	✓✓	XX	✓✓	✓✓	✓✓	✓✓	XX	✓	✓✓✓
Sagittarius ♐	✓✓✓	✓	XXX	XX	✓✓✓	XX	XX	✓✓	XX	✓	✓✓	✓✓
Capricorn ♑	XX	✓✓✓	XX	XXX	✓	✓✓✓	✓✓	XX	✓	XX	XX	✓✓
Aquarius ♒	✓✓	XX	✓✓✓	✓✓	XXX	✓	✓✓✓	✓	✓✓	XX	✓✓	✓✓
Pisces ♓	✓✓	✓	✓✓	✓✓✓	✓✓	XXX	✓	✓✓✓	✓✓	✓	✓✓	XX

Key to Symbols

✓ These two signs are not particularly compatible but will have no real problems. They will probably simply ignore each other.

✓✓ This combination is not bad at all. Two people with these signs will get along fine and are likely to become very close.

✓✓✓ Very compatible. Lovers for life – good business partners – good marriage partners – good friends.

XX Bad move. These two signs are not at all compatible in a relationship. These two will certainly not like each other much.

XXX Sparks will fly. These two positively dislike each other – they wouldn't even stay in the same room. They will be deadly enemies.

birth chart

A natal chart is drawn up for the moment a person is born. An astrologer would need your birth date and the exact time and place for accuracy. The chart below was compiled for Alex, who was born in the United States on 17th June 1943. Alex is an entertainer who travels the world. He was brought up by his father after his parents divorced. He has never married and enjoys a large income. He lives alone but has a global audience.

Reading the Chart

The inner circle, marked 1–12, indicates the positions of the houses. Within it, aspect lines link up any planetary positions that are of interest, such as oppositions, conjunctions, trines (120° angles) and squares (90° angles). The middle ring shows the planets and the outer ring gives the positions of the constellations at the time of Alex's birth.

To the right of the chart, the first two tables shows what the symbols mean. The third shows in which constellation and in which house each planet is to be found. The fourth table explains where the houses fall. You can see that the ascendant is in the first house, the descendant in the seventh and the midheaven in the tenth.

At the top are listed Alex's name and date of birth; the house system that is being used (in this case the equal system); the time zone he was born in; which aspects are being shown (in this case, "strong orbs" means that only the most dominant aspects, such as oppositions, conjunctions, trines and squares, have been plotted); and the longitude and latitude of his place of birth.

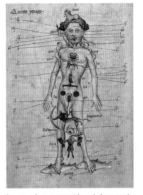

It was always considered that each astrological sign ruled a particular part of the body.

Interpreting the Chart

An astrologer could gain a considerable amount of information from this chart. For instance Alex's Sun is in Gemini in the 11th house. This would give him a very visible public image, with clear objectives and great personal success – someone who brings happiness to others by their personality, charisma and ability to entertain.

Alex has his Sun and Moon in opposition: this means he is a person in whom the sun is a very powerful focus; someone who will have extreme tendencies, which may be theatrical or political; it can also indicate problems between his parents.

His mid-heaven (career) is in Taurus which indicates someone who is comfortable, successful and would do well in farming or the arts. His ascendant (rising sign) is in Leo, which again indicates someone who enjoys the spotlight and will be in the public eye. His Moon is in Sagittarius in the fourth house – this shows someone who won't settle into a relationship easily but enjoys travel a lot, and likes their own company but still needs a very comfortable luxurious home base to return to.

Alexander	Thursday	Equal	Strong Orbs
	17/06/43 09:00:00	Time Zone:5:00W	Summer Time: 0:00
			40N38 73W56

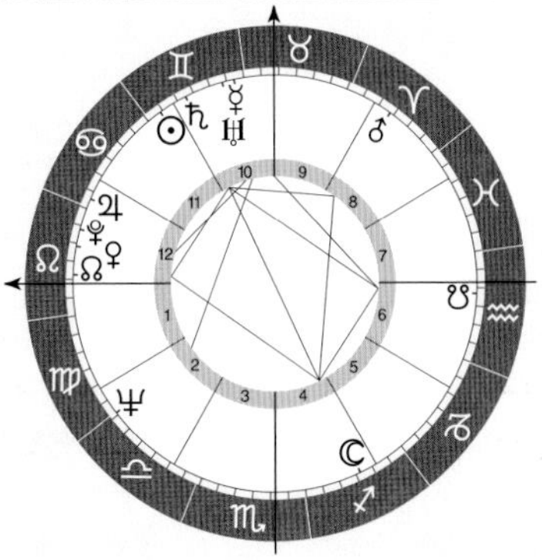

Planetary symbols		Constellation symbols		Planetary position with houses		House position	
☉	Sun	♈	Aries	☉ 25.30 ♊ 11		Aˢᶜ 21.21	♌
☽	Moon	♉	Taurus	☽ 16.40 ♐ 4		2 21.21	♍
☿	Mercury	♊	Gemini	☿ 2.46 ♊ 10		3 21.21	♎
♀	Venus	♋	Cancer	♀ 10.32 ♌ 12		I꜀ 21.21	♏
♂	Mars	♌	Leo	♂ 15.32 ♈ 8		5 21.21	♐
♃	Jupiter	♍	Virgo	♃ 27.13 ♋ 12		6 21.21	♑
♄	Saturn	♎	Libra	♄ 17.17 ♊ 10		D˸ᶜ 21.21	♒
♅	Uranus	♏	Scorpio	♅ 5.54 ♊ 10		8 21.21	♓
♆	Neptune	♐	Sagittarius	♆ 29.17 ♍ 2		9 21.21	♈
♇	Pluto	♑	Capricorn	♇ 5.40 ♌ 12		M˸ᶜ 21.21	♉
☊	N.Node	♒	Aquarius	☊ 18.38 ♌ 12		11 21.21	♊
☋	S.Node	♓	Pisces	☋ 18.38 ♒ 6		12 21.21	♋

chinese astrology

According to legend, when the Buddha found enlightenment under a fig tree he invited all the animals in creation to share in his joy. Only 12 accepted, however, and it is these who are honoured by being included in the Chinese zodiac. Each animal was allotted its own year to govern.

Chinese astrology is very old. Although the Buddha lived two and a half millennia ago (563–483 BC), the truth is that no one actually knows how old it is and it may well predate him. There are some who date its origin as far back as the reign of the legendary Yellow Emperor of China, who lived around 2630 BC. What we do know is that the system, still in wide use today in China and other eastern countries, has remained unchanged for several thousand years. Until even quite recently, it would have been unthinkable for anyone in these countries to have married, moved house, changed jobs, conceived a child or even celebrated a happy event without first getting advice from an astrologer.

Astrological studies reached their peak in China during the Han dynasty (200 BC–AD 200), but at one time, the Emperor banned "ordinary" people from using astrology at all on the grounds that it was dangerous. He considered the information it imparted so accurate that it could be used to plot against him and his court. So he simply banned its use – except for himself, naturally.

the philosophy of chinese astrology

Chinese astrology was influenced by Taoism, one of the ancient religions of China. The Tao (the Way) says that everything in the universe has a quality or aspect which is either male or female, advancing or retiring, light or dark. Everything is in a state of constant change between the two opposites, which are not in conflict with each other but are complementary.

Yin and Yang

The opposites are called yang (male) and yin (female) and they are represented by a symbol in which each half contains a tiny seed of the opposite aspect, indicating their interdependence. Both qualities are essential and balance each other: together they make us complete.

The Five Elements

The basic qualities are further defined by one of the five elements – water, wood, fire, metal or earth. Each animal and each year is either yin or yang and is governed by an element. The animals are divided into four groups: water – rat, ox and pig; wood – tiger, hare and dragon; fire – snake, horse and goat; metal – monkey, rooster and dog. Earth rules no animals but it lends its qualities to some of the years.

The yin-yang symbol.

The Sixty-year Cycle

As there are 12 animals and five elements in the Chinese astrological system, they give rise to 60 different animal types, succeeding one another in rotation through a 60-year cycle, with half of the years being yin and half being yang. This 60-year cycle is important as it makes each year special and unique – you are not just a particular animal (one of 12) but a particular type of animal. If you happen to be a yang water tiger, for example, your character and life will be very different from that of a yang wood tiger. If you then add in the 12 months of the year, which also affect Chinese horoscopes, and the 12 divisions for the times of day, you can see that this gives a total of 8640 possible combinations of horoscopes (five elements × 12 animals × 12 months × 12 times of day).

Clockwise from top

Water is associated with the north: communication, sensitivity and intuition.

Wood is associated with the east: nurturing, creativity and growth.

Fire is associated with the south: passion, intelligence and movement.

Metal is associated with the west: useful and dependable.

Earth is the centre: balance, reliability, foundations.

using chinese astrology In addition to lending its

characteristics to people born during a particular year, each animal also influences the quality of the year itself. So knowing which animal rules a future year can help you to plan for the trials and triumphs that year might bring. For instance, dragons are usually associated with expansion and prosperity, so a dragon year might be an auspicious time to start a new business.

Inner and Secret Animals

You have more than one animal sign which governs your life, and it is important that you work out your inner and secret animals too. Your inner animal is worked out by the month in which you were born – the lunar month. This controls your love life, so if you want to find out whether you are compatible with another sign, you need to know both your own inner animal and your potential partner's. Your secret animal is determined by the time of your birth, and it is this animal which will reveal the true you – to yourself only of course. So if you were born at 08.00 in February 1963, outwardly you are a hare, your inner animal is the tiger, and your secret animal is the dragon.

Use this chart to check your compatibility.

Compatibility

This information helps you to find out what each year (and each month) could bring you, and it can also be informative when you are thinking about the people around you. Suppose you are considering going into business with a friend, for instance. You can find out what animal he or she is, and you know what sort of animal you are – so are the two compatible? Would a pig make a good business partner for a rat? Look at the compatibility chart on the left for a quick at-a-glance check, and use the same information for personal relationships; are you compatible with your lover? You can even use the chart to look at friendships: the compatibilities don't change.

How to Use the Chart

Each of the animals is said to have two close friends and one deadly enemy. The two close friends are identified on the chart by counting round four animals in each direction from your own sign; the deadly enemy is the animal directly opposite yours. The two other signs that make up that particular element group are not too good to associate with either. Once you know what each animal represents you can use that information to plan better, more rewarding and fulfilling lives for yourself and your family.

Animal Months and Hours

Rat: December, 11pm – 1am

Ox: January, 1am – 3am

Tiger: February, 3am – 5am

Hare: March, 5am – 7am

Dragon: April, 7am – 9am

Snake: May, 9am – 11am

Horse: June, 11am – 1pm

Goat: July, 1pm – 3pm

Monkey: August, 3pm – 5pm

Rooster: September, 5pm – 7pm

Dog: October, 7pm – 9pm

Pig: November, 9pm – 11pm

A close group of friends will often find that there are three or four signs predominating. Sometimes there are more than this, which is accounted for by the subtle influence of the elements of each sign.

year charts
Each of the animals has five different and distinct personalities depending on which element governs it – and that depends on the year in which you were born. Look up your birth year and read the introduction to that animal, and then read about the individual characteristics of the animal governed by the relevant element.

The Rat

The Ox

The Tiger

The Years and Their Signs

Year	From – to	Aspect	Element	Animal
1900	31 Jan 1900 – 18 Feb 1901	Yang	Metal	Rat
1901	19 Feb 1901 – 7 Feb 1902	Yin	Metal	Ox
1902	8 Feb 1902 – 28 Jan 1903	Yang	Water	Tiger
1903	29 Jan 1903 – 15 Feb 1904	Yin	Water	Hare
1904	16 Feb 1904 – 3 Feb 1905	Yang	Wood	Dragon
1905	4 Feb 1905 – 24 Jan 1906	Yin	Wood	Snake
1906	25 Jan 1906 – 2 Feb 1907	Yang	Fire	Horse
1907	3 Feb 1907 – 1 Feb 1908	Yin	Fire	Goat
1908	2 Feb 1908 – 21 Jan 1909	Yang	Earth	Monkey
1909	22 Jan 1909 – 9 Feb 1910	Yin	Earth	Rooster
1910	10 Feb 1910 – 29 Jan 1911	Yang	Metal	Dog
1911	30 Jan 1911 – 17 Feb 1912	Yin	Metal	Pig
1912	18 Feb 1912 – 5 Feb 1913	Yang	Water	Rat
1913	6 Feb 1913 – 25 Jan 1914	Yin	Water	Ox
1914	26 Jan 1914 – 13 Feb 1915	Yang	Wood	Tiger
1915	14 Feb 1915 – 2 Feb 1916	Yin	Wood	Hare
1916	3 Feb 1916 – 22 Jan 1917	Yang	Fire	Dragon
1917	23 Jan 1917 – 10 Feb 1918	Yin	Fire	Snake
1918	11 Feb 1918 – 31 Jan 1919	Yang	Earth	Horse
1919	1 Feb 1919 – 19 Feb 1920	Yin	Earth	Goat
1920	20 Feb 1920 – 7 Feb 1921	Yang	Metal	Monkey
1921	8 Feb 1921 – 27 Jan 1922	Yin	Metal	Rooster
1922	28 Jan 1922 – 15 Feb 1923	Yang	Water	Dog
1923	16 Feb 1923 – 4 Feb 1924	Yin	Water	Pig
1924	5 Feb 1924 – 24 Jan 1925	Yang	Wood	Rat
1925	25 Jan 1925 – 12 Feb 1926	Yin	Wood	Ox
1926	13 Feb 1926 – 1 Feb 1927	Yang	Fire	Tiger
1927	2 Feb 1927 – 22 Jan 1928	Yin	Fire	Hare
1928	23 Jan 1928 – 9 Feb 1929	Yang	Earth	Dragon
1929	10 Feb 1929 – 9 Jan 1930	Yin	Earth	Snake
1930	10 Jan 1930 – 16 Feb 1931	Yang	Metal	Horse
1931	17 Feb 1931 – 5 Feb 1932	Yin	Metal	Goat
1932	6 Feb 1932 – 25 Jan 1933	Yang	Water	Monkey
1933	26 Jan 1933 – 13 Feb 1934	Yin	Water	Rooster
1934	14 Feb 1934 – 3 Feb 1935	Yang	Wood	Dog
1935	4 Feb 1935 – 23 Jan 1936	Yin	Wood	Pig
1936	24 Jan 1936 – 10 Feb 1937	Yang	Fire	Rat
1937	11 Feb 1937 – 30 Jan 1938	Yin	Fire	Ox
1938	31 Jan 1938 – 18 Feb 1939	Yang	Earth	Tiger
1939	19 Feb 1939 – 7 Feb 1940	Yin	Earth	Hare
1940	8 Feb 1940 – 26 Jan 1941	Yang	Metal	Dragon
1941	27 Jan 1941 – 14 Feb 1942	Yin	Metal	Snake
1942	15 Feb 1942 – 4 Feb 1943	Yang	Water	Horse
1943	5 Feb 1943 – 24 Jan 1944	Yin	Water	Goat
1944	25 Jan 1944 – 12 Feb 1945	Yang	Wood	Monkey
1945	13 Feb 1945 – 1 Feb 1946	Yin	Wood	Rooster
1946	2 Feb 1946 – 21 Jan 1947	Yang	Fire	Dog

The Hare

The Dragon

The Snake

The Horse

The Goat

The Monkey

Year	From – to	Aspect	Element	Animal
1947	22 Jan 1947 – 9 Feb 1948	Yin	Fire	Pig
1948	10 Feb 1948 – 28 Jan 1949	Yang	Earth	Rat
1949	29 Jan 1949 – 16 Feb 1950	Yin	Earth	Ox
1950	17 Feb 1950 – 5 Feb 1951	Yang	Metal	Tiger
1951	6 Feb 1951 – 26 Jan 1952	Yin	Metal	Hare
1952	27 Jan 1952 – 13 Feb 1953	Yang	Water	Dragon
1953	14 Feb 1953 – 2 Feb 1954	Yin	Water	Snake
1954	3 Feb 1954 – 23 Jan 1955	Yang	Wood	Horse
1955	24 Jan 1955 – 11 Feb 1956	Yin	Wood	Goat
1956	12 Feb 1956 – 30 Jan 1957	Yang	Fire	Monkey
1957	31 Jan 1957 – 17 Feb 1958	Yin	Fire	Rooster
1958	18 Feb 1958 – 7 Feb 1959	Yang	Earth	Dog
1959	8 Feb 1959 – 27 Jan 1960	Yin	Earth	Pig
1960	28 Jan 1960 – 14 Feb 1961	Yang	Metal	Rat
1961	15 Feb 1961 – 4 Feb 1962	Yin	Metal	Ox
1962	5 Feb 1962 – 24 Jan 1963	Yang	Water	Tiger
1963	25 Jan 1963 – 12 Feb 1964	Yin	Water	Hare
1964	13 Feb 1964 – 1 Feb 1965	Yang	Wood	Dragon
1965	2 Feb 1965 – 20 Jan 1966	Yin	Wood	Snake
1966	21 Jan 1966 – 8 Feb 1967	Yang	Fire	Horse
1967	9 Feb 1967 – 29 Jan 1968	Yin	Fire	Goat
1968	30 Jan 1968 – 16 Feb 1969	Yang	Earth	Monkey
1969	17 Feb 1969 – 5 Feb 1970	Yin	Earth	Rooster
1970	6 Feb 1970 – 26 Jan 1971	Yang	Metal	Dog
1971	27 Jan 1971 – 15 Jan 1972	Yin	Metal	Pig
1972	16 Jan 1972 – 2 Feb 1973	Yang	Water	Rat
1973	3 Feb 1973 – 22 Jan 1974	Yin	Water	Ox
1974	23 Jan 1974 – 10 Feb 1975	Yang	Wood	Tiger
1975	11 Feb 1975 – 30 Jan 1976	Yin	Wood	Hare
1976	31 Jan 1976 – 17 Feb 1977	Yang	Fire	Dragon
1977	18 Feb 1977 – 6 Feb 1978	Yin	Fire	Snake
1978	7 Feb 1978 – 27 Jan 1979	Yang	Earth	Horse
1979	28 Jan 1979 – 15 Feb 1980	Yin	Earth	Goat
1980	16 Feb 1980 – 4 Feb 1981	Yang	Metal	Monkey
1981	5 Feb 1981 – 24 Jan 1982	Yin	Metal	Rooster
1982	25 Jan 1982 – 12 Feb 1983	Yang	Water	Dog
1983	13 Feb 1983 – 1 Feb 1984	Yin	Water	Pig
1984	2 Feb 1984 – 19 Feb 1985	Yang	Wood	Rat
1985	20 Feb 1985 – 8 Feb 1986	Yin	Wood	Ox
1986	9 Feb 1986 – 29 Jan 1987	Yang	Fire	Tiger
1987	30 Jan 1987 – 16 Feb 1988	Yin	Fire	Hare
1988	17 Feb 1988 – 5 Feb 1989	Yang	Earth	Dragon
1989	6 Feb 1989 – 26 Jan 1990	Yin	Earth	Snake
1990	27 Jan 1990 – 14 Feb 1991	Yang	Metal	Horse
1991	15 Feb 1991 – 3 Feb 1992	Yin	Metal	Goat
1992	4 Feb 1992 – 22 Jan 1993	Yang	Water	Monkey
1993	23 Jan 1993 – 9 Feb 1994	Yin	Water	Rooster
1994	10 Feb 1994 – 30 Jan 1995	Yang	Wood	Dog
1995	31 Jan 1995 – 18 Feb 1996	Yin	Wood	Pig
1996	19 Feb 1996 – 7 Feb 1997	Yang	Fire	Rat
1997	8 Feb 1997 – 27 Jan 1998	Yin	Fire	Ox
1998	28 Jan 1998 – 15 Feb 1999	Yang	Earth	Tiger
1999	16 Feb 1999 – 4 Feb 2000	Yin	Earth	Hare
2000	5 Feb 2000 – 23 Jan 2001	Yang	Metal	Dragon
2001	24 Jan 2001 – 11 Feb 2002	Yin	Metal	Snake
2002	12 Feb 2002 – 31 Jan 2003	Yang	Water	Horse
2003	1 Feb 2003 – 21 Jan 2004	Yin	Water	Goat
2004	22 Jan 2004 – 8 Feb 2005	Yang	Wood	Monkey
2005	9 Feb 2005 – 28 Jan 2006	Yin	Wood	Rooster
2006	29 Jan 2006 – 17 Feb 2007	Yang	Fire	Dog
2007	18 Feb 2007 – 6 Feb 2008	Yin	Fire	Pig

The Rooster

The Dog

The Pig

the animal signs

the animal signs

The ancient Chinese sages believed that the universe was exactly 3,600 years old, and they divided this time into 300 60-year cycles, which they considered the perfect human lifespan. Each human cycle was divided by the five elements to give 12 years, which were originally referred to as the Twelve Earthly Branches. Eventually these acquired the characteristics of 12 distinct animals. Although, according to legend, the zodiac animals were chosen by the Buddha, it is thought that the names arrived in China from Turkey or Central Asia, possibly not until after astrological studies reached their peak during the period of the Han dynasty (200 BC–AD 200).

Many of the qualities attributed to the animals differ markedly from Western ideas of their characters. The rat, for instance, has a largely negative image in the West, and you may not welcome the idea of such an animal presiding over your life. However, in Chinese astrology the rat is seen as hard-working, loyal to its partner and a good and responsible parent. The snake is regarded not as treacherous or dangerous, but as wise, sophisticated, well-organized and good at solving problems.

The animal signs do not just govern the years. They are also each allotted a month and a time of day over which they preside. So, for instance, you would not be just a tiger, the animal corresponding to your birth year. You might also show some of the characteristics of a monkey if that animal ruled the month in which you were born, and perhaps a goat according to your time of birth. Each of these animals would bring their own qualities to your astrological chart.

The same qualities apply to each animal whether it is the year, month or time of day you are considering. Their combination makes you unique. Your year animal is the outer you – the part seen by the outside world. Your month animal (known as your lunar animal) is you in relationships and love – your inner animal of the heart. And finally, your time of day animal is the real you – the dark, secret animal that you do not show to the rest of the world.

A Chinese astrologer draws up a personal horoscope using the exact moment of your birth, not just the year. Traditionally, before the arrangement of a Chinese marriage, an astrologer would check on the compatibility of the two people concerned, using additional information such as the birth dates of their parents. The descriptions of the animals on the following pages include notes on each animal's compatibility with the other signs.

the rat

Rats are cheerful and industrious. They bounce back quickly from setbacks and even when down they manage to keep smiling. Because of their reputation for being self-motivated they are often mistrusted, but they provide well for their family and make loyal partners and good parents. They love to haggle for bargains and genuinely adore collecting money. Rats do always have a hidden agenda and fend primarily for themselves.

RAT CHARACTERISTICS

Rats do not have a wider social conscience. They look after their own first and foremost. They are passionate and sentimental, and regard a close, big family, well provided for, as their paradise. Rats like company and are not given to much introspection. They can be very generous to their loved ones and have good taste. They may also be very practical, and are able to cope with most tasks quite easily.

Love, Sex and Relationships

Rats are sentimental, sensual and warm lovers. They will go out of their way to please their lovers and like to take the initiative when it comes to seduction. They are naturally faithful but need to be kept interested. As rats are naturally curious, spicing up your love-making with dark secret places, candlelight, good wines and plenty of surprises will ensure a rat stays with you forever. Allow it to be boring and the rat will vanish.

Business, Friends and Children

Rats are the hard-working entrepreneurs of the animal kingdom, and are clearly focused on money and success. They are outwardly charming and quick, and can fool people into thinking that they have the best interests of others at heart, but that is far from the truth. Rats are only interested in themselves and what they can acquire, steal, buy, obtain and accumulate. They hate to fail at anything and will always strive for success, measuring that success by how much they have acquired in material terms. This

The rat likes secret meetings and intrigue, and will indulge in illicit affairs and dangerous liaisons if they get bored.

doesn't make rats bad people – merely greedy. They can turn any situation to their own advantage. Despite these traits, rats are usually popular and genuinely well liked, and usually have many friends. They adore their own children.

	Years of the Rat	Characteristics	Careers
	1900 • 1912	Curious	Auctioneer
	1924 • 1936	Intelligent	Money lender
	1948 • 1960	Practical	Lawyer
	1972 • 1984	Passionate	Antique dealer
	1996 • 2008	Self-interested	Car salesperson
Element: *Water*	2020 • 2032	Sentimental	Financial adviser

Water Rat
This intuitive, adventurous rat likes to travel, but once it finds a safe haven, it will settle and won't be shifted. The water rat is creative, enjoys literature, and is a good diplomat.

Wood Rat
Although hard-working and successful, this is the least dynamic of the five rats and can be indecisive and prone to worry.

Fire Rat
This quick-witted, passionate rat has a flair for business, and the energy and enthusiasm to match. Unless it learns to curb its recklessness, it can be rather dangerous.

Earth Rat
This serious, prudent rat likes practical problems with practical solutions. Although a bit of a plodder, it is usually successful, and makes a good accountant or financial adviser.

Metal Rat
Strong, with fixed ideas, this rat can be stubborn, although it is helpful and hard-working. An ambitious rat, with the ability to see things through, it will be successful in all it undertakes.

All rats like to travel, but they also enjoy homecomings and don't like to be away from their families for long periods of time.

The rat likes to be part of a big, sociable family.

Rat Compatibility Chart

RAT WITH:

RAT	A good combination as rats need a lot of attention – and are capable of giving lots in return. These two do well together in business or a relationship.
OX	A well-balanced and harmonious partnership. The ox is a good listener and the rat will entertain him or her extremely well.
TIGER	As neither of these two knows how to compromise, this combination will create sparks and the relationship will be stormy.
HARE	The rat is a control freak while the creative and intuitive hare dislikes control of any sort. Not a good combination.
DRAGON	A good relationship despite the apparent differences. Each will support the other in their schemes and will be able to give the other the attention they crave.
SNAKE	The snake's love of secrets and mysteries will inflame the rat to fits of jealousy and distrust. Not a good combination.
HORSE	Neither partner will get a word in edgeways – but if either can learn to listen the relationship does have potential.
GOAT	If the rat is allowed to control and be in charge then this could be a successful union. However, if the goat wants any freedom, the relationship is doomed.
MONKEY	These two characters are similar in personality and do well together. They are both starters rather than finishers and so will need to make allowances for that to do well together.
ROOSTER	With two control freaks, this combination just can't work. Neither partner will be interested in the other and both will demand to be in charge.
DOG	A good team. The rat's control and the dog's loyalty make a good combination, although they both like to talk a lot so the relationship could be a noisy one.
PIG	If the rat can earn it, the pig can spend it. As long as both know where they stand, this is a good partnership.

the ox

The gentle giant of the animal world, the ox is a patient, kind character who takes responsibilities seriously, and expects everyone else to do so as well. The fact that they often don't puzzles the ox, who derives a lot of pleasure from doing things the right way – actually their own way. Oxen can be a bit set in their routines. They like to get up early and get on with their work, and they are tidy and well-organized.

OX CHARACTERISTICS

The ox is a determined character with boundless energy and enormous capacity for hard work. Totally reliable, an ox friend will always be there for you. Also patient, consistent and conscientious, an ox can sometimes be a bit dull and will occasionally need livening up. Basically happy, with few worries, the ox occasionally suffers from irrational fears, and needs lots of exercise and fresh air to prevent introspection. Oxen like to be appreciated and have their advice taken seriously. This is a sensible, sober, traditional type with an understanding of good old-fashioned virtues and hardly a vice at all.

Love, Sex and Relationships

Being wary of emotion and too much excitement, the ox is careful to avoid falling in love. But once an ox does fall in love, it's for life. Just don't expect too much romance – the ox is too down-to-earth for that and, being straightforward about sex, regards it as a practical necessity.

Business, Friends and Children

In business the ox can be ruthless and efficient, preferring to get on with the job in hand and hating any waste of time, energy or money. Ox personalities make good parents as they have infinite patience and kindness. They also have many true friends who know they can depend on the ox in times of trouble. The ox is a very stable animal, and children, business partners and friends can all rely on the ox with total confidence.

All oxen know how to work hard, but the earth ox is the hardest worker of them all.

Element:	**Years of the Ox**	**Characteristics**	**Careers**
	1901 • 1913	Reliable	Gardener
		•	•
	1925 • 1937	Purposeful	Judge
		•	•
	1949 • 1961	Patient	Teacher
		•	•
	1973 • 1985	Conscientious	Estate manager
		•	•
	1997 • 2009	Determined	Chef
		•	•
Water	2021 • 2033	Faithful	Police officer

Water Ox

The diplomatic ox knows how to listen and makes a good counsellor. Advice is freely given when asked for, and is usually good
advice – especially about matters relating to love.

Wood Ox

Blessed with a sense of humour, this laughing ox can be very
witty. It is more adaptable than the other ox types, with a need
to try new things, but the wood ox also has a volatile temper.

Fire Ox

Unpredictable and dangerous, this is the bull in the china shop.
When it has its head down and is working, the fire ox is fine, but
once it becomes bored or restless it can be extremely volatile.

Earth Ox

Earth oxen are resourceful and reliable. They make good
researchers and scientists. They don't like to take risks and are
careful and methodical. They accumulate great wealth through
their hard work and endeavours.

Metal Ox

With considerable talents for organization, this very serious ox
makes a good office manager or a writer of business books.
When a metal ox gives advice you'd better listen, for it knows
what it is talking about, especially when it comes to business.

Choose a water ox to talk to when you need a sympathetic ear.

The ox applies itself to its work and is hard-working and methodical.

Ox Compatibility Chart

Ox with:	
Rat	Well balanced and harmonious. The ox is a good listener and the rat will entertain them both extremely well.
Ox	Neither one of these two will have anything to say, and they will suffer each other in silence. This is not a good partnership.
Tiger	Unless the tiger allows the ox to be in control and set the rules this combination can't work. As tigers don't give in easily, expect fireworks.
Hare	The hare has a natural optimism that won't suit the ox, who is pessimistic by nature. These two are badly suited.
Dragon	A powerful combination. The ox can curb the dragon's impetuosity, and if they work as a team they can achieve anything together.
Snake	A good long-lasting and stable relationship. The snake understands the ox and will encourage them to lighten up – the ox gives the snake stability.
Horse	This is not a good combination. The ox is thorough and methodical, while the horse is impulsive and rash. These two will irritate each other continually.
Goat	These two won't agree on anything, and the ox will be appalled by the goat's apparent lack of morals.
Monkey	The monkey constantly seeks change and the ox hates it. This combination can't work under any circumstances.
Rooster	The rooster sets things in motion and the ox will see them through. A good combination.
Dog	If both partners share the same goals, this can be a good partnership, but in business rather than love.
Pig	The ox will never tolerate the pig's spending habits, and the pig will consider the ox dull. Not a promising union.

the tiger

Rash, impulsive and dynamic, tigers don't know how to sit still, and take fearsome risks. But if you need a hero, then a tiger will do fine. Tigers like to take on the cause of the underdog and will fight against any injustice imaginable. They are invariably charming and persuasive. They are born leaders, not because of any natural leading abilities, but because they can talk anyone into following them – no matter how ill-advised the project may be.

TIGER CHARACTERISTICS

The tiger is one of the most tenacious characters in the Chinese zodiac and very little will daunt tigers – or keep them down for long – they will always bounce back. They are not invulnerable, however, and need lots of emotional support, as they are basically insecure and can feel unloved.

Love, Sex and Relationships

Tigers have infinite resources of energy and imagination and will inevitably tire any lover they tangle with. They are promiscuous and have absolutely no moral sense whatsoever, with no compunction about finding new excitement once the current relationship has begun to fade. They are great romantics and fall in love easily and often. They do have a great capacity for intense relationships and are devastated when these fall apart, even if they are the cause. A tiger in love can be a rogue or simply perfect – and you'll never know which sort you're getting until it's too late.

Business, Friends and Children

Tigers are loners with few really good friends, but those they do have they keep for life. They make good parents; not because they set good examples, but because children just adore these exciting and charismatic personalities. They can be very strict and demanding, and do tend to expect a lot of their offspring. In business, tigers are adventurous speculators, full of new ideas. They are good at starting new projects with enthusiasm and energy, but they hate routine and get bored easily.

The metal tiger protects itself well – it can be ruthless and shouldn't be crossed, but is a pussy cat at heart.

	Years of the Tiger	Characteristics	Careers
	1902 • 1914	Daring	Film star
	1926 • 1938	Passionate	Army officer
	1950 • 1962	Heroic	Writer
	1974 • 1986	Tenacious	Athlete
	1998 • 2010	Reckless	Politician
Element: *Wood*	2022 • 2034	Foolish	Restaurateur

Water Tiger

Possessing a greater sense of moral responsibility than the others, this calm tiger will often set a good example and be fair and just. It can be a bit pompous, though, and is very self-assured.

Wood Tiger

This social big cat is the life and soul of the party, full of bright, entertaining ideas, but it's all a front – this tiger is deeply insecure and feels unloved a lot of the time.

Fire Tiger

The quickest and most ferocious of the tigers, the fire tiger races everywhere as if it were on fire, which internally it may well be. It needs to learn to slow down and relax or it will burn out early.

Earth Tiger

A tiger of extremely good taste, this self-indulgent character recognizes quality and likes to enjoy all the fine things in life. It can run to fat if not careful, as it does enjoy good food and fine wines.

Metal Tiger

This roaring tiger is the most opinionated of all. Very ambitious, it can be ruthless about its career. Don't stand in the way of a metal tiger and never invest in any of its schemes. This is a tiger for whom the word "diplomacy" simply doesn't exist.

The earth tiger is the refined tiger of good taste – it can also be rather self-indulgent though.

Children adore tigers – and tigers are very fond of children too – no matter how many.

Tiger Compatibility Chart

TIGER WITH:

RAT	As neither of these two knows how to compromise, this combination will create sparks and the relationship will be stormy.
OX	Unless the tiger allows the ox to be in control and set the rules, this combination can't work. As tigers don't give in easily, expect fireworks.
TIGER	Expect a lot of heat – the heat of passion and ferocious lust. These two will fight and reconcile, laugh and love – a lot.
HARE	The hare makes a good meal for the tiger unless it learns to move fast to stay out of trouble. Although not a good combination, it can work.
DRAGON	Excitement and fun all the way. Dramatic and volatile. A super-charged dynamic team who together can move the earth.
SNAKE	The snake thinks the tiger is over-emotional, while the tiger distrusts the snake's secretive ways. This relationship is bound to end in disaster.
HORSE	A good combination. The tiger will respect the horse's loyalty and the horse will love the tiger's impulsiveness.
GOAT	Could be good together in bed, but there is not a lot else going for them. This partnership is not recommended for business.
MONKEY	As neither will compromise, this is not a good combination. Both suffer ego problems and neither will understand the other at all.
ROOSTER	In spite of the fact that these two will bicker and quarrel, criticize and argue, this match is quite a good one.
DOG	The dog is clever enough to handle the tiger, so these two will do extremely well together.
PIG	These two blame each other when things go wrong and aren't really suited.

the hare

Intuitive, psychic, sensitive and creative, hares care about others. They are lone souls who feel the pain of the world and often try hard to put it right. They love mysteries and hidden knowledge, and are seekers after Truth. Invariably calm and moderate, quiet and refined, hares like to know secrets, which they are capable of keeping. They make good counsellors and clairvoyants. They are eloquent, with good taste and a strong sense of style.

HARE CHARACTERISTICS

Hares like to express their emotions and can be volatile if roused by cruelty or suffering. They have a strong sense of fair play but like to break rules themselves, and they can be arrogant, seeing themselves as a little superior to others. Hares possess genuine intuitive powers and need a calm stable atmosphere to thrive.

Love, Sex and Relationships

Hares get hurt easily, often in love, so they can be very wary of becoming involved. Considerate, gentle lovers, with a true sense of kindness and romance, they will listen to a lover's problems and needs and do what they can to meet them. Hares are traditional and reserved in their sexual habits and are easily frightened by too much tension or intrigue. They prefer a romantic candlelit supper with their true love to an affair or a one-night stand. They are very moral and can be prudish.

Business, Friends and Children

Because of their sensitive nature and inherent good taste, hares will thrive in any business where they can use their flair for style. They suffer in routine jobs and need to work for themselves. They have many friends, but are likely to feel let down by all of them because no one can meet the high standards that hares set. As parents, hares are wonderfully calm and kind. They are not very good with rowdy or badly behaved children, though, and can be very strict. They do inspire children to work hard, however, and children will adore them.

The hare parent is very loving, calm and kind.

	Years of the Hare	Characteristics	Careers
	1903 • 1915	Intuitive	Accountant
		•	•
	1927 • 1939	Sensitive	Pharmacist
		•	•
	1951 • 1963	Caring	Historian
		•	•
	1975 • 1987	Stylish	Art collector
		•	•
	1999 • 2011	Calm	Librarian
Element:		•	•
Wood	2023 • 2035	Creative	Diplomat

Water Hare

Doubly intuitive and doubly sensitive, the water hare can take on too much of others' troubles and get bogged down in suffering. It is prone to irrational fears and can become reclusive and withdrawn. It needs to be livened up occasionally.

Wood Hare

Truly artistic with immense creativity, this hare is good with anything that lets it express emotion – poetry, literature, painting. It is the most adventurous hare, with a flair for exotic travel.

Fire Hare

This passionate hare has a very strong social conscience, works tirelessly for the good of the world and is good in political debates. It is very expressive and people will listen, and quite rightly so for it does know what's what.

Earth Hare

This serious, studious, hard-working, quiet hare gets on with the job in hand and possesses a fine set of moral principles. It makes a good judge or social worker. This is a sensible, pragmatic, realistic and down-to-earth hare who sets achievable targets.

Metal Hare

Ambitious, with courage and perseverance, this least emotional of the hares will rise to lofty heights in any field where its vision and confidence can be put to good use.

The wood hare likes culture, art and travel – an adventurous and exotic hare.

The earth hare is studious and hard-working.

Hare Compatibility Chart

HARE WITH:

RAT	The rat is a control freak while the hare dislikes control of any sort, so this is not a good combination at all.
OX	The hare has a natural optimism that won't suit the ox, who is pessimistic by nature. These two are badly suited.
TIGER	The hare makes a good meal for the tiger unless it learns to move fast to stay out of trouble. Although not a good combination, it can work.
HARE	These two understand each other perfectly which can make the union very good – or very bad. They will both walk away when things go badly.
DRAGON	The hare helps calm the dragon and they work well together as a team, especially as business partners.
SNAKE	With a lot in common, these two have a natural affinity. Not a lot of passion though.
HORSE	The horse is too impulsive and the hare too thoughtful – they will irritate each other. Not a good combination.
GOAT	As long as nothing goes wrong these two are harmonious and beautiful together. At the first sign of trouble they will not support each other, however.
MONKEY	These two characters are so completely alien to each other, a union can't work. They have nothing in common.
ROOSTER	The hare's stand-offishness will infuriate the rooster and the rooster's arrogance will alienate the hare. Not a good combination.
DOG	A nice combination. They understand and respect each other so the partnership works extremely well.
PIG	For some strange reason, these two always seem to get on well. Perhaps it is true that opposites attract – it is in this case.

the dragon

Big, bright and bold, the dragon is life's good luck symbol. Dragons are glorious and mythical, confident and glamorous. They can also be vain and arrogant, but are so wonderful that you cannot help but be impressed. They are also fickle and erratic, they love new things but quickly tire of them. Dragons are usually extremely energetic, full of life and fun. They like to be surrounded by friends and admirers, sycophants and lovers.

DRAGON CHARACTERISTICS

Dragons are bright, showy creatures, always buying new clothes. They have an endless enthusiasm for life, parties and kindness. Although they are generally very friendly and considerate of others, you must be careful never to anger one because you won't like the results – dragons really do breathe fire.

Love, Sex and Relationships

Dragons need more lovers than the world can provide. They get bored so quickly that anyone falling for a dragon had better know it will be short-lived. The only really true companion with any chance of a long-term relationship for a dragon is another dragon. If a dragon does ever fall in love – which may be a rare thing indeed – it will worship the loved one with a deep, possessive, jealous love that is almost suffocating in its intensity. Dragons like sex, a lot, and will wear out any lover, except another dragon, with their demands.

Business, Friends and Children

Dragons perform well in any field where they can be adored and admired – acting is good for them and they also make good fashion designers, impresarios and producers. They are best heading a large corporation rather than working for someone else. Dragons will have many friends. They never think badly of children, but they try to avoid having any of their own – they simply can't stand the mess and noise. Other people's children are fine for a while as they can be handed back to their parents.

The glamorous dragon likes to be the centre of attention.

	Years of the Dragon	Characteristics	Careers
	1904 • 1916	Successful	Managing director
		•	•
	1928 • 1940	Independent	Tycoon
		•	•
	1952 • 1964	Confident	Film star
		•	•
	1976 • 1988	Energetic	Producer
		•	•
	2000 • 2012	Kind	President
		•	•
Element:	2024 • 2036	Ostentatious	Fashion designer
Wood			

Dragons perform well in any field where they can be adored and admired.

Water Dragon

The idealistic water dragon can be very egotistical – it alone has the solution to the world's problems and can't understand why we aren't all listening to it.

Wood Dragon

This beautiful dragon is an exquisite beast that is admired by everyone. A great trend-setter and leader of fashion, it is aloof and sophisticated, cool and stylish.

The dragon loves dressing up and showing off.

Fire Dragon

Bigger and brighter than any other dragon, this one is very entertaining, witty and warm-hearted, but it does possess a temper.

Earth Dragon

The only dragon who can work as part of a team, the earth dragon is more realistic and self-knowing than the other types. It is very conservative and traditional.

Metal Dragon

The theatrical metal dragon, although bombastic and opinionated, is very entertaining and colourful – truly eccentric.

The earth dragon can be an effective teamworker.

Dragon Compatibility Chart

DRAGON WITH:

RAT	A good relationship despite the apparent differences. Each will support the other in their schemes and will be able to give the other the attention they crave.
OX	A powerful combination. The ox can curb the dragon's impetuosity, and if they work as a team they can achieve anything together.
TIGER	Excitement and fun all the way, dramatic and volatile. A super-charged dynamic team who together can move the earth.
HARE	The hare helps calm the dragon and they work well together as a team, especially as business partners.
DRAGON	If they can learn to work together (unlikely) they get on very well. If not they fight (more likely).
SNAKE	A mystic union. They are both reptilian and each understands the other well. A good combination.
HORSE	These two are a lot of fun together although they will fight and argue a lot. A very interesting pairing.
GOAT	Goats are attracted to dragons but get hurt in the process as dragons fail to see them – the indifference is hurtful.
MONKEY	A brilliant combination. These two are both clever, versatile and active. They both like to live by their wits and together they make a formidable partnership.
ROOSTER	A dramatic but good partnership. They both have big personalities but are sufficiently different to make the union interesting.
DOG	Bad news. These two positively dislike each other on sight. The relationship can't and won't work.
PIG	The dragon inspires the pig and the pair bounce off each other. The pig can get roasted, though, so it should keep a little in reserve.

the snake

Snakes are the philosophers and deep thinkers of the Chinese zodiac. They are mysterious, sensual, indulgent and sophisticated. They can be cruel and remote, but if given the right start in life (a sound education and good moral guidance) they are extremely practical. Snakes can see solutions where others might not even see a problem. They have wisdom, exploring the deep mysteries of life, and are clever without ever appearing to work.

SNAKE CHARACTERISTICS

Snakes are perpetually curious about the world and love to investigate anything esoteric and secret. They are incredibly well-organized and will always find quick and efficient ways to get things done – they never seem to have to make very much effort in their accomplishments, but one of their best points is that they always finish the tasks they begin.

Love, Sex and Relationships

Snakes are sensuous and enjoy their relationships. They delight in sex, particularly in all its darker aspects, and can be considered extreme by some. They can be cold lovers, though, because they have an innate aloofness and remoteness that could be considered arrogant. It's not arrogance, however, it's just that they are always busy thinking. Snakes are passionate and very intense. They feel things deeply and analyse everything. They can become too intense and overwhelming. They love to flirt and will often be unfaithful, but it's not because they don't love their partners – they just need to check occasionally that their old magic charm is still working.

The sinuous snake moves with ease and grace. It is languid, stylish and effortlessly clever.

Business, Friends and Children

Snakes do well in any field of research, science and discovery. They make good scientists, philosophers and lecturers. They acquire a large number of friends because they do like to hear confessions and have secrets revealed to them – they are brilliant listeners. As parents, snakes can be rather vague, as they find it hard to concentrate on the trivia of children's needs, but they do inspire children to become educated and thoughtful and they will teach their children to love books. They are generally kind parents, if a little abstracted and remote.

Years of the Snake	Characteristics	Careers
1905 • 1917	Mysterious	Professor
1929 • 1941	Sophisticated	Astrologer
1953 • 1965	Practical	Psychologist
1977 • 1989	Indulgent	Interior designer
2001 • 2013	Wise	Personnel officer
2025 • 2037	Organized	Philosopher

Element:
Fire

Water Snake

This honest snake possesses integrity and a well-developed sense of fairness and honour. The ability to see other people's problems from all points of view makes this snake a wise counsellor or a good arbitrator.

Wood Snake

Imaginative and creative, the wood snake is often a writer with a wonderful sense of beauty and finesse. It may appear lazy, however, and can be self-indulgent.

Fire Snake

A dynamic snake with boundless energy, this snake isn't quite so philosophically minded as the others, and can do well in public life as it has a clearer appreciation of reality.

Earth Snake

A friendly, harmonious snake with a great love of culture and social functions, this is the party snake with charm, wit and sophistication. It is amazingly vague and forgetful.

Metal Snake

This strong, perfectionist snake is serious and hard-working with a quick sharp brain. The metal snake is invariably honest and moral – even to the point of being fanatical.

Wood snakes have a natural sense of beauty and finesse.

Fire snakes are dynamic and can fire people's imaginations.

Snake Compatibility Chart

SNAKE WITH:

RAT	The snake's love of secrets and mysteries will inflame the down-to-earth rat to fits of jealousy and distrust. Not a good combination.
OX	A good long-lasting and stable relationship. The snake understands the ox and will encourage it to lighten up – the ox gives the snake stability.
TIGER	The snake thinks the tiger is over-emotional, while the tiger distrusts the snake's secretive ways. This relationship is bound to end in disaster.
HARE	With a lot in common, these two have a natural affinity. Not a lot of passion though.
DRAGON	A mystic union. They are both reptilian and understand the other well. A good combination.
SNAKE	They get along fine but shouldn't get romantically involved – they're both much too jealous.
HORSE	A good combination. They spark each other off and as long as they both know what the other is doing they get on fine.
GOAT	Only in exceptional circumstances can this combination work. It's much more likely to end in indifference as the two have different agendas.
MONKEY	These two mistrust each other, are jealous of each other, and have no real understanding of the other. Yes, the relationship is doomed to failure.
ROOSTER	Despite their differences these two get along just fine. There is friction but it is manageable.
DOG	The dog trusts the snake, which suits the snake just fine. An unlikely combination but one that works.
PIG	These two never make a good combination and will never be able to see the other's point of view.

the horse

Friendly and communicative, horses are great givers and incurable gossips. They are kind, generous, supportive and well-liked, and appreciate openness and honesty. Horses talk a little too much, however, and they're always so cheerful it can be irritating. They can also be somewhat irresponsible and careless. As long as they're in the limelight, everything is fine, but if they lose your attention they can become sulky and bored.

HORSE CHARACTERISTICS

Horses shy away from anything subversive or dark and prefer plain-speaking to any coded messages – they're not very good at picking up hints. This doesn't mean that they're thick-skinned, just unaware of subtleties: they have little notion of tact or discretion. They can be a bit boisterous and overpowering, but they have hearts of gold and are genuinely nice people.

Love, Sex and Relationships

A happy horse is one that is in love – and horses are usually happy. They do love to be in love. They are big softies, very romantic and charming. They can be impatient as lovers, however, and have a tendency to rush things. Although enthusiastic and exciting lovers, they can become bored easily if the magic and romance begins to wane. They enjoy all the physical aspects of love-making and are energetic lovers.

Business, Friends and Children

Horses and money never go well together. Horses are frivolous and, as they never think of tomorrow, they do not accumulate any savings. Being creative and talented, anything to do with business does not appeal to them. They are social and popular – especially among other horses, and have many friends – good ones. They can be very good with children as long as they are outdoors and where nothing can get broken. Horses are notoriously clumsy and their boisterousness can sometimes frighten timid children.

The horse is eternally cheerful and well-meaning, but not very perceptive of other people's feelings.

Element:
Fire

Years of the Horse	Characteristics	Careers
1906 • 1918	Hard-working	Reporter
1930 • 1942	Friendly	Inventor
1954 • 1966	Generous	Technician
1978 • 1990	Talkative	Comedian
2002 • 2014	Cheerful	Wine expert
2026 • 2038	Boisterous	Racing driver

Water Horse

This truly artistic horse is very communicative and witty, with a tremendous sense of fun. Although very charming, the water horse can be a little insensitive.

Wood Horse

Calmer and more reserved than the water horse, the wood horse is slightly gullible and can get teased a lot. But it is always jolly and rarely gets depressed.

Fire Horse

In Chinese horoscopes this extreme horse is either feared or famed. It either rises to incredible heights or sinks to the lowest depths. The fire horse year occurs only every 60 years and the next isn't until 2026.

Earth Horse

This is a stable and conventional horse with traditional views and a rigid set of morals. Earth horses can be rather pompous but do pay attention to detail and are relatively well-organized.

Metal Horse

Headstrong and easily bored, this horse needs a lot of excitement and passion. It is the Don Juan of horses and needs many admirers and lovers.

The boisterous horse enjoys rough-and-tumble play and gets on well with children.

The water horse is very communicative and often has many friends.

Horse Compatibility Chart

HORSE WITH:

RAT	Neither partner in this noisy combination will be able to get a word in edgeways – but if either can learn to listen, the relationship does have potential.
OX	The ox is thorough and methodical, while the horse is impulsive and rash. These two will irritate each other continually. Not a good combination.
TIGER	A good combination. The tiger will respect the horse's loyalty and the horse will love the tiger's impulsiveness.
HARE	Not a good combination. As the horse is too impulsive and the hare too thoughtful they will irritate each other.
DRAGON	These two are capable of having a lot of fun together although they will inevitably fight and argue a lot. A very interesting pairing.
SNAKE	These two spark each other off and as long as they both know what the other is doing they get on fine. A good combination.
HORSE	Not a very emotional pairing but one that can work extremely well. They both love their freedom and trust one another.
GOAT	These two can learn a lot from one another, and they have the potential to give a lot to each other as well. A good combination.
MONKEY	After the initial cut and thrust for dominance has taken place, this is a very long-term, lasting relationship.
ROOSTER	The horse hates arguing and the rooster loves arguing, so these two can never really get on.
DOG	A brilliant relationship under any circumstances. These two understand each other almost telepathically.
PIG	The horse's popularity will enhance the pig's social standing – which the pig will appreciate. A good combination.

the goat

Of all the animal signs the goat is the one best able to live in the moment. Goats don't fret about the past and they don't worry about the future. They are relaxed, happy-go-lucky creatures who like to enjoy what they have now rather than strive for what might be. Goats are creative and friendly and certainly like to meet people and talk a lot. They are kind, honest and imaginative. Nothing is too much trouble if it helps other people.

GOAT CHARACTERISTICS

Goats can be fiercely independent creatures and they hate being hemmed in or having their freedom curtailed. They need new people, fresh horizons and new experiences and excitements. They like to partake of all that life has to offer – they are perpetually curious and this can lead them into trouble.

Love, Sex and Relationships

Goats have a capacity for making lovers feel very special – as if they are the only and true one. However, the goat will have many lovers and will try very hard never to settle down or be in a permanent relationship, which looks like a trap to them. They are adventurous when it comes to sex and like a lot of variety and experimentation. Goats aren't particularly moral and shouldn't be judged by conventional standards.

Business, Friends and Children

Because of their charm and elegance, people are sometimes jealous of goats, but those who know goats well realize they have a good heart and care a lot about their friends. Goats in business are rare – in fact goats who work hard for long hours are rare. They are not lazy; just not motivated by money. They can be extremely busy and industrious when they want to be, but the project has either to be creative or to benefit humankind in some way. Children adore goats as they will take time and trouble to talk to them without patronizing, and will go out of their way to treat them with the same respect as an adult.

Untroubled by needless worries, goats like to relax and be peaceful. They have a certain elegance and style.

	Years of the Goat	Characteristics	Careers
	1907 • 1919	Adaptable	Television presenter
		•	•
	1931 • 1943	Sexy	Sex counsellor
		•	•
	1955 • 1967	Creative	Musician
		•	•
	1979 • 1991	Friendly	Artist
		•	•
	2003 • 2015	Independent	Garden designer
		•	•
	2027 • 2039	Curious	Actor

Element:
Fire

Water Goat
This conservative goat dislikes change or any other kind of upheaval in its life. It is very sympathetic and has a tendency to take the world's worries on its own shoulders. It is sensitive and emotionally perceptive in its dealings with others.

Wood Goat
A very sensitive, generous goat with great compassion, its impressive talents for inspiring other people would make it an excellent leader of a new religion.

Fire Goat
Courageous and intuitive with a good sense of drama, this goat would make a fine actor. It can be reckless and foolhardy, however, and should never be trusted with large amounts of money – its own or anyone else's.

Earth Goat
This goat likes fine, rare and beautiful objects and enjoys good art. It would make an excellent art critic or collector of antiques.

Metal Goat
Determined and ambitious, the metal goat enjoys a particularly thick skin and is impervious to criticism. This goat will go at anything relentlessly.

The earth goat has a very discriminating eye and likes to be surrounded by unusual and beautiful objects.

Water goats are sensitive and do not like change, so farming is a good career as it keeps them close to nature.

Goat Compatibility Chart
GOAT WITH:

RAT	If the rat is allowed to control and be in charge then this could be a successful union. However, if the goat wants any freedom, the relationship is doomed.
OX	These two won't agree on anything, and the ox will be appalled by the goat's apparent lack of morals.
TIGER	Could be good together in bed, but there is not a lot else going for them. This partnership is not recommended for business.
HARE	As long as nothing goes wrong these two are harmonious and beautiful together. At the first sign of trouble they will not support each other, however.
DRAGON	Goats are attracted to dragons but are likely to get hurt in the process as the egotistical dragons fail to see them – the indifference is hurtful.
SNAKE	Only in exceptional circumstances can this combination work. It's much more likely to end in indifference as the two have different agendas.
HORSE	These two can learn a lot from one another, and they have the potential to give a lot as well. A good combination.
GOAT	One of this pair will need to take control – and that's the problem. Neither is any good at being in charge and together they will go nowhere.
MONKEY	This isn't a bad partnership. The monkey motivates the goat and the goat curbs the monkey's excesses.
ROOSTER	The rooster will never allow the goat time off, while the goat will be irritated by the rooster's flamboyance.
DOG	These two can tolerate each other well but there's little passion between them and little understanding.
PIG	Each of these leads the other astray, which can be fine but is not really conducive to a lasting relationship.

the monkey

Inquisitive, bright, energetic and highly competitive, the monkey is the liveliest of the animal signs – full of new ideas. Monkeys are very good at manipulating other people. They make fine leaders – as long as people realize that where they are being led is entirely at the whim of the monkey – and they always have their own agenda. Monkeys have quick, sharp brains and are usually extremely sharp-witted, though not necessarily wise.

MONKEY CHARACTERISTICS

Monkeys are social creatures who love having lots of people around them. They are also, however, independent characters, and are always optimistic. They like to take risks and will always rise to a challenge – or a dare. The monkey is loud and communicative, full of itself and very entertaining.

Love, Sex and Relationships

Monkeys have voracious appetites, both for relationships and for sex. They enjoy the challenge of new conquests and love the experience of being in love. They seem to achieve their best potential while in a relationship, but their interest, as in all things, will quickly turn to something – or someone – else if their interest isn't kept up – they need fresh excitement continually. Monkeys have no moral code and will stray at any opportunity that arises. They hate conflict in any relationship and will run at the first sign of trouble.

Business, Friends and Children

Monkeys collect large numbers of friends, and small children will follow them to the ends of the earth. Business partners will drop them quite quickly, however, when they attempt to follow any of the monkey's crazier schemes – of which there will be many. Monkeys and money are easily separated. Monkeys change careers often and quickly, as they hate routine. They can shine in any occupation where they can use their wits, be entertaining and not work too hard. The monkey is, by nature, quite indolent.

The monkey is a mercurial trickster, full of ideas and schemes.

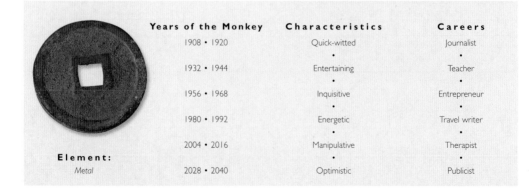

	Years of the Monkey	Characteristics	Careers
	1908 • 1920	Quick-witted	Journalist
	1932 • 1944	Entertaining	Teacher
	1956 • 1968	Inquisitive	Entrepreneur
	1980 • 1992	Energetic	Travel writer
	2004 • 2016	Manipulative	Therapist
Element: *Metal*	2028 • 2040	Optimistic	Publicist

Water Monkey

You won't ever understand this secret monkey, full of hidden agendas and complex mysteries. It is a monkey from another planet. It is affectionate but keeps its distance. It can be a worrier and take slights to heart.

Wood Monkey

A truly resourceful monkey, very talented, artistic and creative, this is the cleverest of all the monkeys. It is the friendliest monkey too, and is very warm and lovable.

Fire Monkey

This passionate lover monkey is very dynamic, charming and ruthless, and needs more lovers than there are available. It is very dangerous, but very attractive.

Earth Monkey

More harmonious than the other monkeys, this is the great communicator. It is extremely witty and very funny, although its humour can verge on the cruel. Its parodies are extremely accurate, if unkind.

Metal Monkey

This monkey loves to take risks. It may well be a gambler and may be the only monkey that can make money. It is very independent, hates to be tied down and will escape any traps laid for it.

The energetic monkey likes plenty of stimulation and adventure, and relishes an element of danger.

The monkey is quick-witted and can use this to its advantage. As it thinks well on its feet, it could do well in buying or selling.

Monkey Compatibility Chart

MONKEY WITH:

RAT	These two characters are similar in personality and will do well together. They are both starters rather than finishers and so will need to make allowances for that to do well together.
OX	The monkey constantly seeks change and the ox hates it. This combination can't work under any circumstances.
TIGER	As neither will compromise, this is not a good combination. Both suffer ego problems and neither will understand the other at all.
HARE	These two are so completely alien to each other, a union can't work. They have nothing in common.
DRAGON	These two are both clever, versatile and active. They both like to live by their wits and together they make a formidable partnership. A brilliant combination.
SNAKE	These two mistrust each other, are jealous of each other, and have no real understanding of the other. Yes, the relationship is doomed to failure.
HORSE	After the initial cut and thrust for dominance has taken place, this is a very long-term, lasting relationship.
GOAT	These two can learn a lot from each other, and they have the potential to give a lot as well. A good combination.
MONKEY	Too much rivalry. Too much competition. This combination could settle into a team but it is unlikely.
ROOSTER	If they share any interest they can get along – but that is not really a basis for a love match.
DOG	If these two have any common interests they get on well but basically they do not make a good combination.
PIG	A good team for indulgence. They both like pleasure and excitement and get on well together. Not a good combination though if there are any serious problems.

the rooster
Roosters like to show off. They are flamboyant, colourful people with outgoing, friendly personalities. They are good communicators and enthusiastic. They do like to be independent although they are fond of their families. They can be very entertaining as they are never still or quiet, but most of their stories will be about their own prowess. Roosters are far more sensitive than you'd ever know, and they can be deeply hurt by criticism.

ROOSTER CHARACTERISTICS
Roosters put great store by education, and will read and learn a lot by themselves. They often know more than you think, although they don't like to appear too clever. They often play the part of the buffoon when they don't need to – it's just another way of getting attention.

Love, Sex and Relationships
Love is a serious business for roosters and when they take a partner they expect it to last – for life. They are not, however, necessarily completely faithful themselves but they do expect their partners to be. They are dramatic and exciting lovers and have endless sexual energy but little imagination. Roosters expect a lot from their partners, and can be quite hard to be with in a relationship, especially as they don't like to give too much away about themselves in return.

Business, Friends and Children
Roosters like to be surrounded by people, but while they certainly have many acquaintances, they don't really ever open up sufficiently for close friendships to develop. Roosters adore children and can give them considerable attention while still working hard themselves – a unique skill. Roosters have an infinite capacity for hard work which makes them very popular with employers. They love a challenge and will often enter an occupation for which they seem unsuited, and will then slog heroically away at it until it is conquered.

Though outgoing and apparently confident, the rooster can be insecure deep down.

	Years of the Rooster	Characteristics	Careers
	1909 • 1921	Protective	Engineer
		•	•
	1933 • 1945	Honest	Beautician
		•	•
	1957 • 1969	Flamboyant	Surgeon
		•	•
	1981 • 1993	Entertaining	Company director
		•	•
	2005 • 2017	Sensitive	Hairdresser
Element:		•	•
Metal	2029 • 2041	Noisy	Public relations

Water Rooster

One of the few roosters that can work in a team, this is a sympathetic, caring rooster who takes on world causes. A kinder, calmer rooster.

Wood Rooster

With masses of enthusiasm, the very extroverted wood rooster can be highly creative but is also prone to live life excessively and may overdo anything it takes on.

Fire Rooster

This dramatic, flamboyant rooster can be very successful if it can curb its aggressive streak. It has a unique ability to be able to see into the future and plan accordingly, which can make it a bit reckless as it thinks it is all-knowing.

Earth Rooster

The earth rooster is a very determined, blunt rooster of few words. It can be disliked for its forthright opinions but it is usually right. It takes its responsibilities seriously and can be ambitious.

Metal Rooster

As it sets very high standards indeed, this rooster won't tolerate fools and expects everyone to live up to its ideals. It is rather inflexible and can suffer as a result. This rooster needs to learn to relax and will find times when it needs to be on its own.

The metal rooster sometimes needs periods of quiet, solitary contemplation.

Roosters can give children a lot of attention but are able to work hard at the same time.

Rooster Compatibility Chart

ROOSTER WITH:

RAT	With two control freaks, this combination just can't work. Neither partner will be interested in the other and both will demand to be in charge.
OX	The rooster sets things in motion and the ox will see them through. A good combination.
TIGER	In spite of the fact that these two will bicker and quarrel, criticize and argue, this match is quite a good one.
HARE	The hare's stand-offishness will infuriate the rooster and the rooster's arrogance will alienate the hare. Not a good combination.
DRAGON	A dramatic but good partnership. They both have big personalities but are sufficiently different to make the union interesting.
SNAKE	Despite their differences these two get along just fine. There is friction but it is manageable.
HORSE	The horse hates arguing and the rooster loves arguing, so these two can never really get on.
GOAT	The rooster will never allow the goat time off, while the goat will be irritated by the rooster's flamboyance.
MONKEY	If they share any interests they can get along but that is not really a basis for a love match.
ROOSTER	This couple will bicker and criticize each other but they can get on well – they can also fight. Overall, not really a good match.
DOG	The dog will eventually get bored waiting for the rooster to calm down, and the rooster will be irritated by the dog's patience. Not a good combination.
PIG	Although different, these two can be friends. They share similar interests and can have an interesting, if passionless, relationship.

the dog

Of all the Chinese animals the dog is the friendliest and kindest. Dogs are here to serve us all and they love being of use. It is no accident that the dog was chosen to represent this group of people, for the dog is a firm, dutiful, noble beast indeed. Dog people are unselfish and moral. They love to be with other people and are extremely honest, trustworthy and tolerant. They are easy to take advantage of, and they can overdo their good aspects.

DOG CHARACTERISTICS

Dogs are eager to please, perhaps too ready to help, too anxious to serve. They can also be a bit unadventurous and can suffer from a kind of victim mentality where everything that goes wrong is endured with fatalism and stoicism. If left to their own devices they can run wild – they need to be supervised and led.

Love, Sex and Relationships

Although dogs are into romance and love in a big way, they enjoy friendly relationships much more. They seek companionship rather than sex and would be quite happy to keep all their affairs platonic. Their need to please, however, makes them good lovers as they go out of their way to be approved of and praised. They are quite faithful but do need a lot of reassurance that they are still loved. They can be very jealous and suspicious lovers, which can lead them to destroy a relationship unintentionally.

Business, Friends and Children

Children would rather be with a dog than any other zodiac sign. Dogs are big kids at heart themselves. They have few really close friends but everyone loves a dog in their own way. Dogs are very outgoing, social people who need constant contact and company. This is probably best seen in their love of children, whom they adore. Dogs are extremely hard workers and can rise to any challenge. They work well in teams and will shoulder responsibility well. They don't particularly like to lead and need to be encouraged by their colleagues, and given specific tasks.

Dogs understand loyalty better than any other animal.

	Years of the Dog	Characteristics	Careers
	1910 • 1922	Loyal	Critic
		•	•
	1934 • 1946	Trustworthy	Lawyer
		•	•
	1958 • 1970	Friendly	Doctor
		•	•
	1982 • 1994	Kind	Priest
		•	•
	2006 • 2018	Unselfish	Professor
Element:		•	•
Metal	2030 • 2042	Fatalistic	Charity worker

Water Dog

The water dog has the happiest, most easy-going character. It likes being outdoors and makes a good farmer or gardener. This is a more relaxed, charming dog, and one who can afford to be slightly more liberal with other people than the other types.

Wood Dog

The creative wood dog is extremely talented and has the ability to put together a most wonderful home environment for itself and its family. It is very intuitive and can empathize with the needs and problems of others.

The relaxed and happy water dog finds satisfaction in creative outdoor pursuits like gardening.

Dogs are keen on romance and the world of love, but enjoy friendly relationships as much, if not more.

Fire Dog

This mad, flamboyant and colourful dog is loved and idealized for its kindness and warmth. It is brilliant with children, as it has infinite patience and resources when dealing with them and with all its friends and acquaintances. In spite of making time for everyone, it still has time to pursue an unusual career.

Earth Dog

Well-balanced and with materialistic ambitions, the earth dog is capable of considerable success in fulfilling them. It is especially well suited to a career in the world of entertainment, as it possesses natural charisma.

Metal Dog

This guard dog can bite. It is never happier than when prowling around, making sure that everything is safe for others. Although it can be very principled, strong and determined, it is still essentially a dog and likes to be liked.

Dog Compatibility Chart

DOG WITH:

RAT	A good team. The rat's control and the dog's loyalty make a good combination. They both like to talk a lot though.
OX	If both partners share the same goals, this can be a good partnership, but in business rather than love.
TIGER	The dog is clever enough to handle the tiger, so these two will do extremely well together.
HARE	A nice combination. They understand and respect each other so the partnership works extremely well.
DRAGON	These two positively dislike each other on sight. The relationship can't and won't work.
SNAKE	The dog trusts the snake, which suits the snake just fine. An unlikely combination but one that works.
HORSE	A brilliant relationship under any circumstances. These two understand each other almost telepathically.
GOAT	They can tolerate each other well but there's little passion between them and little understanding.
MONKEY	If these two have any common interests they get on well but basically they do not make a good combination.
ROOSTER	The dog will eventually get bored waiting for the rooster to calm down, and the rooster will be irritated by the dog's patience. Not a good combination.
DOG	They may love each other forever – or fight on sight. The union is risky but worth it if it works.
PIG	No real conflicts, although the pig's spending habits may baffle the thrifty, honest dog.

the pig
Pigs love pleasure, but what their pleasures are may be hard for other signs to understand. Pigs need to know all about themselves emotionally, which can result in emotional turmoil. But they do have big hearts and care a lot about other people. They are very forgiving and always seek a quiet and peaceful life, even to the point of being withdrawn from the mainstream, preferring instead to stay at home and indulge themselves.

PIG CHARACTERISTICS
Pigs are moral beasts; clean in their habits and avoiding anything dark or dangerous. They expect others to follow their strict virtuous guidelines and are surprised when they don't. Pigs have good common sense and their advice will often be sought and followed. Pigs are natural mediators and diplomats.

Love, Sex and Relationships
Pigs will do anything to keep their partners happy – until they have had enough and then they become boars. A roused pig is dangerous and should be avoided. Pigs are happy in love and need a good partner who will allow them the space and freedom to explore their own emotional needs – they will, however, rarely find this. Because of their own inward turning they will often miss the warning signs of a relationship dwindling due to lack of attention.

Business, Friends and Children
Pigs have many friends as they are popular and keep a good table. They love to cook for friends and their advice will often be asked for. Children find pigs a bit hard to take as they can be very strict and set such high standards. A pig in business is a rare sight indeed. Pigs think it better to let others do all the hard work and keep them well supplied with everything they need. Pigs do expect a lot from others, including being looked after. Pigs need security and will plan for it. They don't take risks and they like comfort and harmony in their lives.

Pigs like to roll around in the mud, and can seem rather self-indulgent in their tendency to withdraw into themselves.

Element: Water

Years of the Pig	Characteristics	Careers
1911 • 1923	Sensual	Chef
1935 • 1947	Eager	Healer
1959 • 1971	Pleasure-seeking	Counsellor
1983 • 1995	Moral	Diplomat
2007 • 2019	Virtuous	Civil servant
2031 • 2043	Self-indulgent	Architect

Water Pig

This self-indulgent pig needs to be got out of bed and made to work hard or it will wallow forever and its love of home may become obsessive, leading to melancholia. In spite of its lazy, good-for-nothing habits, however, this is a charmer.

Wood Pig

Wise and ambitious, this powerful pig can achieve great success, if it is not taken advantage of along the way.

Fire Pig

Brave and adventurous, this pig likes to take risks – although these may initially appear to be small ones, they can eventually lead to dramatic consequences.

Earth Pig

Whatever happens outside, in the big wide world, this prudent, home-loving pig will invariably do whatever is necessary to make sure it is safe and secure inside.

Metal Pig

Witty and entertaining, this party pig doesn't like to stay at home for too long. As long as there are good food and fine wines on your table, you'll not be rid of the metal pig. It is very sociable and friendly – until your cupboard is bare, and then you will find that it will quietly slip away, only to return another day when your stocks are replenished.

Pigs enjoy their home life and like to make it comfortable.

Pigs love entertaining their many friends and are often good cooks.

Pig Compatibility Chart

PIG WITH:

RAT	If the rat can earn it, the pig can spend it. As long as both know where they stand this is a good partnership.
OX	The ox will never tolerate the pig's spending habits, and the pig will consider the ox dull. Not a promising union.
TIGER	These two blame each other when things go wrong and aren't really suited.
HARE	For some strange reason these two always seem to get on well. Perhaps it is true that opposites attract – it is in this case.
DRAGON	The dragon inspires the pig and the pair bounce off each other. The pig can get roasted, though, so it should keep a little in reserve.
SNAKE	These two make a good combination if they ever manage to see the other's point of view.
HORSE	The horse's popularity will enhance the pig's social standing – which the pig will appreciate. A good combination.
GOAT	Each of these leads the other astray, which can be fine but is not really conducive to a lasting relationship.
MONKEY	A good team for indulgence. They both like pleasure and excitement and get on well together. Not a good combination though if there are any serious problems.
ROOSTER	Although different these two can be friends. They share similar interests and can have an interesting, if passionless, relationship.
DOG	No real conflicts, although the pig's spending habits may baffle the poor thrifty dog.
PIG	These two can be friends but nothing more. They both rather like to over-indulge, which isn't an ideal basis for a lasting love affair.

palmistry

The "hands-on" approach used in palmistry makes it one of the kindest and friendliest methods of divination. All the time you are looking into the palm to interpret the lines and markings found there, you are touching and holding someone's hand. This intimate and caring gesture can have a profound effect in lifting any personal barriers to communication; it allows the person to feel comfortable and cared-for, enabling them to open up and express whatever is really on their mind at the time. When you are going to read someone's palm, it is important to look at both the hands to judge the various changes that have occurred between childhood and adult life. The palm-reader reads the major hand (the one used to write with) to find what an individual has made of their life up to the present time, and what is in store for them in the future. The minor hand reveals their past history and family background and shows what talents or assets are inborn.

Choose a setting that is comfortable both for you and the other person. Try to clear your mind, and then look clearly at the hands, always listening to your sixth sense or intuition. You will also find it helpful to have a notebook, a magnifying glass, a ruler, and a pair of compasses. Put them within easy reach so that you do not have to interrupt the reading once it has begun.

Once you have discovered how much information is on the palm, you will look at hands in a different light. Palmistry is a wonderful way to discover more about yourself and others.

general aspects of the hand

Before studying the lines and markings of the palm itself, some general indications of personality can be drawn from various aspects of the whole hand. This information should be collected as a whole to give you a general picture of the person whose palm you are interpreting. More advanced palmists will also take into consideration the undertones of the skin and the texture of the hand itself.

SHAPE OF THE HAND

Ascertain the overall shape of the hand by holding it up with the palm facing you and using an imaginary outline to gauge its shape.

Pointed or "Psychic" Hand

Narrow hand; middle finger peaks higher than others. These individuals tend to have keen intuitive faculties and a sixth sense. Usually very good-looking, they strive for perfection around them and within themselves.

Conical or "Artistic" Hand

This gently rounded shape is so-called because these people are extremely visual, and artistic; they are sensual by nature. They want to see all the beauty in life, and they see life as something to be enjoyed.

Square or "Useful" Hand

This shape belongs to individuals who need to be needed. They have a logical pattern to their thinking, and usually have a good mechanical sense. They are often very busy physically.

Spatulate or "Necessary" Hand

The palm widens out from a narrow base. These people get things done. They will do whatever is necessary to succeed, and are persistent and bright enough to carry it off. These individuals hate to waste time.

A musician is likely to have a palm longer than the fingers, showing creativity and dexterity.

PROPORTIONS OF THE HAND

Differences in length between the palm and the fingers can usually be seen with the naked eye, but if necessary simply measure the difference using a ruler. By holding the ruler lengthwise alongside the whole hand you can assess at a glance the proportions of fingers to palm.

Palm is longer than fingers

This indicates people who have difficulty in saying no to their whims; people of ideas and dreams who can conjure up great schemes but need to watch out for the "Oh, I'll put it off until tomorrow" syndrome. They are creative people, and are likely to be artists or musicians.

Palm is same length as fingers

Very balanced individuals have this balanced hand. They find it relatively easy to cope with the highs and lows in life and are usually stable in character, both mentally and physically. They are determined individuals who have the ability to see things out to the end and have a logical approach to life. They are very fortunate in that they suffer few health problems.

Palm is shorter than fingers

These individuals will always use their gut intuition to guide them through life. They are very imaginative and sensitive. They have a delicate constitution and may suffer health problems.

Conical hand

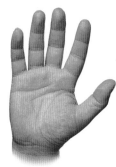

Spatulate hand

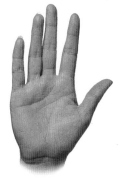

Pointed hand

Square hand

FINGER SHAPES

When assessing the shape of the fingers, examine them with the palm facing you, looking only at the overall shape of the fingertips while ignoring the shape of the fingernails. Many people will have a mixture of finger shapes, so look for the shape which occurs most frequently. At this stage you should also take into account the settings, spacings and patterns on the fingers and thumb, all of which are dealt with later.

Pointed fingertips

Finicky, precise personalities, these people have a good eye for colours, shapes and designs. They are refined, with a highly developed aesthetic sense and good taste, which will be evident in their dress and homes.

Conical fingertips

These individuals carry certain instinctive beliefs about themselves and possess a great inner knowledge of other people's circumstances and concerns. They are generally wise souls with a gentle nature, always willing to lend a hand and help out. They are usually very attractive.

Square fingertips

These people prefer to lead a simple life, with simple pleasures to keep them happy. They are excellent workers, who are always able to make money easily, and so do well in the field of business. They are always scrupulously fair in their approach and in their dealings with others.

Spatulate fingertips

Highly intelligent and witty, these people have a dry sense of humour and are mentally versatile. They enjoy travelling. They are very active and will generally go for a career in which they will work non-stop around the clock. They are adaptable, capable of handling most situations and other people.

Most people are likely to have more than one shape of fingertip on their hand. If this is the case, base your reading on the shape which occurs most frequently. Finger shapes (left to right): pointed, conical, square and spatulate.

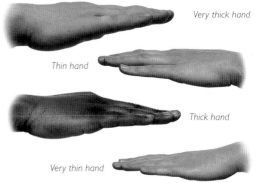

Very thick hand

Thin hand

Thick hand

Very thin hand

HAND THICKNESS

Tilt the hand sideways to judge its depth and suppleness.

Very thick and very hard

These individuals tend to behave in a very rough, tough manner, following their own basic needs and crude thoughts.

Thick and hard

These people have very basic needs: food, shelter and love. Free from ambition, they have no desire to keep up with the rat race.

Thick and medium hard

These people are good workers, always reliable and trustworthy. Life does not come too easily for them, but they usually enjoy it.

Thick and medium soft

These people work hard and play hard; they really want to enjoy themselves with other people. They need to be needed.

Thick and soft

These people are artists, poets or musicians, but are not usually very good workers. They tend to dream and ponder on life.

Thin and very hard

These individuals have strategic skills and can be quite calculating. They may seem cold, but it takes time to get to know them.

Thin and hard

These people tend to be selfish and self-opinionated. They are possessive and stubborn and do not make friends easily.

Thin and soft

These people are always the last to leave a party. They find it difficult to say "no", so they are susceptible to temptations.

Thin and very soft

These individuals have a keen intuition, but tend to focus on the negative, which may lead them to react harshly or snap at others.

the size of the hand

When ascertaining the size of the hand, you should consider it in relation to the person's size and build. Ask yourself if it is in proportion. For example, a small person who has small hands would be considered to have hands of average size. The hands of a tall and broadly built man might be larger, but if they look dainty compared to the rest of his body you should consider them as small.

Very Small Hands

Individuals with hands that are very small in proportion to the rest of their body tend to be free thinkers. They often have a fiercely strong sense of moral politics and will stick firmly to their beliefs and stand up for them. They like to fight for the underdog against dishonesty and injustice. However, this may lead to a tendency not to listen to the other side of a story, so their support can be misguidedly given. If a man has exceptionally small hands, it can indicate that there is a cruel side to his nature.

Small Hands

Individuals who have proportionally small hands are ideas people. They often come up with bright and broad-reaching ideas, but they usually need the support of others to help carry them through to fruition. People with small hands make very good committee members and fundraisers because they possess an ability to gather the support and enthusiasm of others in their endeavours. They are usually very dear and sweet in nature, and would not hurt a fly.

People with large hands are often surprisingly dextrous.

Average Hands

People with average-sized hands are down-to-earth individuals who usually possess good common sense. They have balanced, healthy attitudes and are good-natured. Any mental or physical problems are easily overcome.

Large Hands

People with large hands have a surprising aptitude for doing fiddly things with great patience, and may use this talent to earn their living. They have excellent analytical talents and are mentally strong and good-natured. They can usually be found figuring out detailed projects or pursuing hobbies.

Very Large Hands

These individuals are very bright mentally. They love trivia and mental exercises which sharpen their minds. They can be the mavericks and trendsetters and are unlikely to accept the status quo. They often possess a great strategic ability. They like to be constantly in charge of life, and object to being told what to do.

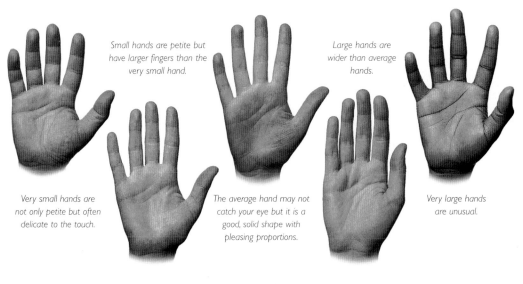

Small hands are petite but have larger fingers than the very small hand.

Large hands are wider than average hands.

Very small hands are not only petite but often delicate to the touch.

The average hand may not catch your eye but it is a good, solid shape with pleasing proportions.

Very large hands are unusual.

elemental hands

There are four basic types of hands, each of which corresponds to one of the four elements: water, air, fire and earth. Assessing this aspect gives an overview of a person's character based on astrological principles. This then complements the detailed interpretation of the palm and fingers made during the reading. The elemental hand often corresponds with the individual's astrological zodiac sign.

Water Hand

The person who has a Water hand has a delicate structure with long fingers and a long palm which features a fine mesh of linear markings. Often, though not always, the water hand belongs to those people born under one of the three water signs: Cancer, Pisces and Scorpio. They possess emotional natures, with very sensitive and sensual personalities. They are often artistic, enigmatic, esoteric and intuitive. The water hand usually accompanies an attractive face with large, intense eyes and soft lips. These people have a love of music, art and culture, and seek relationships: they feel the need to belong to someone or something, in order to be fully content with their lives.

Air Hand

Those people with an Air hand have a robust hand structure with long fingers and a fleshy, though square, palm, with well-defined linear markings. The air hand frequently belongs to those born under one of the three air signs: Libra, Gemini and Aquarius. They are intellectual in their pursuits and possess well-balanced minds. They are literate and not overly sensitive to visual stimuli. They need facts and figures to help guide their decision making, and they look for mental challenges. They are strong-minded individuals with a powerful sense of self. For their relationships to work and not become bogged down or boring, these people need to retain their independence and personal freedom. They need a strong sense of self to be content in life.

Individuals with a Fire Hand tend to be fiery characters who like responsibility as long as it involves action and excitement.

Individuals with an Earth Hand are down-to-earth, reliable characters with a useful ability to detect fakes and swindlers.

Fire Hand

The Fire hand is an energetic hand structure with short fingers and a long palm, and has lively linear markings. Often, though not always, the fire hand belongs to those people born under one of the three fire signs: Aries, Sagittarius and Leo. These individuals have strong instincts, and act on gut feelings. Often they are assertive and quick to rise, but also quick to cool down. They usually prefer action to excuses; they need to be kept busy, otherwise they are easily bored. These people can handle the stresses of a battle but cannot always cope with the more mundane responsibilities of life. They like to be life's leaders and do not enjoy following on behind others.

Earth Hand

The Earth hand is a heavy, thick hand with short fingers and a coarse, square palm; the lines on the palm are few but are deeply incised. The earth hand frequently belongs to people born under one of the three earth signs: Capricorn, Taurus and Virgo. They are well-balanced and logical by nature and make good problem solvers. They have an inherent wisdom. They are sure-footed in their dealings with people and have a useful ability to detect fakes or liars. Once committed to a personal relationship, they are normally very devoted. Earth types need a purpose in life and usually feel a need to be relied upon. They are not afraid of, nor do they mind, good, honest hard work in order to reach their goals.

The Water Hand indicates an artistic, sensitive character with strong emotions.

The Air Hand indicates that the character is strong-minded and well-balanced.

reading the palm

reading the palm

A good palm-reader is one who also brings intuition and common sense to their reading. You are dealing with a whole person, and that includes their feelings. To begin, take a moment before the other person enters the room to clear your mind. Invite the other person in. Focus on your unity with them. Maintain a calm silence until you feel ready to begin. Then explain briefly that the lines and mounts can change, so that everyone has control over their own life. Ask your subject if they are right- or left-handed, and ask their age.

While you are looking at the hands, keep half your attention focused in on your intuition and half of it focused out towards the hands. Ask yourself what the main themes of this person's life are. Scan the hand, noting the relative strength of the mounts and the length and proportions of the fingers. Look for the main lines and any special marks. There are six major lines of the hand. At least three will be found on every hand, but remember that, whether you find only three or all six, the hand must be interpreted as a whole. So, while you are looking at these major lines, you will still be considering the shape and size of the hand, the mounts, other lines, and the fingers. The major lines are normally assessed in their order of importance, which is as follows.

The life line, or "vital line" is read first. It is never absent. Next is the head line or "cerebral line", which deals with the mind. Serious mental illness may be indicated by its absence, although this condition is very rare. The heart line or "mesal line" deals with love and the emotions. The longer the line and the more it reaches towards the Jupiter finger, the longer a relationship is likely to last. Its absence is rare, but it can be a grave

omen. If you do not detect this line, be tactful with your subject and ask a professional reader for advice.

The fate line, or "line of luck", which deals with career and ambition, frequently takes the place of the line of the Sun or Apollo, also known as the "line of fortune and brilliancy". This line deals with luck, talent, and money. The longer it is, the greater the luck. The line of Mercury, or "health line" deals with health issues which may be hereditary. It is often absent, but this is auspicious as it indicates good health.

After looking at, and listening to, everything, take a deep breath and let the information come together naturally in your mind. When you have a general idea of what you're going to say, assess the person and decide on the best way to express yourself. Remember, be kind! Speak clearly, letting your intuition guide you, and ask if they understand you. As long as you touch on the meanings of all the major lines and mounts in the context of the hand, you will do fine. Think carefully and be sure that what you say is exactly what you mean. Open up your intuition and listen to what the palm is telling you.

Ask the person if they have any further questions, and see if the questions can be answered directly from the palm. As long as you make it clear that the hands represent probabilities, not certainties, and that the person's lines can often alter with time, you can answer the questions. If a person asks about death, do not answer the question directly. Above all, take your time and keep yourself open and receptive. Bring the reading slowly to a close. Take time once your client has left to go over the reading in your mind. Was there anything else you could have said?

the life line

The life line is the measure of vitality and life force. It deals with the length and strength of life, family ties and the generalities of life. It is always present in the hand. It starts above the thumb and is then read downwards towards the wrist, where it ends. You may notice one or more thin horizontal lines cutting directly across the life line. These indicate slight obstacles at a given time period.

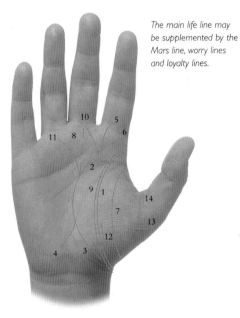

The main life line may be supplemented by the Mars line, worry lines and loyalty lines.

1 Life line close to the thumb
This indicates someone who has a close relationship with their family and is content with family life. They are happy spending time at home, with no great ambition or urge to travel.

2 Life line towards middle of hand
This indicates a person who wants to achieve great things and break new ground. They will have a keen sense of adventure and want to travel.

3 Line ends near thumb side of wrist
When the life line veers around the thumb to end at the side of the wrist, this indicates an individual who yearns for home and wants to end their years on home ground.

4 Line ends towards other side of wrist
When the end of the life line veers away from the thumb towards the opposite side of the hand, this indicates a person who will emigrate, or move away from their family.

5 Line starts at base of Jupiter
When the life line starts below the index finger, the individual seeks a change of lifestyle for the better. They are strong-willed and very ambitious.

6 Line from side of hand near Jupiter
These people are ambitious and will single-mindedly achieve success. They are proud characters who make good leaders.

7 Line cuts close to thumb
This person lives a restricted life under a strong religious or cultural influence, in prison or in the place where they were born.

8 Breaks in the life line
Breaks signify starts and stops in life resulting from big changes such as marriage, divorce, or the death of a close relative.

9 Double life line
This can mean three things: the person may be a twin; they may have a guardian angel or they may lead a double life, such as being a mother during the day and working in a club at night.

10 Effort line
When the life line veers upwards towards the mount of Saturn, a person is working hard and not taking no for an answer. But this does not necessarily mean success.

11 Success line
If the life line veers upward towards the mount of the Sun, it indicates success and good fortune. It may also be a sign of fame.

12 Mars line
This line, running inside the life line, indicates that the person has a guardian angel or protective spirit looking after them.

13 Worry lines
Horizontal lines in the pad of the thumb indicate stresses and worries. The deeper the lines, the more serious the worries. Many faint lines indicate someone who is prone to anxiety.

14 Loyalty lines
Vertical lines creased in the pad of the thumb indicate loyalty to family and friends.

the head line

This line deals with the mind, indicating weak or strong mentalities, possible career directions, and intuitive and creative faculties. Look first to see whether the line is thin and faint, indicating a person who is highly strung, or thick (wide and deep), which is a sign of someone who is methodical. They seem to lack enthusiasm and drive at times; they are solid and sound but stubborn in nature.

1 Line starts high near Jupiter
A head line that starts on the mount of Jupiter, under the index finger, indicates an ambitious individual who is a self-starter and very focused. They can be very competitive and determined in their efforts to achieve their goals in life.

2 Head and life lines tied
This usually indicates an individual beset by doubt and confusion which leads to a lack of independence. They are very involved with the family. They have little self-confidence and doubt their abilities. This may be due to upbringing or early environment.

The head line deals with an individual's strength of character.

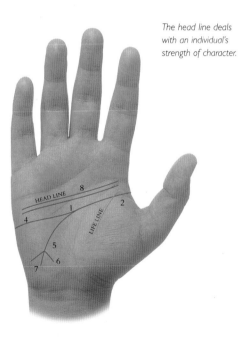

4 Line cuts straight across palm
When the head line touches both sides of the palm, this indicates a self-centred individual who has the ability to stay very focused on their needs and goals. They must have secure material foundations, such as house ownership, insurance policies, and a healthy bank balance. The good news is that they are good citizens and will often give money or time to charity.

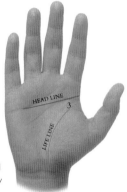

The head line may be positioned separately from the life line.

5 Line dips
A head line that forms an arch, dipping downward into the palm, indicates a very sensitive individual with a highly developed intuition. They are imaginative and perhaps rather eccentric. This may lead them to artistic pursuits or into a profession that involves caring for others.

6 The "writer's fork"
A head line that splits in three directions at the end (like a chicken's foot) indicates an intuitive nature similar to the previous example. People with this characteristic are inclined to communicate cerebral ideas, thoughts and information to others by using their hands. They are likely to be writers, journalists or computer programmers.

7 The "communicator's divide"
When the head line divides into a two-pronged ending, it indicates a person who has great communication skills, and is an able public speaker. They may work in radio or television, as a professional after-dinner speaker or be an actor or singer.

3 Head line separate from life line
When the head line is clearly segregated from the life line, it indicates an individual who possesses great independence and self-will. This is a free thinker who does not follow others but will make their own road in life.

8 The double-headed line
Two head lines lying close together indicate an individual with outstanding mental abilities. The double-headed line is so rare that when it does exist the person is likely to be in a very studious and analytically-driven career, such as an eminent mathematician, scientist or other scholar.

the heart line

This line deals with all matters relating to the heart: love, romantic interests, and relationships with family and friends. It indicates degrees of contentment and happiness in life, as well as the nature of a person's relationships: whether they are likely to be steady or stormy, short-term or long-term. The longer the line, the longer a relationship is likely to last. In general, the heart line deals with a person's emotional and romantic life.

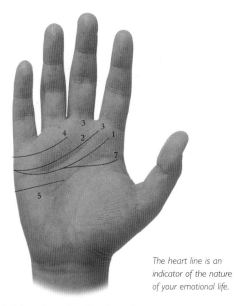

The heart line is an indicator of the nature of your emotional life.

1 Line low in the hand
The heart line starts below the underside of the knuckles in the palm. These individuals are lovers; feminine and romantic, they believe in love and are looking for "fairy-tale" perfection. In matters of the heart they can become perfectionists and expect too much from their partners. This high expectation can lead to them feeling let down.

2 Line high in the hand
The heart line starts on or above the underside of the knuckles in the palm, and appears to rest near the base of the fingers. These individuals are extremely sensitive to what others think of them. As a result they can become quite destructive with their self-criticism. They tend to be very reserved with their emotions.

3 Line veers to middle or index finger
This heart line indicates a dominant and demanding person, who expresses their emotions bluntly. Someone whose line veers towards Saturn (under the middle finger) will have a very contented family life. They keep family members close to them, both physically and in their heart. Veering towards Jupiter (under the

index finger) the heart line indicates a person who is very successful in love. They will end their years in love, and the love they bestow will be returned.

4 Short, high line
This person's loyalties and morals are expendable: they believe that sex is the answer. If they are feeling unloved or neglected, or if someone pays a lot of attention to them, they can give themselves over too easily.

5 Short, low line
This individual cannot be faithful: they think that sex is a game or a sport. They are very self-indulgent and assume that if they do not talk about their activities then no harm will be done. So, they are quite self-deceptive too.

6 Line touches head and life lines
When the heart line drops down to touch the head and life lines, it indicates a person who wants the best of both worlds: to be happy both at home and at work. They need love but also have a strong sense of independence. At times they can feel divided between family and career. More often they will find a way to juggle both and find a happy medium in their own way.

7 Line runs straight across the palm
A heart line which runs in an almost straight line right across the palm of the hand indicates a humanitarian with a great sense of purpose in life. This type of person will put a great deal of time and effort into working hard for the good of the community. He or she will experience great luck in life due to their selfless nature.

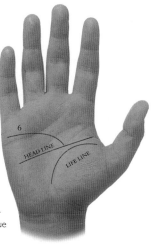

the fate line

This line deals with career, work, ambition, and the direction of a person's life, beginning from their childhood. It also indicates the person's faith in their own abilities. It is read from its starting point at the bottom of the palm, near the wrist, and leads up the palm towards the base of the fingers. It often takes the place of the line of the sun, and ends in varying positions between the index and middle fingers.

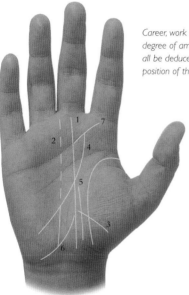

Career, work and degree of ambition can all be deduced by the position of the fate line.

4 Line starts on Lunar mount

When the fate line starts from the side of the palm opposite the thumb, it normally indicates an independent individual who will break away from family traditions. It may also indicate someone who is likely to move overseas to work.

5 Line of milieu

If a separate line runs vertically alongside the fate line for a short distance, it indicates outside pressures or responsibilities. These may be slowing down the individual's way forward, so that they are thwarted in their ambitions.

6 Influence lines

If short lines veer upwards in a feathering motion from the fate line, they indicate positive influences from other people. Feathery lines veering downwards indicate negative influences.

7 Line veers upwards to Jupiter finger

The individual possesses great determination and keen leadership qualities. The will to win is second nature.

Double line

A double fate line means one individual with two careers. They may be running two companies, or have one job in the daytime and a different one in the evening.

1 Fate line runs up middle of palm

This vertical line indicates an individual who has had a keen sense of direction and purpose in their life and career from an early age. It could also indicate that they will pass down their trade or business to their family members.

2 Breaks in the fate line

When the fate line is full of breaks it indicates changes in life and career. These people have never really been able to become fully involved, so may be able to achieve only mediocre success.

3 Fate line begins by veering away from, or touching, the life line

Family commitments were important early in the life of this individual. Before they reach middle-age they will have great family responsibilities or will be heavily involved in a family business. They tend not to want to travel and are inclined to stay close to home in later life.

A keen sense of purpose in life is apparent when the fate line is deep and unbroken up the middle of the palm.

lines of the sun and mercury Also known as the

line of Apollo, the Sun line deals with luck, success in life, talents, and money. It is seldom seen below the heart line. The longer the line, the more luck will be found. Two or three lines together also increase a person's chance of luck and good fortune. The Mercury line is also known as the health or liver line as it deals with health issues, including hereditary ones.

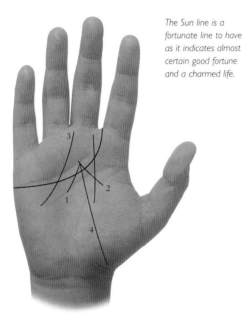

The Sun line is a fortunate line to have as it indicates almost certain good fortune and a charmed life.

MERCURY LINE
The absence of the Mercury line indicates good health.

1 Mercury line cuts across life line
This indicates a weakened constitution. It is a clear sign of hereditary illness such as diabetes, heart disease or arthritis. This individual needs to pay special attention to their health in order to combat the likelihood of this kind of illness. (It must be stressed that this line does not show the possibility of a fatal illness.)

2 Intuition line
A reversed crescent shape indicates a strong sixth sense. It is always present in the hand of the highly intuitive. These are people who have a deep interest in all things esoteric. They are peace-loving and do not like loud noises, big changes or chaos.

3 Mercury line does not touch life line
This is an extremely fortunate line to have in the palm. It indicates very good health and longevity, together with success in business ventures, and good financial fortune.

SUN LINE
This line is also known as the line of fortune and brilliancy.

1 Short line
A short Sun line (less than 1cm/½in) indicates an individual who has so far been unable to achieve their goals and dreams.

2 Line curves towards thumb
This individual works very hard to achieve their goals. No one else does the work for them, and, as a result of this self-reliance, they are quite capable of holding on to their achievements.

3 Line curves away from thumb
This line is a good omen if the individual works in the public eye, as it indicates public prestige, and possibly eventual fame.

4 Long line runs vertically
A long Sun line indicates a gilded life, with good luck falling into one's lap. Life will come very easily and successfully.

The Mercury line is also referred to as the health or liver line. If present, it can indicate good or poor health or an intuitive nature.

markings

As you read along the major lines of the palm – the life, head and heart lines – you are likely to come across various markings created by the many small lines that cross or abut them. These may include distinctive shapes, such as stars and squares, which will help you in your reading. It must be said that these markings do not imply anything grave or fatal, but simply indicate stresses or irritations. Indeed, some are signs of protection or good fortune.

Bars and dots

These signify hindrances preventing the individual from moving forward. It will be hard work to recover momentum, and willpower must be kept up throughout this period.

Cross

This is a sign of a more significant or longer-lasting problem such as divorce or the loss of a job or home. On the life line, one cross may indicate a non-fatal accident in early life. Two crosses indicate an individual who is sensuous and willing to learn. Crosses at the end of the life line indicate poverty or ill health in old age.

Square

This wonderful marking represents protection and good health, and indicates being saved at the last minute. A square containing a cross is a sign of preservation: there will be danger but it will not be harmful. Any square on the life line indicates safety.

Chain

This marking indicates confusion, and comes on to the lines when someone is trying to do too much at once.

Island

An island is a sign that the person's energy temporarily diverges in two directions. The mark shows that the individual has bitten off more than they can chew, but also shows they have the ability to pull it all back together. On the life line, islands indicate serious but treatable illnesses.

The islands on the palm offer a temporary respite from a situation.

Tassel

This mark appears at the end of a line and indicates a scattering of the power of the line.

Fork

A fork in a major line shows increased possibilities of success in life, love or career.

Star

On the life line, this can indicate the gain (birth) or loss (death) of a relative. For each gain there is a loss and vice versa.

Circles

On the life line, a circle could indicate problems with the eyes.

Marks of the three principal lines

Bars (above) and dots (below)

Fork

Cross

Square

Chain

Island

Tassel

Star (left) and circle (right)

lines of special interest

These lines complement the major lines of the palm. They are each unique in their meaning and everyone has at least one, although some people have all of them. They give valuable additional information to the reader about an individual's character, personality and situation, whether it is an indication of courage, psychic ability or a long-lasting romantic commitment.

Line of Mars

Situated on the side of the palm, between the heart and head line, this line indicates great courage. People who have this line make excellent protectors – it is often to be found on courageous military leaders.

Rascettes

These lines, also known as the "Bracelets of Life", are found running across the underside of the wrist just below the palm of the hand, and this is one of the most important areas to check for longevity. The lines can be very faint or very deep, or somewhere in between. Their depth does not matter; it is the number of lines that counts:

1 rascette is equal to 15 to 35 years of life;
2 rascettes are equal to 35 to 55 years of life;
3 rascettes are equal to 55 to 85 years of life;
4 rascettes are equal to 85 to 105 years of life.
5 rascettes are equal to 105 to 135 years of life, though this is very rare except in some parts of the world. The more rascettes a person has on their hand, the longer the life expectancy of that individual.

Girdle of Venus

This can either be one continuous line forming the shape of an upturned crescent moon, or the shape of a saucer; or it can be made up of two lines, one under the other. This marking indicates an individual who can empathize with the deep sorrows of others. Unfortunately, this can lead to them becoming too involved with other people's problems and this can sometimes lead to depression. On a lighter note, these individuals often need to reach for tissues or comforting chocolates when they are watching a sad film on the television and they find this quite enjoyable!

Sympathy Lines

These lines are always straight and are angled upwards. They indicate a caring nature. They can be found on the hands of nurses, doctors and people who feel a strong need to alleviate pain and suffering in others.

Medical Stigmata

This mark, which is found on the hand of a healer, is made up of no fewer than three lines, with a slash cutting through the middle of them. People with these lines have a healing touch or healing hands. They may be doctors, nurses or other professional carers.

Ring of Solomon

A ring around the mount of Jupiter, which starts at the side of the index finger and sweeps around to end between the first and second fingers, indicates wisdom and a deep interest in the occult, the supernatural and other psychic phenomena. On a less psychic level, the ring of Solomon indicates someone who has good leadership skills, is very good at managing people, and will usually achieve success in life.

Ring of Saturn

This semicircular mark beneath the middle finger is rarely found. Whether it is continuous or made up of two or more lines, it seems to isolate and overemphasize the negative Saturnian qualities in a character. Someone with this line will tend to be too serious about life and its problems, and this may lead to depression at times.

Marriage or Union Lines

There may be one line, indicating one serious involvement and commitment, or two or more lines indicating additional emotional involvements. The longer the line horizontally, the longer the relationship in question will last. Nearly everybody's hand bears at least one of these lines, which represent any serious, committed relationships, not just marriage.

LINES OF MARRIAGE

PLAIN OF MARS

This is the area in the centre of the palm of the hand. The plain of Mars shows how sensitive an individual is. In most people, this area will appear concave. If it is slightly raised, or even if it is flat, it is therefore described as "high". Only if it is very markedly indented is it defined as "low".

Average Plain of Mars

When the area is slightly concave, it indicates that the person is balanced emotionally, with good sensibilities and a practical approach to life.

Shallow Plain of Mars

Individuals with this kind of palm can be stubborn, proud and overbearing. They are single-minded and can do one thing at a time very well. Their lack of sensitivity, however, can make them unaware of the problems of other people around them.

Deep Plain of Mars

These individuals will always try to help others, and are highly sensitive to other people's opinions and feelings. They feel other people's pain very personally, and make strong efforts not to upset or offend anyone. If the plain of Mars is too low, it can indicate a tendency towards depression.

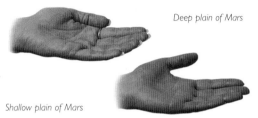

Deep plain of Mars

Shallow plain of Mars

THE PERCUSSIVE OR PALM EDGE

The edge of the palm is a unique area of the hand. It is not a part of the palm itself but rests at the outside edge of the hand. When interpreting this area, you need to take into account that it concerns the aspect of the individual's personality that is projected to the outside world and shows how others may view them. Have the palm facing you when considering this area.

Creative Percussive

This individual tends to be colourful, with a great imagination and creative tendencies; they set their own trends and fashions. They usually have a knack for creating attractive domestic surroundings.

Active Percussive

This person is nearly always busy, with a very active social life. Ever the perfectionist, they search for the best that they can achieve. However, they can have a highly strung nature and be prone to nervousness. These active people are often very physically attractive.

Physical Percussive

This person has excellent physical health with a physique designed for sport and endurance. They are usually involved in physical activities, such as gardening, walking and sport. They need to feel useful and productive.

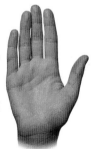

Independent Percussive

This person is independent and follows their own instincts. They will usually be leaders. They have good intuitive faculties.

Intellectual Percussive

This person prefers mental activity to physical labour. They are problem solvers with an analytical nature. They tend to be physically weak and need to take rests between bouts of exertion.

the mounts of the hand

The mounts are the fleshy mounds present in different segments of the palm. Personality types and even physical traits are indicated by the dominant mount, which is found by looking at the palm from various angles and taking note of which mount is raised highest. As the mounts of Venus and the Moon are the widest, you must compare the height rather than the width to establish dominance.

Predominant Mount of Venus

Physically, the Venusian is likely to be of above average height with a round face, large, clear eyes, a small mouth, thick lips, white teeth and small ears. They will have a high instep, with small, neat ankles and long thighs. Venusian men will usually keep their hair until late in life.

They have a strong and healthy constitution, with a generally cheerful disposition. Venusians are happy and sensually inclined people who love life and social interaction. They are the souls of kindness, and hate quarrelling, strife and warfare.

Predominant Mount of the Moon

Individuals with a predominant mount of the Moon tend to be tall, with a round head and broad forehead. They have very fine hair on their heads and hardly any body hair. Large, yellowish teeth, a small mouth with thick, full lips and large, round bulging eyes are all typical characteristics of these individuals.

Lunar subjects are constantly anxious about their health, which does give some cause for concern. They suffer from poor circulation, have bursts of energy followed by a need for rest, and may also experience problems with their kidneys or their bladder.

Temperamentally, moon subjects are very charming and live their life to the full. They are fond of travel and new and exciting experiences, but also enjoy relaxation. They have a fickle nature, and will tend to start a new job before completing the previous one.

When looking at the mounts on the palm, the reader usually works clockwise, beginning with the mount of Venus.

Alma-Tadema's painting, The Years at the Spring, *has a sensual feel and shows a woman with large, clear eyes and a small, full mouth. She is typical of Venusians, who tend to be life's romantics.*

Predominant Mount of Mars

Martians tend to be of above average height with a strong bone structure; their most noticeable physical characteristic is their prominent cheekbones. They have a large mouth and eyes, thin lips, small, yellowish teeth and small ears. Their head may be proportionally small and the nose may be beak-like. Their voice is powerful and generally attracts attention.

The fiery temperament of the Martian may manifest itself physically in feverishness. With this heated character, Martians are at a great risk of accidental injury when they get into an argument. Martians are amorous individuals by nature with a generous personality, and they enjoy social occasions. They can be domineering, and are often unwilling to listen to reason once they have a fixed idea in their head. Though their hot temper may get them into trouble sometimes, they are courageous but without being vicious.

Predominant Mount of Mercury

The Mercurian is small in stature with good bone structure. They stay young-looking longer than others. Their hair is curly and the skin is soft. They have deep-set, penetrating eyes, a long pointed chin and large hands with long thumbs.

Mercurians do not have a very strong constitution. They are susceptible to weakness of the liver and digestive organs. They often have a nervous temperament.

Quick in thought and action, Mercurians are skilful at all games, good students of mathematics and medicine and excellent in business. They are great judges of human character. Usually of an even-tempered nature, they love the closeness of family life. Their acuity and enjoyment of others makes them natural observers and born actors.

Predominant Mount of the Sun

Those individuals with a predominant mount of the Sun, also known as the mount of Apollo, are usually above average height and have a shapely figure. They tend to be muscular and fit, and are seldom stocky. Their hair is soft and wavy, their mouth is of an average size, and one of their best features is their beautiful, large, almond-shaped eyes.

Apollonians, or solar subjects, have good general health. Their eyes are their weak point. Their below-average eyesight may make them prone to injury stemming from silly accidents like tripping over the carpet.

Solar subjects have versatile minds, with clear, logical thought processes and understanding. They love everything that is beautiful in art and nature but are also, in contrast, very competitive and assertive, always wanting to be ahead of the pack. They make ardent and trustworthy friends, but you should beware of falling out with a solar subject, as they can be bitter enemies.

Sun types can often be found watching people with great interest. Auguste Renoir's painting, Femme à la Rose, also shows the solar subject's soft hair and large, almond-shaped eyes.

Predominant Mount of Saturn

Saturnians are tall and thin. They have a long face with a pale complexion. Their eyes are deep set and slope downwards so that they take on a sad appearance. They have a wide mouth with thin lips, a prominent lower jaw, and fine teeth. These people are particularly susceptible to problems with their legs and feet. They are not keen on drinking plain water, so dehydration may be a problem.

Saturnians have a certain sadness in their lives. Conservative and suspicious by nature, they dislike taking orders. They are very prudent, born doubters, good problem solvers, and are interested in the occult sciences. They enjoy country life and love solitude. They spend little and save more, but are passionate gamblers. They like dark colours.

Predominant Mount of Jupiter

Jupiterians have a strong bone structure. They are of average height, usually with attractive curves, and they have a stately walk. They tend to have large, deep-set eyes and thick, curly hair. They have a straight nose, a full mouth, long teeth, a dimple at the base of the chin and ears close to the head. Jupiterian men may lose their hair at an early age. Jupiterians have a tendency to suffer with digestive problems and will often be overweight.

Destined for public life, Jupiterians have confidence in themselves and can be selfish. They like eating out, most social functions and spend money too freely. They love peace, believe in law and order and are, to a degree, conservative.

Alma-Tadema's Portrait of Alice Lewis captures a Mercurian's intelligent air. Their quick and enquiring mind and even temper makes them excellent judges of other people's character.

lines and signs on the mounts

Each mount usually features lines and markings such as crosses, squares, or very strong horizontal lines. These signs give the reader a deeper insight into the person's character than can be found by assessing the dominant mount in isolation. When examining the mounts for these lines and signs, use a magnifying glass to give better definition.

The Mounts Combined

Sometimes two mounts are equally raised. This combination gives you an additional insight into the character.

Jupiter and Saturn	Excellent luck ahead.
Jupiter and Sun	Fame and fortune.
Jupiter and Mercury	Love and success in business and science.
Jupiter and upper Mars	Bravery and success as a commander.
Jupiter and Moon	Imagination.
Jupiter and Venus	Pure and respected love towards others.
Jupiter and lower Mars	Cautiousness.
Saturn and Sun	Deep artistic tendencies.
Saturn and Mercury	Love of science and nature.
Saturn and upper Mars	Argumentative temper.
Saturn and Moon	A gift for the occult.
Saturn and Venus	Vanity and pride.
Saturn and lower Mars	A self-critical and reserved nature.
Sun and Mercury	Brilliant talker.
Sun and upper Mars	Leadership instincts.
Sun and Moon	Imaginative.
Sun and Venus	Love of cultural interests.
Sun and lower Mars	Cheerful.
Mercury and upper Mars	Logical and strategic.
Mercury and Moon	Inventive mind.
Mercury and Venus	Prudent in love.
Mercury and lower Mars	Perseverance.
Moon and Venus	Looking for ideal love.
Upper Mars and Venus	Mentality of a soldier.

Venus equals love in many languages, even in palmistry.

MOUNT OF VENUS
Flat, hard mount

This marking indicates an individual who has grown cold to love, due to difficulties in past relationships.

Lines

Two or three lines indicate an individual who suffers with ingratitude in love. They believe that they can always do better, so can be inconstant in relationships.

Strong horizontal lines

This indicates someone who has an overpowering influence on members of the opposite sex.

Mixed lines

This person's disposition will be of a strong and powerfully passionate nature.

Islands

Islands in the lines are a sign of someone who has a tendency to feel guilty in love.

St Andrew's cross

A large cross of this type is a sign that there will only ever be one true love in this person's lifetime. A small cross indicates a very happy and joyous love affair.

Star

A star by the thumb indicates a wonderful, lifelong marriage. However, if it is at the base of the mount it indicates misfortune for the individual due to the opposite sex, such as divorce or a partner's extreme overspending.

Square at base of mount

This person will live a sheltered and protected life.

Triangle

This is the mark of someone who is calculating in love: they may marry for money to get ahead.

Grille

This is a sign of someone with a dreamy and gentle nature.

When we look at the moon, we are captivated by the mysteries of life.

MOUNT OF THE MOON
Long crossed line
A long line with another crossing it shows a tendency to aching bones and rheumatism.

Cross
Indicates a tendency to heart trouble.

Many lines
Indicate a tendency towards insomnia.

Horizontal line
The person will be likely to travel.

A voyage line
An angled, horizontal line which reaches up towards the heart line indicates someone who might suddenly abandon everything to go on a long voyage, or to live in another country for love.

Mixed lines
This, together with a chained heart line, indicates inconsistency in love – the person cannot make up their mind in matters of love.

Cross
This indicates an individual with a superstitious nature. A large cross can indicate someone who has a tendency to brag a lot. On the upper part of the mount, a cross shows a possibility of trouble with the intestines, while in the middle it indicates rheumatism. On the lower part of the mount it can mean trouble with the kidneys or possibly with the bladder.

Square
This mark signifies protection from bad events throughout a person's life. The more squares, the greater the luck.

Triangle
The triangle indicates great inner wisdom and creativity.

Grille
The grille indicates a tendency towards nerve trouble.

MOUNT OF UPPER MARS
One line
Indicates an individual with great courage.

Several lines
A series of lines in this position indicate someone who may have quite a volatile temper; they can get confused by love, so that they are unable to have a contented relationship.

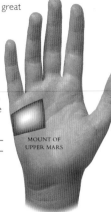

Horizontal lines
One or more lines indicate an individual's susceptibility to bronchial troubles.

Spot
A spot indicates that the individual has been wounded in a fight at some point.

Circle
This indicates that the person has been wounded in, or around, the eye.

Square
This marking indicates an individual who experiences uncannily good protection from bodily harm, even though they may have put themselves at risk.

Triangle
This indicates an individual who is strategically minded, and is especially adept at military operations.

MOUNT OF LOWER MARS
Ill-formed cross
An irregular cross on this mount may indicate that the individual seriously considered suicide in their youth.

Star on line
A star on a horizontal line running across the mount indicates an individual who has experienced a great misfortune, such as the death of a close relation or a good friend, in their youth. In general, any marking on the mount of lower Mars tends not to be as auspicious as one on the mount of upper Mars.

MOUNT OF MERCURY
One line

A single line on the mount of Mercury is generally a good marking to have. Unexpected financial good fortune will come to the person who bears this lucky mark, in the form of a windfall, a lottery win, or an inheritance.

One deep line ───

This marking shows great scientific aptitude: this person is set to carry out valuable research or make an important scientific discovery.

Three or more lines

These multiple lines indicate an individual who has a great interest in medicine and its related schools of study.

Mixed lines

When the lines are above the heart line, the individual is financially very shrewd and good at saving money, to the extent that they may have great difficulty in spending it.

Mixed lines below the heart line

This is the opposite of the example above. A group of mixed lines below the heart line shows that the individual is so generous that they have a tendency to spend too much on others. They should try to curb their desire to spend.

Cross

This person has a tendency to deceive, though this does not always mean that they are doing so in a negative manner. Sometimes you will see this mark on the palms of actors or sales executives, people who sometimes need to present an image which is not their own. However, people who are prone to lying a great deal can also have this marking.

Star

This individual definitely has difficulty telling the truth. More often than not they will be dishonest in their dealings with other people and in their relationships.

Square

The individual with this marking is blessed. They will be saved or preserved from heavy financial losses. This is a wonderful marking to have in your hand.

Triangle

This individual is shrewd in politics and in their dealings with others. They tend to listen to the other side of an argument first and then respond, and they will usually put their point of view with tact and diplomacy.

Mercury

MOUNT OF THE SUN
One line ───

This marking indicates the likelihood of gaining great wealth.

Two lines ───

These lines indicate real talent but without achieving much success.

Many lines

This person has artistic tendencies and may be successful in a creative sphere.

Cross

This marking indicates success.

Star

The star indicates that fame may be nigh but only after the individual has taken many risks to achieve this goal.

Spot

A spot indicates that a person's reputation is in danger.

Circle

This is a very rare mark and indicates great fame.

Square

The square indicates someone with a great commercial mind.

Triangle

This marking indicates a selfless individual who wants to assist in the success of others.

Grille

The grille can indicate that an individual is inclined to vanity.

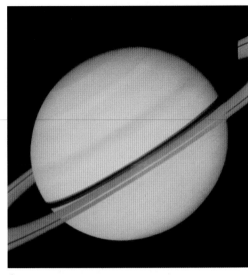

Saturn

MOUNT OF SATURN
One line

A single line signifies that an individual will benefit from very good luck.

One long, deep line

A long, deep line indicates a peaceful ending in old age, perhaps passing away quietly while sleeping at home.

Three or more lines

This marking indicates bad luck. The more lines on the individual's hand, the more bad luck they are likely to face.

Circle

A circle is a good marking to have. It indicates good luck, and protection from most troubles in life.

Square

A square signifies good protection from accidents. For example, this individual could emerge from an accident without a scratch.

Triangle

A triangle indicates an individual who possesses great inner wisdom and strength.

Grille

A grille is a negative marking here. It indicates someone who is likely to lose their luck, especially in old age.

MOUNT OF JUPITER
Two lines

A pair of lines indicates an individual whose ambitions are divided; they are confused over which path to follow. A line on this mount that crosses the heart line indicates that the individual is likely to suffer misfortunes in love.

Cross

The cross is a desirable marking. It indicates a very happy relationship where commitment is usually involved.

Cross and star

A cross with a star is the "soulmate" marking: it shows that the individual has found or will find their partner for life.

Star

The star marking on the mount indicates a satisfying and sudden rise to fame in life.

Square

This indicates an individual who has a natural capacity to lead or command. They may follow a military path or be a teacher.

Triangle

This marking indicates an individual who is extremely clever and diplomatic. It might be found on the palm of a successful business executive, a politician or world leader.

Grille

This marking indicates an individual who tries too hard to please.

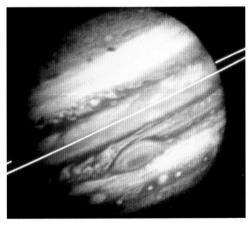

Jupiter

fingers and thumb

The settings, spacings and patterns on the fingers and thumb show the palm-reader the public persona of the individual. This is the personality that they choose to show in the outside world. With the hand raised and the palm facing you, look first at the position and spacing of the fingers. The settings of the thumb have their own meanings, so it is considered separately.

FINGER SETTINGS

The setting of the fingers on the palm varies. They form a distinct shape at the point where they meet the palm.

Fingers arched

These are the fingers of a well-balanced individual, with moderate and tolerant views.

Fingers set straight across; little finger dropped down

When only the little finger is low-set, it is an indication of someone who lacks self-confidence.

Fingers set straight across

This person is very self-confident. with plenty of drive. They can be pushy and feel that whatever they do must be automatically right.

FINGER SPACINGS

The fingers often incline in one of several patterns. It is worth observing this natural spacing of the fingers for an additional character insight.

Fingers held tightly together

This indicates a reserved individual.

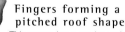

Fingers forming a pitched roof shape

This person has a grudge against other people and an inferiority complex. They lack trust in others and self-confidence in themselves.

Fingers divided in the middle

Those who have this type of hand are resourceful and work quite well by themselves. They are generally loners in life.

Fingers all held apart
These are the fingers of someone who is extrovert, vivacious, and alert to life's opportunities.

First finger set to one side
This is the hand of a person who is intellectually independent.

Fingers form a pacifier
This indicates someone who enjoys security and the company of others. They love domestic peace and harmony.

Little finger set to one side
This person has a need for physical independence and personal freedom.

SETTINGS OF THE THUMB
The thumb is, if you like, the leader of the hand; it covers the fingers tightly when you clench your fist.

The characteristics of the thumb indicate the strength of a person's conviction and their powers of logic. Measure and compare the phalanges (joint settings) of the thumb. The top section relates to willpower and the second section to reasoning and logic. The mount of Venus will usually be equal to the first and second sections measured together.

A thumb that is set low in the hand (close to the base of the wrist) indicates a practical and cautious person. A thumb that is set high in the hand indicates an individual with a passionate approach to life.

Balanced thumb
It is desirable to have a fairly even balance of willpower with reasoning capability. Where one of these areas is lacking, it suggests that the individual will usually be weak in that area: a thumb with a comparatively short first section, for example, would indicate poor willpower. The third section indicates the level of an individual's desire and the tendency to act on it.

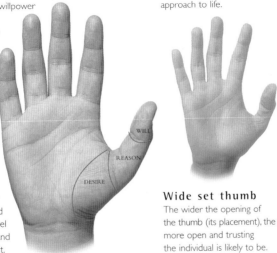

WILL
REASON
DESIRE

Close set thumb
A thumb that is placed close in to the hand indicates an introverted and mistrusting character.

Wide set thumb
The wider the opening of the thumb (its placement), the more open and trusting the individual is likely to be.

fingertip patterns

When looking at the fingertip and thumb-tip patterns, make sure you have good lighting so that you can see the shapes distinctly. Use a magnifying glass if it helps. The patterns will probably not be of the same type on all the fingers. If this is the case, you should interpret the pattern that occurs most frequently. The significance of the shapes may vary, depending on which fingers they are seen.

The Peacock's Eye

This is a rare pattern to find. Its central area looks like the eye of the peacock's tail. If it is on the Sun/Apollo finger it guarantees protection from accidental death. When present on other fingers, it shows that the person is endowed with a high degree of perception or intuition.

The Arch

The arch is not often found. Prominence of this pattern indicates that an individual may have built a bridge to cross the gap between themselves and the rest of the world. They have a need to provide security for their family and the community. Dedication and loyalty are their watchwords. Their chosen path is that of the saint. Physically, they will probably have a predisposition to digestive weaknesses, ulcers and blood disorders.

The Tented Arch

This is the least common pattern, and is usually only found on the index finger, if at all. Four examples on ten fingers would be a high count. It suggests emotional sensitivity which verges on instability. This person is very sensitive to stimuli and needs peaceful surroundings. Artistic and idealistic, they have impulsive tendencies. They are highly strung and predisposed to nervous disorders.

The Composite Loop

These two loops reflect two paths to choose from, and indicate an indecisive individual who will weigh up a problem for hours. The pattern is most often found on the thumb or index finger: indecisiveness will be greater if it is on the thumb. The person has a practical and material mind, but can be inflexible, repressive, critical and resentful. There is a predisposition to malignant conditions and mental troubles.

The Whorl

This pattern can be found on any finger or the thumb, but is most often seen on the Sun/Apollo finger. On the thumb, it indicates stubbornness and dogmatism; someone who will not back down in an argument, even when they have been proved wrong.

When it occurs on the Sun/Apollo finger, the whorl shows a fine sense of discrimination, with fixed likes and dislikes in such things as clothes and food. It indicates a nonconformist who individualizes everything. They are prone to nervous digestive troubles, heart disease and other nervous disorders.

The Loop

This is the most commonly found of all patterns and is also known as the "Lunar loop", because it points in the direction of the Moon side of the hand. On any finger, this marking indicates adaptability and versatility in the face of changing circumstances.

People with this pattern predominating are emotionally responsive and not confined by a narrow viewpoint. They have broad horizons and liberal ideas.

maps of time
Palms can be divided into time maps that are used to give the palm-reader a clearer idea about when events and situations will take place. They are drawn by dividing the major lines into short sections that roughly correspond to periods of years. The periods are often gauged by marking the increments of time directly on to the hand with a pen. If you are a beginner, it is probably safer to mark the increments using a pair of compasses.

Older Map of Time
The older map is used to interpret the ages in the life and head lines. The line is broken down into sections which represent increments of ten years. Starting from a middle point at the heart of the thumb pad, divide the life line as shown in the diagram. Begin the reading at the start of the life line, just above the thumb, and move downwards.

The newer map of time is a less accurate, but quick and easy, guide to the timing of life events.

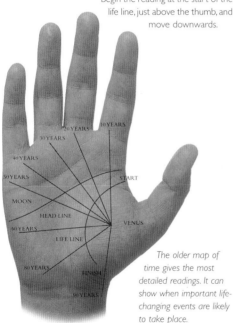

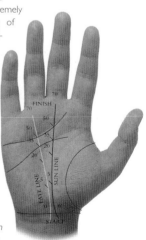

The older map of time gives the most detailed readings. It can show when important life-changing events are likely to take place.

Ageing Map of Time
This guide to ageing is extremely useful in judging the timing of events and occurrences indicated on the fate line, such as changes of job or career, or a spell of good fortune. It works on a similar basis to the other two maps but, here, you take the point at the beginning of the fate line, just above the wrist, and work downwards towards the base of the fingers. The same technique can be applied to the Sun line.

The ageing map of time can pinpoint important changes in an individual's life, such as a change of career or spells of good luck.

Newer Map of Time
This is used to interpret the ages on the life line only. It is a more general, and therefore less precise, way of measuring time on the palm and is often used as a quick reference guide to the timing of events in a life. The life line is broken down roughly into increments of six years. Although more generalized than the older map, this works on the same basis. By reading from the start of the life line, the palm-reader gets a quick idea of the timing of events in the individual's life. If necessary, they can then use the older map of time to look at certain points in depth, giving a more accurate picture of when events are likely to take place.

energylines

inner peace

growth

earth secrets

The spiritual web of life on earth binds together an amalgamation of human beings, animals, plants, rocks and water. All are fundamentally linked by energy. Energy suffuses all things, and each part of creation vibrates at its own particular frequency and has its own natural rhythm which means it harmonises with all other things. By allowing yourself to become more receptive to this spirit that surrounds you, you can tune in to the earth's secret energy, reaching new depths of insight and understanding which will help you to find your own place and path to achieving your true life's goals in the great pattern of creation.

shamanism

Shamanism is essentially a state of mind, a way of viewing life as a whole. The shaman gains insights and wisdom by connecting with other parts of creation and sets out to heal the divisions that exist between its separate pieces. Such divisions can occur any-where: within the self, within groups of people, between human beings and the environment, and so on.

The word "shaman" comes from the Tungusic dialect of the Ural-Altaic tribes of Siberia. Shamans were the priest-doctors of the tribes, responsible for officiating at ceremonies and rituals, advising the elders, tending the sick and injured and caring for the spiritual well-being of the people. More recently, the term has become a more or less generic word, used in reference to anyone who fulfils that role in traditional societies all around the world.

Shamanism does not recognize differences of age, gender, race or religious doctrines and so is available to all. Indeed, many people have had shamanic experiences without labelling them as such. Like everything else on earth, human beings are part of creation, and shamanism is the human way of connecting with the whole. It is a fundamental part of our heritage and, although the connection may be weakened by the pressures of modern life, the ability to connect and the inclination to do so is still present. This introduction to shamanic practice will guide you towards wisdom and insight through the use of rituals, spiritual journeying, and working with dreams.

tradition and spirit
When communities were much more isolated and self-reliant than modern society, shamans played an integral part in their cultures. They treated the sick and injured, but they were not specifically healers. Although they communed with ancestors, spirits and gods, they were not priests, and while they offered counsel to their communities, they were not solely sages. Rather, they fulfilled a combination of these roles.

The Shaman's Role
To understand the function of a shaman, it is necessary to adopt a world view relative to traditional peoples. Typically, older cultures more in touch with the natural world have been animistic societies. Animism is a term derived from the Latin *anima*, which means soul, and these older cultures held the belief that all things possessed a soul or spirit. The fundamental role of the shaman was to act as an intermediary in relating to the other spirits of the earth: the animals, the land, the rain, the crops and so on. Because humans were so dependent on the forces of nature and the other beings of the planet, communicating with them was seen as a way of predicting problems or finding a way out of them. The

Wearing animal skins helped a shaman commune with the spirits.

shaman could send his or her soul out on a journey to meet with these other spirits, and ensure a successful hunt or determine why a crop was failing, or if there would be a drought. These journeys of the soul could also lead shamans to other dimensions where they would commune with gods, find special knowledge or acquire powers.

It was this ability to travel to other realms that marked out the shaman. Often it was unlooked for, with visions occurring spontaneously, or caused by traumatic experiences. What is often now termed "madness" was seen as being "touched by the gods". Shamans usually lived apart from the community, but individuals who could hear voices and experience realities beyond normal perception were regarded with respect. Altered states of consciousness could be induced by a shaman seeking to go on a journey. The drum was a very powerful shamanic tool, seen as a mode of transporting the soul on its regular beat as it opened gateways for the shaman. Dancing was another method employed to achieve a trance state, usually to contact a specific animal spirit. By moving the body in a way that mimicked the animal in question, the shaman became that animal and was able to relate directly to it. Costume was also important in this respect and the use of feathers, skins, bones and significant designs was seen as a way of linking with spirits and journeying to other dimensions.

Sacred plants have long been used as a means of accessing spirit worlds. In Europe, fly agaric, psilocybe mushrooms and doses of hemlock were all used as vehicles by which a shaman could enter an altered state of consciousness. In Mexico, the peyote cactus was, and still is, eaten to bring the shaman into contact with the spirit of the universe. Such plants induce visionary trances and heightened telepathic abilities which allow the shaman to "tune in" to the different levels of creation or travel to otherworlds. Because of the powers of these sacred plants, they need to be approached with respect and ceremony.

Traditional shamans, then, held a position of influence but also one of great responsibility. The people would turn to them first in matters of importance, and the shamans would use their abilities and powers to find a satisfactory outcome.

A North American Blackfoot shaman in ceremonial robes.

Merlin dictates his history to a scribe.

Legendary Shamans

In the European cultures there are many myths of shamans and shamanic adventures. Ceridwen was a great Celtic shaman who brewed a magic potion to confer infinite knowledge on her son, but the kitchen boy drank it and acquired all her wisdom. During a shapeshifting chase to catch him, she became a hen and he a grain of corn. Ceridwen ate the corn and became pregnant with the Celtic bard, Taliesin. In the Arthurian legends, Merlin possessed divinatory powers and could shapeshift, commune with animals and spirits and travel to the otherworlds.

Odin, the chief god of the Scandinavian Pantheon, was another famous shaman. He gave up one of his eyes in return for a drink from the well of Mimir, the source of all wisdom. He also sacrificed himself on the World Tree to learn the wisdom of the dead, bringing back runes from the underworld.

Modern Shamanism

Traditional shamanism still exists in many places in the world, especially where the old cultures remain strong. It is not uncommon for people to seek the assistance of a shaman in the lands of the Arctic, Africa, Australasia, Indonesia, North and South America, Mongolia, China and Tibet. Although in modern Western societies there seems to be little need for a shaman to help with problems about food, the weather or disgruntled gods, there is a place for shamanism on a personal level. Shamanism is a way to find our place in the universe. By embarking upon a shamanic journey to other levels of consciousness, the modern shaman can reach depths of insight that can lead to enlightenment.

Connecting with Spirit

What is spirit? How can it be defined? Spirit is the omnipresent energy possessed by all things. It is the essence of creation, the unifying force that is present throughout the universe. Spirit connects us one with another, but also with animals, plants, rocks, water, air, the stars and the space between the stars. It is the skein of being beyond the physical that can be accessed for communication, for healing and for understanding.

Imagine a spider's web, a beautifully delicate construction designed to catch flies and transmit vibrations. The structure is continuous, so that the whole is affected to some degree wherever an insect is trapped in it. Moreover, the spider can differentiate between the struggling of a trapped fly and the vibration set up by, say, the wind or an airborne seed. The simile of a web is used in many traditional societies to illustrate the principle of connectedness, and the same analogy is used in the modern world – in the World Wide Web, the information superhighway, which permits worldwide communication in virtually no time at all. Just think of the energy incorporated here – energy that is an extension of the universal energy, the spirit of creation.

All of us are aware of energy on an instinctive level. We have all experienced atmospheres; in a room after an argument has occurred so much energy has been emitted that the air is thick with it. On a more subtle level, there is the instinctive feeling that you are liked or disliked by someone. Because humans have closely linked vibrations, the energy is readily sensed by other humans. A shaman can extend this sensitivity to feel the vibrations of other parts of creation.

Energy is apparent all around us.

sacred space

Do you have a place that you find especially conducive to meditation or relaxation? Perhaps a tree in a park or in your garden, a certain rock outcrop or a wood where you often walk. Anywhere that you feel comfortable can be a sacred space, and that can include a place within yourself: sometimes it's not possible to travel physically to a special place to unwind just when you need to, so why not carry it with you?

Sacred Sites

There are many examples of sacred sites around the world that have special significance to particular societies: Stonehenge for the Druids; Mount Olympus for the Greeks; the San Francisco Mountains for the native American Zuni tribe; the Black Hills of South Dakota for the plains tribes; and Uluru (formerly known as Ayers Rock) for the Australian tribes. These sites are usually powerful places associated with the ancestors, gods or spirits of a given culture. Their power has been augmented by the accumulated energy of many generations who have assembled there for sacred rites or meditation, and over time they have become increasingly important to the collective psyche of the society. Sacred space approaches the concept on a more personal level.

Your sacred space is a safe, secure place.

Your Own Sacred Space

The inner sacred space is a place that you can create inside yourself. You can use this special place as a sanctuary, a retreat from the outside world, where you can relax and recoup your spiritual energies. The place you create can resemble anything in the physical world that makes you feel comfortable: a desert island, a hut on a mountain, a cave, anything. Maybe it's a place that you already know; somewhere you have visited before, either in a dream or in this world. The more you visualize your sacred space, the more real it will seem, so try to feel textures, see details, hear sounds and smell scents.

Your sacred space is a safe place and, because it is always there, you can visit it at any time. It can evolve as much as you want it to, because you created it and the control over it lies only with you. The only limitations on it are ones that you, as the maker, impose yourself. So, be aware of what comes into being in your visualization, for that can offer important insights into your subconscious. This private place is a good jumping-off point for beginning journeys.

Experiencing Nature

The natural world is a great place to find peace, tranquillity and inspiration, and to practise visualizing details to put into your own sacred space. Get out and walk in beautiful, wild places as much as possible to experience the benefits that a natural environment can bring. When you are out walking, be receptive and aware of your surroundings: admire the beauty of a tree, a flower or a bird in flight and always be grateful. Remember that life is a precious gift to be appreciated now.

Nature can give us many things to help remind us of our connection. While you are out walking you may find stones, feathers, sticks, intricate patterns and images, but if anything is taken, remember to leave something else in return as an offering, an exchange of energy to signify your appreciation of the gift that has been given to you. Shamanism is about relating to the natural world and your place in it.

Take time to stop, relax and meditate on the incredible complexity of the creation around you. To help your meditation, close your eyes and see how much sharper your other senses become. Extend that receptivity to feel the land, and blend with it. Feel what is around you: the vitality of the earth, the immensity of the world and the universe beyond. You are a part of it, be aware and accept the experience for what it is: humbling and precious.

Visualizing Sacred Space

Before you begin journeying or dreamwork you need to work on visualizing a place in your mind that becomes your own personal sacred space. The sacred space you create will be your place and only people you invite may enter. It can be any kind of place in which your spirit feels happy and at home: a woodland clearing, a cave, a deserted beach, even a corner of your own garden. The more times you visit your sacred space the more real it will seem and the easier it will be to get there. Concentrate on creating and remembering detail; love the place, care for it, plant flowers and trees and tend them as they grow, decorate it as you would your home. Work out rituals for arriving and leaving and, from time to time, imagine making an offering there to help express your gratitude.

Expanding the Visualization

Now picture an opening: a natural doorway such as a hole in the ground or the mouth of a cave. This will lead you to the sacred space you seek. When you pass through, pay attention to details that will make the place seem more real. Utilize all your senses to give the place solidity. This is tricky to achieve at first, but with a little practice it will get easier.

Expand your senses. Touch trees and feel the texture of the bark; sit on a rock and feel its surface – is it smooth or rough? Feel the warmth of the sun as you walk through the place. What is beneath your feet? Grass, sand, a path? Pause to smell the delicate fragrance of a flower, the bloom redolent with its essence of attraction. Look into it and notice how bright the colours are and how the petals and stamens are arranged. Hear the birdsong and the sighing of the wind. Sit down by a stream, taste the

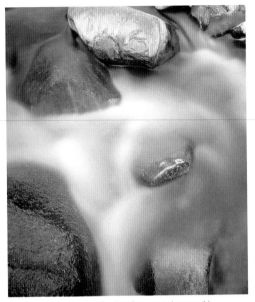

Use all your senses to make the place as real as possible.

refreshing coolness of the water and absorb the beauty and peace around you.

When you feel it is time to leave, give thanks and promise to return. Retrace your steps through the entrance, back into your physical body. Come slowly back to this world.

Entering Sacred Space

Use these simple steps to begin to build and enter your own inner sacred space. As with all shamanic practices, it is good to concentrate on achieving a calm, grounded and open state of mind before you begin. Breathe slowly and deeply from your diaphragm and use your breathing to help you release any worries that are distracting you.

When you feel relaxed, picture your spirit body stepping out of your physical body. Your spirit body is beautiful, glowing, solid and real, connected to your earthly body by a thin filament. Look down at yourself, sitting or lying peacefully, before you start the journey.

Develop a ritual that feels right for you, and repeat the same steps whenever you enter your sacred space at the beginning of future journeys. Practise a similar ritual for returning to this world.

1 Take five deep breaths to centre yourself and focus on what you are about to do. Voice your intent out loud. Light a candle and burn some incense, holding your intention in your mind.

2 Contemplate the candle flame quietly for a while. As you watch it, imagine that it is lighting up the recesses inside you so that you may find a way to the place you seek more easily.

altars

We're all familiar with altars, and the term probably conjures up some richly decorated object that is the focus of attention in a temple or church. A small personal altar, made using a natural object such as a stone or a log, can be placed in your home or garden and will serve the same purpose for you. It needn't be showy, although bright colours have a greater impact on the subconscious, and therefore a greater power.

Natural Altars

You may come across a special place when out walking, such as a tree or a rock, which you can use as a temporary altar on which to leave an offering to celebrate that particular moment in time. Being in a more public place, a natural altar also has the advantage that others might see it too, and add their energy to the place.

Trees make very beautiful natural altars, pleasing to the eye and very calming when attention is focused upon them. Being firmly rooted, a tree has a deep connection with Mother Earth and that energy can be tapped into when you talk to it, leave offerings and pray or meditate there. You can tie things in the branches for decoration, or place tiny items in the trunk. A flat rock placed at the base of the trunk can serve as an altarstone. Be aware of which trees attract you, because they all have their own attributes and symbolism. For example, oak is the keeper of wisdom and possesses great strength; willow represents love and regeneration because it is able to grow a new tree from a cut branch; the very tall and

Natural altars can show appreciation for the moment.

graceful beech symbolizes aspirations to higher ideals; yew, associated with ancient burial sites, represents transformation and inner wisdom.

Rocks are the bones of the Mother, supporting her and therefore us. Because they take millions of years to form, they hold within them a rich store of ancient earth wisdom and knowledge, power and strength. They aid in connecting with the earth because they are so much a part of it, being formed deep within. Call upon this strength when you pray at a rock altar and feel it helping you, supporting you and connecting you.

Indoor Altars

An altar in your home can be made using a flat rock or a piece of wood or a small table. Whatever you use, look after it, keep it clean and give it your attention for a few minutes each day. The altar will help to focus your awareness and strengthen your spiritual connections.

Making a Cairn

The beauty of making something to use as an altar is that the maker's energy is blended with the materials in a focused way. A cairn serves very well as a natural altar. It can look like a haphazard pile of stones but, to make it stable, care must be taken in selecting stones that fit together well. Take your time as you gather the stones and lay them in position.

1 Begin by selecting a few large, flat, roughly circular rocks to act as the base.

2 Build up a tapering dome by laying smaller flat rocks in an overlapping pattern.

3 As you work, keep the intent of honouring creation, to help focus your energy.

4 When the cairn is complete, decorate it with objects found close by.

Stone Circles

There are many examples of these ancient structures, especially in the British Isles and other parts of Northern Europe. The full purposes for their construction are unclear, although they are accurate astronomical calendars in which certain stones align with celestial bodies at significant times of the year, such as the summer and winter solstices. In North America there are large circles, outlined in stone, at a number of sites. These wheels are orientated to the compass and constructed on sacred sites where people still come to pray and leave offerings.

The intent behind ancient stone circles is obscure, but they have a simple, awe-inspiring majesty such as this one at Castlerigg, Cumbria, England.

Blessing the Stones

The east is the place of illumination, the place of conception. It is the direction represented by spring with all its vigorous new growth. Call on this energy as you bless the stone and place it in the east position.

The south is the place of consolidation, the place of the child. It is the direction represented by summer when the burgeoning life progresses into fullness. Call on this energy as you bless the stone and place it in the south position.

The west is the place of fruition, the place of the adult. It is associated with autumn when the growth reaches its ripeness. Call on this energy as you bless the stone and place it in the west position.

The north is the place of calm reflection, the place of the elder. It is represented by winter, the season when the strength is drawn in. When the growth cycle is past, the elder has the wisdom of experience to reflect upon. Call upon this energy as you bless the stone and place it in the north position.

The stone for Mother Earth is to honour her and thank her for the gifts she gives, the food and shelter she provides, the air she breathes into us and the water that supports us. Recognize her and give thanks as you bless the stone and place it in the circle at the 11 o'clock position, near the centre.

The stone for the spirit is to honour and give thanks for all of creation of which we humans are a part. Recognize the bond as you bless the stone and place it in the circle at the one o'clock position, near the centre.

The stone for the self is to acknowledge the individual's part in the whole and to give thanks for all the things that come to you. Honour the connection as you bless the stone and place it in the circle at the six o'clock position, near the centre.

Making a Stone Circle

Create a sacred space to honour the circle of life and your place in it with your own stone circle. Select seven stones, one each for the four directions, one for Mother Earth, one for the spirit and one for the self.

1 Bless and place the direction stones first, beginning with the one in the east. Each of the directions has its own symbolism and energy.

2 Bless each stone before you lay it in place. Put the three remaining stones inside the circle formed by the four direction stones.

3 The completed stone circle can be used as an altar: as a place to pray, and to give thanks and gain insights into the progression of your life-path.

using herbs and incense

When performing shamanic practices, it is good to begin by preparing yourself spiritually and physically to approach the undertaking in an open and honest manner. Purifying is a very positive act which both cleanses the spirit and relaxes the body. In many cultures, herbs or incense are burnt for this purpose, the scent acting at a physical level while the smoke washes negative influences from the spirit.

PURIFYING HERBS

Native Americans use several herbs in purifying ceremonies, notably sage, sweetgrass and cedar, either separately or together.

Sage

The term "sage" is a catch-all for the main herbs used in spiritual cleansing. Many varieties of sage and sage-like plants are used, including White Mountain sage, which grows mainly in California, and the sagebrushes and wormwoods, which also favour dry conditions but are found more widely. Sage has a transformative property, working upon negative energies that are somehow clouding an aura. It changes these negative influences to enable them to act for the benefit of the person, place or object whose aura is being cleansed.

Cedar

A purifying incense, cedar is very beneficial for healing on both physical and spiritual levels. The small, flat leaves can be burned alone on a hot rock – as in a sweatlodge – or on a hot coal, or they can be mixed with loose sage into a ball for burning. The

Burning white sage transforms negative energies.

sharp, sweet smoke produced is very refreshing and calming, having an uplifting effect on the spirit and enhancing clarity of mind.

Sweetgrass

Also called "Hair of the Mother", sweetgrass is a tough, fibrous plant that grows in wetland conditions. It is often used to make braids, and attracts beneficial energies to the user, calling on spirits to give strength and guidance.

INCENSE

Burning a joss-stick is a familiar use of incense: you may be in the habit of lighting one simply for its pleasing effect, but when the burning is performed with conscious intent the effect is magnified.

There are many different incenses to choose, with different aromas and properties. Frankincense has been prized for thousands of years. It is a natural tree resin which is often used as a meditation aid. Piñon is a tree resin from North America with cleansing and clarifying properties. Temple Balls are a blend of gums, herbs and oils including elemi, juniper and sandalwood. They cleanse the air, affect atmospheres and relax the body.

Making Sweetgrass Braids

Bundles of sweetgrass are plaited into long braids, which produce a sweet-smelling smoke when burned. Where sage works upon influences that are already present in a person, sweetgrass has the effect of attracting new energy. Native American shamans use sweetgrass in their sweatlodges, where it is rubbed on the red-hot stones to get it smouldering, to invite spiritual allies to join the ceremony. Sweetgrass braids can be bought from alternative and New Age stores, but making your own braid gives greater significance to its burning. Waft the braid in front of your face to inhale the smoke, and repeat four times.

I Tie up one end of the bundle of sweetgrass, divide into three equal sections and braid.

2 Once the sweetgrass braid is lit, extinguish the flame so that the grass smoulders for a short while.

smudging

When you are smudging, you are cleansing the aura, the energy shell of a physical body. Your aura can become dirty, just like your body. You can wash your body to clean it and you can do the same for your aura. Smudging can be performed on places and objects as well as on people. Visualization, altars and smudging are all ways of creating a sacred space, within and without, and are powerful aids in aligning with universal forces.

Smudge Sticks

Smudge sticks are densely packed bundles of herbs, often including mixtures of white sage, sweetgrass and cedar, which can be obtained from most alternative or New Age stores. When lit, they smoulder slowly and produce clouds of fragrant smoke. This smoke can be used for smudging, or just to scent a room with natural incense. When smudging, the smoke is wafted over the body using a smudge fan, or just a single feather.

Smudging a Place

You can smudge places and objects as well as people. The smoke from smudging will help to cleanse or purify a small area of a room or an entire building, and can also be used on an object, perhaps before using it in a ceremony. When you first move into a new home, smudging can help clear any residual influences of the previous occupants, especially if you can perform it when the place is empty. Whenever or wherever you feel it is appropriate, smudging can be performed.

The principle is the same as that for smudging a person: cover the whole area and try to feel if there are any particular areas that need a little extra attention. You can finish off by drawing a circle in the air with the fan to close the ritual and seal the cleansing.

Smudging can be used to cleanse an area or place.

Smudging a Person

When used to clean a person's aura, the smoke from the smouldering herbs acts like the soap when washing, picking up the negative grime that accumulates. Following the same analogy, the wind from the fan acts like the water, in that it carries away the grime as it blows through the aura and leaves the smudgee feeling refreshed and uplifted.

Light the smudge stick and use a smudge fan or feather to fan it until glowing strongly. While smudging, focus on the cleansing action of the herbs and hold the intent of cleansing the recipient in your mind as you perform the act. Imagine the smoke carrying away the grubbiness as it blows through the aura.

1 Your partner should stand with arms outspread, focusing on the cleansing. Fan the smoke over the body, starting at the head and finishing with the feet.

2 When you feel the ritual is complete, finish it by stroking down the aura with the fan, ending each stroke with a flick to preen the aura and signal the end.

shamanic ritual
We are all creatures of habit, with certain ways of performing routine tasks, but what differentiates habit from ritual is intent. Performing an act with conscious intent increases its efficiency, because the intent carries to other levels of your being. If you take a shower with the intent of cleansing your spirit as well as your body, the overall cleansing effect will be greater. Rituals help strengthen our connection with the universe.

Morning Ritual
Greeting the morning is a great way to start a new day. Work out your own simple ritual involving a few stretches followed by a moment of quiet or meditation to collect yourself for the day. If you can be outside, your morning ritual will have greater significance. The yoga moves called "Salute to the Sun" require little time or space and the movements invigorate the body while the ritual strengthens the spiritual bond you have with creation.

Eating as Ritual
Food preparation and eating are powerfully symbolic activities, and a good time to incorporate ritual. Prepare food with love and appreciation of what is supplied by the bountiful Mother.

Eat natural foods in preference to processed ones, and organically produced food in preference to intensively farmed products. This is not only beneficial to your health but also to your spirit. Fresh, organic foods have more goodness and flavour, and a closer connection with the earth, therefore more of those attributes are entering your body. As you prepare food, endow it with love and appreciation every step of the way, and do the same when you eat it. While eating, the food nourishes the body and the ritual nourishes the spirit.

Greeting the day outside has particular significance.

The Breath of Life
Deep-breathing exercises help to awaken a sleep-fuddled mind and vitalize the body. Scoop up armfuls of energy as you breathe in. As you repeat this sequence, begin to visualize a flow of energy, so that you are both gathering it in and giving it out, returning it to its source. Visualize gathering energy in your arms as they rise up above your head and, as you exhale, picture the energy filtering through your aura as you let your arms sink slowly down with your hands.

The fundamental characteristic of energy is movement, and if it is blocked it becomes stagnant in much the same way that still water does. By giving out you are allowing room for more to come in: the more you give, the more you will receive.

1 Stand relaxed with knees slightly flexed and arms at your sides, hands cupped loosely in front of you. Slowly take three deep breaths to centre yourself.

2 On the fourth breath, circle your arms up, keeping them rounded. Now exhale, and let your arms sink slowly down with your hands in front of you as before.

shamanic offerings

When you make an offering you are exchanging energy, as well as giving thanks. Leave an offering on your altar with gratitude for the day and your life. Tobacco is often used, as it is regarded as sacred by native Americans and is used in their ceremonies. Salt, which is regarded as sacred by Celts, is also used for offerings. It doesn't matter what you leave, as long as it is significant to you, and your intent is clear.

Making an Offering Inside

Your indoor altar may be permanently set up in a corner of your home that you have set aside for this purpose, or it may be a very simple collection of stones, candles and incense that you assemble when you feel it is needed.

Use your altar for offerings at particular times of the day, or leave an offering whenever you feel it is right to do so. A good ritual before you go to bed each night is to give thanks for the day that has passed, and to ask for dreams in the coming night to be clear and that you may remember them. Make an offering on your altar last thing at night, using incense and candles, and voice your request aloud to reinforce the intent with which you perform the ritual.

An offering of tobacco on an indoor altar.

Making an Offering Outside

Natural items can be used for offerings, such as a pretty shell or pebble, a single flower or a few nuts or berries that you have gathered on a country walk.

You can leave an offering on an outdoor altar, such as a log or a flat stone, which may be a temporary altar or a place that you visit regularly. As you make your offering, keep in mind your sense of the connection in spirit between yourself and everything else in creation.

Present your offering to Mother Earth, to the sky and to the four directions before leaving it in your chosen place. Say these words as you place it on your altar: "I offer this in gratitude for the gifts given, in honour of creation and my part in it." Speaking aloud helps to focus your attention and energy.

1 To make an offering, gently hold whatever you wish to give in your hand and present it up to the sky.

2 Lower your hand and present your offering to the earth to show appreciation to the Mother.

A stone left as an impromptu offering on a tree.

3 Hold it out to each of the four directions, north, south, east and west.

4 As you leave the offering in your chosen place, voice your thanks and intention.

shamanic symbols

People have used symbols for millennia, as charms for luck, protection and inspiration. Every symbol has its own energetic vibration, which influences the spirit. In ancient rock art, there are certain symbols that appear repeatedly in many places and from many periods, indicating their universal importance for the human spirit. Among these powerful signs, or sigils, are the spiral and the circle in their various forms.

The Role of Symbols

Rock art has been found all over the world, some as much as 35,000 years old. Before writing was developed, information was passed on orally, but our ancestors used symbolic representations to reinforce aspects of their lives, such as successful hunting or good harvests, using positive visualizations. Certain symbols, such as masks or totems, were boundary markers. Other scenes show human figures with animal characteristics, representative of shapeshifting in shamanic journeys, where a shaman will adopt an animal form for learning, healing or communication.

Symbolism remains powerful today, from graffiti to national flags, from religious icons to currency signs and club insignia: each one is a symbol that conveys a wealth of meaning.

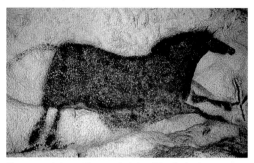

The cave paintings at Lascaux include wild, galloping horses.

The Medicine Wheel

Also known as the sacred hoop, the medicine wheel is used to help meditation. It is a circle bisected by two lines, which symbolize the blue road of spirit (east to west) and the red road of life (south to north). The resulting four sections of the circle represent the seasons. Each cardinal point is associated with particular attributes. The east is the place of inspiration and the inception of a new idea. The south is related to consolidation of the cycle. West is the place where the fruits of an endeavour can be harvested. North is the place to recuperate and reflect.

The circle can help you find the best course of action to take: to decide whether you should be starting something new, or to concentrate on nurturing what you have at present, accepting gains from a situation or drawing your strength in.

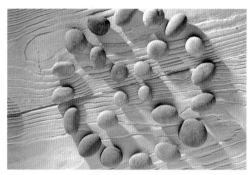

A medicine wheel simply marked out in stones.

Spirals and Circles

The spiral is an evocative image, symbolic of a life path that is moving simultaneously out and around. It relates both to the cyclic nature of existence, and to spiritual and emotional growth through life, apparently repeating experiences, but always moving to new levels. The spiral is also representative of a pathway, usually downwards and inwards, that a shaman may take to reach another realm.

The circle is the line without end. It represents birth, death and rebirth, all intimately linked. The circle symbolizes the cycles which are present in all of creation, the relentless progress of life in all its forms. Circles that incorporate another solid circle inside, speak of the totality of creation, showing that all things are connected and that creation encompasses the individual.

Triple spirals relate to three life stages: maiden, mother and crone.

shamanic tools

The shaman can use a number of natural tools, to assist in connecting with the spirit that weaves through creation. A feather can assist a shaman to fly on a journey; a staff or wand cut from a certain tree can allow insights into the properties of that tree; a stone or crystal can give access to the strength and wisdom of the earth. Other tools are hand-made for specific purposes, and the most universal are the drum and the rattle.

Natural items can be potent shamanic tools.

The Shaman's Drum

The drum carries deep primal undertones that reach into the atavistic recesses of the soul. The heartbeat is the first sound the unborn child hears and the drumbeat evokes the link between mother and child. But it reaches deeper and, representative of the heartbeat of Mother Earth, is full of vibrancy and energy.

The most desirable drum is one you have made yourself by hand, using natural materials, which holds the energy of both the materials and its maker. Make an offering to the drum's spirit before using it for a ceremony, ritual or journey. When journeying, a drum helps to focus the traveller in entering the spirit body. Research indicates that the optimum drumbeat is around 200 beats per minute (bpm), so practise your drumming until this is your automatic rhythm.

Smudge fans can be elaborate or simple.

The Shaman's Rattle

A rattle is a useful tool to signal intent to any spirit you may wish to call upon. Because of this, using a rattle is a good way to open a ceremony or ritual, in addition to voicing your desire aloud. Shamans use it to great effect to coax a damp sweatlodge fire into roaring life by calling on the spirit of the fire. Of course it is also a good complement to any singing and chanting that may occur to you. The rattle can be used for healing purposes, to call in allies to aid with a problem or cure. A very simple rattle can be made by putting dried peas in a jar or tin but, as with the drum, you can buy one, or you may be able to find a workshop where you can learn to make one from hide mounted on a wooden handle and filled with dried beans or pebbles.

In journeying, the drumbeat opens gateways to other worlds.

Smudge Fan

A smudge fan is a very simple tool to make and is very pleasing to use. It can be as elaborate or as simple as you wish, consisting of feathers mounted on a handle or just bundled together and decorated with small beads and bells. Feathers make very good smudge fans and have the advantage of holding within them some of the energy of the birds that gave them. For example, eagles and associated birds of prey symbolize the ability to fly high and see far; owls, with their renowned night vision, represent the ability to see inside or beyond the veil of reality; ravens and crows have a long history of occult links; turkeys symbolize abundance. You can always find feathers while out walking in the country, so pick them up and see if they convey any sense of their properties to you.

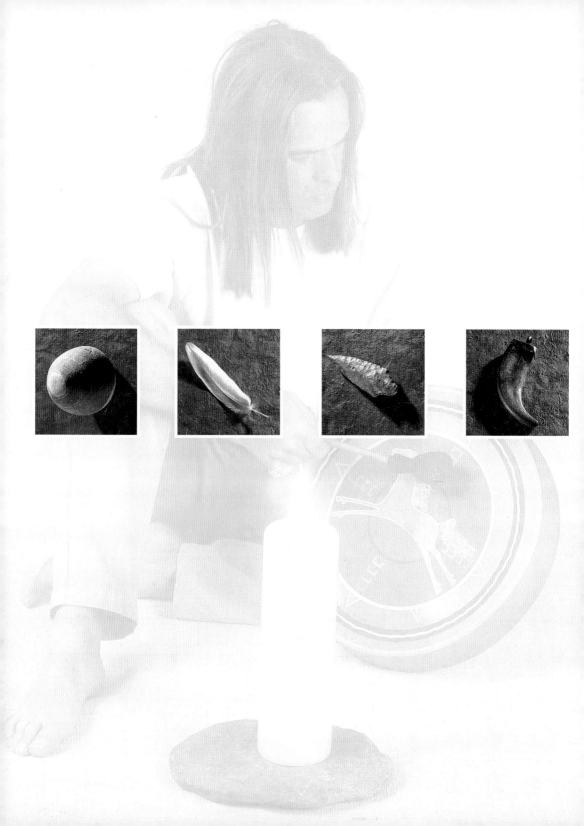

dreamworlds and journeys

dreamworlds and journeys

To enter a dreamworld is to enter a place where anything can happen. It is a magical world of limitless possibilities, where the dreamer will find that they can fly, shapeshift, walk through solid objects or swim in the sun. And, especially while the dream is going on, it is every bit as real as this common reality that we all share from day to day.

A dream is a way for the spirit self to communicate with the physical body, relaying information in allegorical frames that relate to the dreamer's life and experiences. Because the inner dreamworld reflects the outer world of the dreamer, it follows that a change in the outer world will result in a change in the inner dreamworld.

To go a step further, because all worlds are dreams, a change in the inner dreamworld will effect a change in this outer world. This idea that we all dream our own world into existence is not a new one, and if we are the creators of that reality we must, by extension, have the ability to change it by changing the dream. Dreaming is an important human activity and changing a dream is a self-empowering way of altering circumstances, behaviour and responses. A shaman recognizes the validity of those other worlds and also accepts that this world, which we inhabit, is the dreamscape of some other reality. This is how strong, experienced shamans can perform magical or superhuman feats; they can enter other worlds at will and project them to such an extent that they can be experienced by an observer.

We all have the ability to journey to different worlds: indeed, this is what we are doing each night when we dream. These otherworlds are places of limitless possibilities, where information is relayed in a format the journeyer can relate to. But in shamanic journeying, unlike dreams, the journey to a different world is undertaken with conscious intent and with a specific goal in mind, such as healing or to gain new insight. The journey can begin in your own sacred space. When journeying to another realm it is important to be open to whatever may happen and to anything you might meet. Trust your intuition, because what first comes to you is the right thing, whatever it may be. Just go with the flow and don't try to force anything.

working with dreams

To work with a dream with a view to changing or interpreting it, you need to return to it by recalling it while relaxed and conscious. Being relaxed allows your intuition to flow more freely and enables you to use your creativity to a greater degree. It is this interplay of intuitive creativity that allows you to gain insights from dreams and to effect a beneficial change in them, enabling you to move forward.

Dream Interpretation

The information that dreams are trying to convey can be divined by the simple expedient of questioning whoever or whatever is in the dream. If you can practise lucid dreaming, the questions can be posed there and then. If not, ask them in recollection.

To determine whether or not you can dream lucidly, try to perform a voluntary act in the dream. Attempt something simple, such as looking down at your hands or feet. Just work with it and see what can be done. If you wake with the memory of a dream, run through it to help fix it or, even better, write it down immediately. If possible, go back to it there and then, although it can be done at a later date.

When you are back in your dream, politely question the characters and even the places involved. Go with the first answer that comes to mind but don't accept "No". A character may run or try to frighten you but don't be intimidated. Follow them if necessary – they will lead you to an answer.

More often than not, the main characters in a dream are manifestations of aspects of the dreamer. For example, disturbing dreams – perhaps involving death or violence of some kind – are not necessarily portents that some harm is about to befall the

Dreaming is an important activity.

characters involved. Rather, the injured parties represent aspects of the dreamer that are being harmed, perhaps by not being allowed their full expression.

Record your dreams in a journal for future reference and because they can offer valuable insights. Keep a pad by your bed so that you can write dreams down when they are fresh, because they tend to slip away from the wakening mind very easily.

Returning to a Dream

If you want to return to a dream that seemed particularly significant or curious to you, you can use these simple steps to focus your mind on the dream and explore it. In doing this you may well find that you can then release it.

1 Perform a small ritual beforehand: light candles as a symbol of the inner illumination that will help to guide you back into your dream.

2 Make an offering and voice your intent. Why are you returning to the dream? For understanding? To change it? Or to extend it?

3 Sit or lie comfortably and relax yourself with deep diaphragmatic breathing. Start the dream again and focus on what occurs.

changing dreams
The self-empowering ability to change your dreams has effects in this world, according to the shamanic premise that all worlds are in fact dreamscapes. Invariably, the dreams that we want to change are those that cause a response of fear, pain or anger in us, and by taking control over them in the dreamworld they manifest in, we are affirming our strength here, in the physical, conscious world.

Deciding what to Change
There are a number of ways in which you can change dreams. If the dreams are complete they can be altered by changing what occurs in them or by changing how you, the dreamer, react to what goes on. If the dream is incomplete it can be continued with creative intuition.

When changing a dream don't try to force things to happen, just let your intuition flow and allow your creativity to come to the fore. Remember, anything can happen in a dream, so don't restrict yourself to the physical constraints of this world.

Changing what Occurs
Say you have a dream in which you feel powerless, perhaps chasing someone or something which eludes you. A way of changing that type of dream is actually to catch whatever it is that you are pursuing. They may continue to escape when you re-enter the dream, but be persistent and persevere until you reach your goal. This is a self-empowerment technique which returns the control to you. When you can confront whatever eludes you, it may lead to an altogether unexpected insight.

Belinda's Dream *by Henry Fuseli.*

Changing your Response
In a similar way to changing the dream, changing your response is a method of taking control. Fear dreams are often recurrent, and many feature being chased or stalked by some unseen or barely glimpsed presence. This can cause a great deal of anxiety and the dreamer may wake up short of breath and with a pounding heart. A way of taking control in this situation would be to transmute the reaction: instead of being tense and afraid in the dream, be lighthearted and happy. This will help dispel anxiety.

Extending a Dream
Most of us have experienced dreams that end prematurely when we wake, usually with a fearful start. A good way of changing this type of dream is to allow it to continue and see where it goes. Simply recall the dream and, at the point where you woke up, carry it on using your creative intuition.

A typical situation in this type of dream is that the dreamer is falling, which can signify a leap into the unknown. The dream usually ends abruptly just before impact with the ground (thank goodness), but who knows what might happen if the dream was allowed to continue? Perhaps the ground might open up to allow safe passage, or maybe it would turn out to be soft and resilient. A good way to find out is to return to the dream, allow your creative intuition free rein and take that leap.

A Dream of the East *by Jean-Jules Antoine Lecomte.*

journeying

Unique to shamanism, the practice of journeying is a very powerful way to gain insights into problems, to look for healing, to seek allies or just to relax. When you journey, you enter a different world. It is essentially one that you create and guide yourself through, although your conscious self relinquishes control to your spirit. We have already explored the concept of sacred space and this is a good place to start a journey.

Contemplating a Journey

When journeying to another realm, it is important to be open to whatever may happen and to anything you might meet. Trust your intuition, because what first comes to you is the right thing, whatever it may be. Just go with the flow and don't try to force anything. Remember that you have control over what you can accomplish in this otherworld that you have travelled to and don't be inhibited by fear. Be creative in circumventing any problems and challenges that may arise.

The Role of the Drum

A drum is useful in journeying and it is good to have someone drum for you, as a regular rhythm of around 200 beats per minute aids the focus needed for the opening of a gateway. It is good to build up the rhythm gradually to allow the traveller to become acclimatized to the adventure.

At first it is best to journey for a set time of around five minutes. At the end of this period the drummer can initiate the return by changing the rhythm to give a call-back signal – for example, four one-second beats followed by some very rapid drumming. With experience, the drummer will be able to use their intuition to tell when the traveller's journey is complete. If you are drumming for someone else, your power animal might

Make your own drumming tape if you have no one to drum for you.

be able to tell you when to start the call-back. Making a drumming tape to accompany your journeys can also be very useful, as you can record several drumming sessions of various lengths and incorporate your own call-back signal.

Preparing for a Journey

As with physical travel in this world, if you prepare properly for a spiritual journey, things will go much more smoothly and it will be a much more relaxing and fruitful experience. A simple ritual helps to prepare you by centring you and focusing your attention on the journey you are about to undertake.

Gather your tools together and create a comfortable place where you feel relaxed and safe from disturbance. Light a candle for inner illumination and contemplate it quietly for a while.

As you make your offering, call upon the spirit of the drum to assist you on your journey and express your gratitude for the help you are receiving.

1 Smudge yourself, the tools and your surroundings. Make an offering to the spirit of the drum and voice your intent, for example to meet a power animal or find a power object on your journey.

2 Lie comfortably and breathe deeply to relax. Start the tape, and compose yourself as the drumming begins, maintaining deep, regular breaths as your journey commences.

power animals
You can make a journey to meet your own personal spirit ally, which takes the form of an animal. It is an ally that can accompany you on future journeys and give you guidance and wisdom. Animals have always had great significance to native peoples all over the world and throughout history. In any culture, certain animals are thought to embody traits and strengths that are relevant to the history and geography of the culture.

The eagle flies high, symbolizing the striving for higher goals.

The Symbolism of Power Animals
Whole books have been written on the symbolism of animals. This list represents a few of the more common ones. Nowadays, we are familiar with animals from all over the world, and you may meet a power animal that has no general cultural significance, but the important thing is what that spirit represents to you. What strengths does it convey? What does it teach you?

Eagle: can fly high and free without fear and has the gift of far-sightedness. It symbolizes restless male energy, striving for higher goals. Similar totems include the buzzard and condor.
Bear: retreats in winter to hibernate and renew its earth connection. It represents receptive female energy, able to go within to seek answers. A similar totem is the badger.
Wolf: fiercely loyal and true, still maintains its freedom and independence. A similar totem is the hound or dog.
Coyote: related to the wolf, exhibits the trust, innocence and playfulness of the child in all of us.
Bison: evokes the strength and wisdom of the elders, providers for and protectors of the people. Similar totems include the bull, reindeer and orca.
Horse: covers distance with endurance, symbolizing swiftness, freedom and faithfulness. A similar totem is the elk.
Dolphin: represents understanding and awareness, with a gentle, loving energy. Similar totems are the manatee and deer.
Owl: hunts by night. Symbolically it represents the ability to see that which is indistinct and understand hidden truths.

Journey to Meet a Power Animal
Meeting a power animal is a useful journey to start with because the animal can accompany you on future adventures. It is not a deep journey but it does expand your awareness, taking you to the edge of your sacred space, where it borders the realms of other spirits. Once you have prepared for your journey, enter your spirit body, go to your sacred space and orient yourself.

Begin walking. As you do so, a path will become apparent. Follow the path to the boundary of your sacred space. Take your time to acclimatize yourself and observe your surroundings. Wait, because the ally will come to you.

The animal could be anything and it may not be what you were expecting, but when it arrives, greet it warmly, touch it and give it love. Be aware of what it feels like and feel the love it has for you. Remember, the greater the detail, the more real it will seem. If it feels appropriate, transform yourself into the same animal and run, fly or swim. Above all, have some fun.

When you hear the call-back signal, thank the animal for coming and tell it you look forward to future meetings. Retrace your steps and return to the familiar area of your sacred space before leaving it and coming back to awareness of this world.

When you have returned, go over the journey in your mind or write it down to help fix the details. This will aid you in future travels and make it easier to access the next time you visit.

Follow the path to the boundaries of your sacred space.

journeys to otherworlds

Deeper journeys to otherworlds require going beyond your sacred space. The otherworlds that shamans journey to are many and varied and can encompass any number of features, because each is a construct of the shaman who enters it. Essentially, otherworlds are confined to two realms, and when you journey from your sacred space you can travel downwards to the underworld or upwards to the upperworld.

The Underworld

Most shamanic journeys involve going to the underworld, which is not comparable with the hell of Christianity and other faiths, but represents the inner recesses of the traveller. It is a place of challenges and adventure. A shaman enters the underworld to seek solutions and understanding. The challenges you might encounter are all manifestations of your own fears and problems. By confronting them and finding solutions in the underworld you are facing them within yourself and allowing your spirit to communicate the solutions to your conscious self. Because you are journeying within yourself, you are seeking an entrance that will lead downwards and in. Remember, to gain entry, you can transform yourself to any size and shape required.

At first it is an advantage to have some structure to a journey. A good goal is to meet another shaman, who will give you something. It could be knowledge, such as insight into a problem, or it could be an object. Accept it gratefully and give something in return. If the gift is an object take it back to your sacred space and put it away in a safe place.

The Upperworld

Associated with the higher self or the soul, the upperworld is the place to go to for inspiration and communion with other spirits. Whereas a journey to the underworld is about confronting fears that lie within yourself, the upperworld is more concerned with seeking assistance from others, by meeting other spirits on an equal basis, sharing any knowledge you have gained with them and gaining new insights from them.

This realm is very light and tranquil, with a feeling of limitless space that stretches away forever. Because it is related to the higher self, it is reached by going upwards. As with a journey to the underworld, it is good to have some structure to follow to help maintain your focus so that you do not lose your way. Because going upwards relates to the soul, a good focus to have is to connect with your higher self. This is the part of your being that is calm and all-knowing. It is dissociated from the emotions that have such a strong influence on the physical body, and can therefore give you counsel with a dispassionate objectivity that will cut to the heart of a problem.

Entrances to the Underworld

- A cave or crevice in the side of a rockface
- A recess or a knothole in a tree
- A wormhole
- An animal's burrow in a bank
- A well
- A doorway or gate
- A waterfall or stream

Entrances to the Upperworld

- A gap in the sky which can be reached by flying or leaping
- A cave mouth high up a cliff that you need to scale
- A tall tree to climb
- A mountain that pierces a cloud
- A flight of stairs
- A ladder

After passing through the opening, take note of your surroundings.

The upperworld is a peaceful, tranquil place.

journeying for others

Sometimes a shaman may be required to journey on behalf of someone else, for healing or to seek the answer to a question. The principle is always the same: go with a specific aim in mind and be open to what befalls you on the way to your goal. The meaning of the tests and solutions might not be immediately apparent, but ideas will manifest themselves to the conscious mind and answers will come.

On your journey to find another soul, your path may not be clear, but keep following and it will eventually lead you to your goal.

Soul Retrieval Journey

Journeying on behalf of another person is a mutually beneficial undertaking and can form a close bond between the two people involved. Sometimes a person may be too deeply involved in an issue, or too traumatized, to journey with clarity for themselves. Someone else, removed from the immediacy of the situation, is likely to be more successful in the venture, being able to see with a more objective eye.

A journey to find part of a person's soul is a beautiful journey to undertake for someone else. As the name suggests, the purpose is to return a part of the soul or spirit to its rightful place. We are often careless with our soul: as we go through life we may leave a part of it with someone else or even lose a part during difficult times of our lives. These lost pieces of our soul are of no use to anyone else, but the result is that we are left less than complete – weakened in such a way that it can take a long time to recover. By restoring an errant piece of soul to where it belongs, the healing process is facilitated and the recipient becomes more resilient.

Because you are journeying for someone else, it is beneficial to develop an empathy with that person, so an extra step is incorporated into your preparation. Sit quietly for about ten minutes holding hands with the other person and feeling each other's energy, then perform the preparation ritual. Relax by breathing deeply, enter your spirit body and go to your sacred space. Call for, and greet, your power animal, who will be your ally on the journey. You are seeking another's soul so the journey will take you upwards into the upperworld. Begin walking along the path and look for the entrance. Once in the upperworld, locate the main part of the soul and note the missing area. Is it raw like a cut or has it healed like a scar?

Begin your search for the missing piece of the soul. It could have become attached to someone else's soul, or it could be wandering alone. You may find that it seems lost and afraid or it may be comfortable and happy where it is.

Once you have found it, talk to it. Find out what part of the soul it is and why it left or was given away. Tell it that it has a rightful place where it is needed. Be persuasive and do not leave without it. When it agrees to accompany you, guide it back to where it belongs and see it settled back in and comfortable before you leave.

Retrace your steps to your sacred space, say goodbye to your ally and come back to awareness of this world. Relate the events you have experienced in detail to the person you made the journey for and, if they agree, record your experiences in your journal to help you recall them later.

Spend some time before you start your preparation for your journey "tuning-in" to the person you are journeying for.

receiving a power object
While you are making a journey, you may receive a power object, something that is for healing, inspiration or empowerment. This may be the gift of a shaman whom you meet, or your path may lead you to it. The object itself, once found, should be brought back to your sacred space and left there, but the spirit or energy of it is brought back to this common reality and kept with you.

Journey to Find a Power Object

The power object may take any form. It may be a natural object, or something that has been made from natural materials, carrying the energy of the maker within it. Its significance may become apparent only later, after you have returned from your journey.

Of course, when you obtain the power object, you should remember to leave something in exchange, because that strengthens the link. An offering in this case works the other way around: you leave the physical offering in this world, and you take the spirit of it with you into your sacred space when you make a journey. Making this offering can be incorporated into your preparation ritual as an extra step.

To find a power object, perform the now familiar ritual of preparation, then make your offering to signify the grateful receipt of the object you seek, taking the spirit of the offering with you. Sit or lie down comfortably, relax by breathing deeply, enter your spirit body and go to your sacred space. Call for, and greet, your ally. Power objects are found in the underworld, so look for the opening, enter and look around you.

In the underworld, look for a path or let your ally guide you to the object you seek. Do not allow obstacles or opponents to hinder you on your quest. Be adaptable in circumventing problems and keep an open mind. When you find the object, receive it gratefully and leave the spirit offering. Retrace your path back to your sacred space and leave the power object in a safe place. Thank your ally and say goodbye, then return to this world.

When you have received a power object on a journey, be aware of things that may come to you in this world, objects which may be a physical representation of the power object that you left in your sacred space. These things may not look like the article that was given to you, but they will have a similar feel, or energy, about them. They are often gifts from other people, but they could be things you see when you are out walking, or even while you are shopping. The key is to be aware.

A power object can be natural or man-made or a combination of the two. It will have an energy that is derived from the earth, or the animal from which it comes, or from its maker, and you may recognize this energy in objects you encounter in the physical world when you return from your journey. Some examples of power objects are, anticlockwise from top left: smooth, river-washed stone, eagle feather (or other bird's feather), flint arrowhead, deer antler, bear claw pendant.

receiving a symbol

Symbols are potent images, and it probably won't surprise you to learn that, as a shaman, you can discover or create your own symbols for personal empowerment. Returning to the idea that dreamworlds and reality are essentially the same, symbols that appear in dreams and journeys have their own reality and strength. Any symbol that you receive on a journey or in a dream can be represented physically in this world.

Journey to Find a Symbol

In essence, a power animal is a symbol, as is a power object, and just as you journeyed to find an ally or an object, a similar journey can be undertaken to discover a particular symbol to aid you in healing or self-empowerment. Such a symbol could take any form: a word, a picture, a song, a design or even a person. The important thing is that it is significant to you and that it conveys a strength that you can call upon.

After your journey, you can give physical form to the symbol you received. For example, a design or an image can be drawn; a word or phrase can be written down. These images can be displayed around your home so that you can focus your attention on them to gain the benefits they offer. A song can be sung whenever necessary for the same purpose, and a person can be represented by a drawing or even a photograph.

Whatever forms your symbols take, you need to focus your attention on them to get the maximum benefits. It is not enough just to have them lying around. If the symbol is an image, spend time each day concentrating on it; if it is a word, phrase or song, say it aloud or read it, and if it's solid, handle it and note its detail.

Visualizing a Symbol

You don't need to go on a journey to create a symbol but you do need to be in a relaxed state to let your creative intuition flow freely and to contact your higher self. Symbols are a form of positive visualization, so you need to focus on an area of your life where you would like to see some improvement, such as a new job or a different lifestyle.

Once you have the concept in mind, perform a simple ritual to help focus your attention. When you start receiving images or words, write them down or draw them as they come. Don't worry about fine details at this stage, because the main thing you are after is the form, and you can embellish it later. When you have finished, thank your higher self for helping you and see what you have come up with.

There is no limit to the number of symbols that you can acquire or create, although if you have too many you may become a bit confused about what you are trying to achieve. As with a power object, you need to be aware of things that come to you later that may have a similar feel to them, things that may represent your symbol in this world.

Receiving a Symbol

In order to find a symbol to help you in your quest, you must simply follow the steps below. Create a soothing atmosphere and quietly focus your mind on what it is that you wish to achieve and hold this vision in your mind's eye.

1 To begin your preparation ritual, light a candle to represent inner illumination. Relax and make yourself comfortable as you sit and contemplate the candle flame for a while.

2 Smudge yourself with purifying herbs to cleanse and calm you. Also smudge the tools you will be using to give form to your symbol, and the place where you will be sitting.

3 Holding a pad and pencil, close your eyes. Breathe deeply and concentrate on your objective. Ask your higher self to give you a symbol that will help you to achieve your aim.

dream therapy

dream therapy

By their very nature, dreams are ephemeral and transitory, and therefore difficult to remember. If you do remember them it is often in the form of a confused series of images and feelings, but occasionally a dream is so startlingly vivid that it stays with you for hours, sometimes days, afterwards. To dismiss the significance of dreams and the role they play would be to ignore a regular experience that is not only fascinating but can also be insightful and inspiring. There are ways to help you remember your dreams and lead you to a greater understanding of them. This in turn could lead to a greater understanding of the events that affect and influence your waking life.

Dream analysis is not straightforward. The dream language of symbols and images needs to be interpreted. Sometimes the meaning may be obvious, such as a dream about a supervisor at work turning into a monster, but at other times you need to dig deeper, and you may even discover that themes or patterns begin to recur. Sadly, dreams are more often negative than positive (which is why nightmares tend to be more memorable than pleasant dreams), but this is a good reason to try to understand them as they can help you confront and assess unresolved problems.

Dreams are as individual as people. Exploring yours may reveal different aspects of yourself, offer an interesting perspective on life, or fire your imagination and creative potential. It is an unexplored territory waiting to be discovered.

why you sleep and dream

People spend about a third of their lives asleep, and a quarter of that time dreaming. During sleep, the metabolism slows, the immune system concentrates on fighting infection and the production of growth hormone increases, not only for growth but also for repair of body tissue. On a mental level, sleep deprivation leads to poor concentration, memory failure and irritability.

Sleep Patterns

The sleep cycle is broken up into several distinct phases. The first is a period of "slow-wave" sleep, when brain activity, breathing and heart rate all slow down. Slow-wave sleep goes through four stages, the last of which is the deepest, when the brain waves are slowest. This is the time when it is most difficult to rouse someone. After about 90 minutes, Rapid Eye Movement (REM) sleep begins, when the most vivid dreams occur. Phases of REM sleep recur four or five times during the night, between periods of slow-wave sleep. Each REM phase is longer and more intense, from 15 minutes for the first up to 45 minutes for the last, which is often in the final hour of sleep before you wake up.

Our brainwaves can be monitored during sleep.

Why You Dream

Studies have shown that if people are deprived of REM sleep they become irritable and lack concentration. They try to catch up on dreams as soon as they are allowed to sleep again by dreaming more than usual, even if this means having less non-REM sleep. This suggests that dreams are in some way necessary for mental and emotional health. They may be a sign that the brain is "ticking over", continuing to interpret signals from the outside world. They may be a form of wish-fulfilment or a way of expressing and resolving emotional crises. Dreams may also be a way for the brain to sort information it has received during the day, as well as considering ideas and grappling with problems.

During REM sleep the brain is active but the body lies quite still.

When You Dream

It was once thought that dreams occurred only during REM sleep, but research has found that dreams occur throughout the night during periods of non-REM sleep, although they are less vivid and are usually forgotten. In the lighter phases of sleep (stages one and two), dreams resemble the fleeting images and thoughts you may experience if you simply allow your mind to drift while awake. Dreams from deeper sleep (stages three and four) are often fragmentary sensations, feelings and thoughts rather than images. When people are stirred from these deeper stages of slow-wave sleep they are often groggy, confused and unable to remember what they have dreamed. In contrast, dreams during REM sleep have characters and storylines played out in a series of vivid images. You will usually wake from REM sleep fully conscious and with clear memories of your dreams.

The body also responds to different types of dream experience. During slow-wave sleep you may twitch, talk or even sleepwalk, but during REM sleep you are virtually still. Although the brain remains active, muscle tone is lost, resulting in virtual paralysis. This means there is no danger of physically acting out a dream, and also explains the sense of paralysis often experienced during a nightmare.

Why You Forget Your Dreams

Even though everyone has periods of REM sleep, some people claim never to dream. This is simply because they don't remember them. But if dreams are important, why is this?

About a quarter of sleeping time is taken up with dreaming, approximately two hours a night. That is a lot to remember, especially if you recall your dreams only when you wake up during them or immediately afterwards. Most people lead busy lives, and wake up ready to get on with the day. Taking the time to think about what you were dreaming of during the night would seem a luxury.

Dreams are also difficult to remember – frequently chaotic and confusing, they flash incoherently from one image to the next. Memories of them tend to be partial and imprecise, and it is always easier to remember dreams that are dramatic and colourful or those that have some personal significance.

preparing to sleep and dream

A peaceful night's sleep will create an environment in which dreams can flourish. Make going to bed a pleasurable ritual, a time when you can put the day behind you and concentrate on the relaxing night ahead. If you are in the habit of going to bed late, retire earlier. The natural human sleep pattern is to sleep early and wake early, so don't stay up late "pottering" or watching television.

Relaxation Techniques

Think of your bedroom as a restful haven in your home where you can get away from the stresses of the day. Don't put computers or piles of work in the bedroom. Keep colours and lighting soft and warm, and tidy away discarded clothes and other clutter.

A long soak in a warm bath has a soothing effect on the body, and can be further enhanced by adding aromatherapy oils. Essential oils are concentrated, so add no more than 5–10 drops to a full bathtub (no more than two drops for children) and consult your doctor if you are pregnant. Experiment until you find the fragrances that work for you, but three oils are traditionally considered the best for sleep. Lavender helps with insomnia, tension and tiredness; sandalwood is purifying, warming and soothing; and jasmine is a balancing oil which helps to relieve stress. Bathing by candlelight will also make the occasion more relaxing and special.

Massage a few drops of lavender or chamomile oil into the soles of your feet before going to bed, as both of these will act as a sedative. Putting a few drops of lavender oil on your pillow will also help to induce sleep.

Avoid caffeine drinks such as coffee and tea at least an hour before retiring as they will probably keep you awake. Instead, have a bedtime drink such as hot milk with honey, chamomile tea or lemon balm (a good restorative for the nervous system).

Once you are in bed, unwind physically by concentrating on the different parts of your body in turn, from your toes to your head. Think about each part and make sure that it is relaxed before you move on to the next: "I relax my toes, my toes are completely relaxed. I relax my calves, my calves are completely relaxed. I relax my thighs... I relax my hands... I relax my jaw... I relax my face..." and so on. Alternatively, first tense and then release each group of muscles, starting at your toes and moving upwards through your calves, thighs, hands, arms, bottom, stomach, neck and face, giving your mouth, eyes, cheeks and eyebrows separate attention.

Finally, if you do sometimes have trouble dropping off to sleep, try not to worry about the amount of sleep you are getting; your body will eventually make sure that you get all the sleep you need. However, if you have persistent symptoms of insomnia, consult your doctor.

Relaxing essential oils will help you sleep well.

Preparing to Dream

Before switching off the light, tell yourself that you will relax in body and mind, go to sleep quickly and sleep uninterrupted through to the morning. Or simply repeat to yourself, "I will remember my dreams." Say this as an affirmation, a positive and gentle way of telling yourself that you feel in control.

Just as essential oils can help you to relax, certain herbs are thought to be conducive to dreaming. The following herbs can be put in a small sachet and kept under your pillow. Mugwort is said to aid dream recall and also to induce prophetic dreams. Rose has a relaxing smell and, like mugwort, is supposed to bring prophetic dreams – especially those of a romantic nature. Rosemary is useful for warding off nightmares and bringing restful sleep; it is also said to be effective if you want a particular question answered in a dream.

Finally, hang a "dream-catcher" above your bed. Originating from Native American culture, this is a net woven on a round frame which is usually decorated with beads and feathers. The net is thought to catch bad dreams, which evaporate with the first rays of the morning sun, while the good dreams drift down on to the sleeper below.

Gentle preparation for sleep reduces the likelihood of insomnia.

analysing dreams

You cannot begin to understand your dreams until you remember them. One of the most effective ways to achieve this is to keep a dream diary. Over time, you will find that you begin to gain an insight into your dream world, and into some of the events that influence your life. You will also become more familiar with the images of your unconscious mind and will begin to recognize and understand your own symbols.

Keeping a Dream Diary

Buy a notebook specifically for the purpose and keep it, with a pen, by your bed at all times. This means that even if you wake up in the middle of the night, you can scribble down your recollections of your dream, or dreams, immediately. It might also be useful to keep a torch by your bed.

As soon as you wake up and before you start writing, close your eyes for a few seconds and try to recapture some of the images in your dream. Most dreams are a series of images and remembering one could trigger the recollection of a sequence. If you can't recall any images, try to remember how you were feeling as this, too, could trigger a fragment of a dream.

Now start writing. You could use the left-hand page of the notebook to record the dream, and the right-hand page for your subsequent notes and comments. It is essential that you write your dream diary before you do anything else in the morning, so try to make it a habit. The more conscious you are in waking life, the less conscious you will be of your dream world, and any activity, such as having a shower or making a cup of coffee, will break your concentration and dissipate the dream. Try to include as much detail as possible, even the parts which don't seem to be relevant or don't make sense to you. Writing in the present tense will make the dream seem more immediate.

In dreams objects may be transformed, yet still strangely familiar.

Once the bare bones of the dream have been recorded, you can begin to flesh them out. One approach is to look at the dream in categories. For example, you could analyse it under the following headings:

Significance: Is there a direct link between the dream and the day's events? Or does the dream reflect something from your past life?

Theme: Did the dream have a main theme running through it? Were you running away? Is it a recurring dream?

Setting: Where did the dream take place?

People: List the cast of characters.

Feelings: Make a note of any emotions you experienced in the dream. Were you angry, scared or frustrated?

Symbols: Did any objects figure prominently, such as a bird, a tree or a train?

Words or phrases: Did any words or phrases in the dream jump out, or seem to have particular significance?

Other notes: Was a particular colour, time of day or season important in your dream?

Sometimes dreaming of a problem may force you to confront it.

Both flying and falling are very commonly the subject of dreams.

Methods of Analysis

Once you have started your dream diary, you will have the material at hand for analysis. Remember to leave space on the pages for this. The longer you keep a dream diary, the more you will be able to make associations. Do certain objects make a regular appearance? Do you have a certain type of dream in times of stress? Are there any patterns to your dreams?

The first step is to decide whether a dream is worth studying more closely. Is it simply throwing up an event from the day before which is neither interesting or useful? Or does it have some greater resonance, a feeling that stays with you or an event that seems important? You could assess it by looking at some of the categories you have already used in your diary:

Setting: Is the place in your dream somewhere you have been to recently, or in the past? How does it make you feel? Try to think of words to describe it. For example, if you dreamt you were back at school, the words might be "young, teacher, learning, test". If you dream you are being tested, perhaps you feel pressurized when you are awake?

People: Are they people you know? If so, what role do they play in your life? Or are they figures you have not met before? Again, try to think of words to describe them. For example, you may have dreamt of a child, whom you describe as "young, sweet, helpless, crying". Does this say anything about how you are feeling at the moment? Do you long to return to your childhood? Or do you feel vulnerable in your waking life?

Feelings: How did you feel during your dream? How did you feel after it? Have you felt a lot like this recently? For example, have you been angry, frustrated or stressed? Emotions expressed in dreams can give you clues about your emotional state when you are awake.

Exploring Symbols

The best way to try to unravel a dream is to explore and interpret the symbols within it. You will be bombarded by images, so try to select symbolic ones that seem important and leave a lasting impression. Symbols can appear in many forms and guises – not just as objects but as people, colours, numbers, even words. Some of the following techniques may be useful in trying to decipher what your symbols mean to you.

Look up the definition of a word in a dictionary. This will sometimes trigger associations that you have not previously considered. There are also plenty of dream dictionaries to choose from and they will give you some idea of what your symbols mean, or could lead to other ideas. Don't take their meanings as definitive, as symbols can mean different things to different people. Drawing the images that have been prominent in a dream can give you fresh insights, or you could try explaining your dream to someone else: putting a dream into words can bring out different aspects, and the person you are recounting it to may contribute ideas of their own.

Look at myths, folklore or fairy tales. Some symbols, such as snake, witch and dragon, are dominant in stories. Perhaps a symbol you have dreamt of has played a role in a story or myth, which may give you a new insight.

Free association was the method favoured by Sigmund Freud for dream interpretation. Think of the symbol, then allow your mind to wander through any words that come into your head and see where the train of thought takes you. Carl Jung used direct association. He believed that thoughts and associations should always refer directly back to the symbol. Think of a symbol then, holding it in your mind, write down all the associated ideas and images that come to you. You will find that certain themes recur and certain symbols become familiar. In time, you will learn to understand your own dream language.

Describing a dream to someone else may help you to analyse it.

dreamworlds dreamworking

dreamworking

Once you learn how to understand and appreciate your dreams, you can use them to help you look at things in a different way, to further your self-development and, if not to solve a problem, then at least make you confront or assess it. Sadly, much of what you dream about is likely to be negative rather than positive. Dreams are often about conflict, but this is not necessarily a bad thing: a dream can often make you confront a problem that you may be avoiding or refusing to acknowledge.

Although some of the content of your dreams may be familiar in many ways, the context can be entirely unfamiliar, with a muddled story presented in a series of surreal circumstances. Most dreams exist on two levels. The surface level is made up of the people, events, sights and sounds of the dream. This will probably include fragments from the day – a person you have seen or met, or something you have been thinking about. The second, deeper level holds the meaning of the dream. Not all dreams have meaning – they may be just a regurgitation of images and thoughts from the day. But with time, and by keeping a dream diary, you will be able to identify those that could be interesting or useful to look at.

The most indecipherable, and fascinating, aspect of dreams is the language they use to convey meaning. It is in the form of metaphor and symbol which, like a foreign language, need to be translated and interpreted.

There are a number of theories as to why the unconscious mind should want, or need, to convey information to the conscious mind in symbolic form. One is that the message is something you are not ready to hear, so if it is presented in an incomprehensible way you can easily dismiss it. Freud believed that symbols protect you from the underlying message, which is often so disturbing that it would wake you up if it was presented more clearly. Alternatively, the fact that the message is strange may force you to look at it more closely, and having to decipher and decode a dream could make you feel that you were "solving" a puzzle. Another theory is that you can handle information only in a limited way and that symbols and metaphors are actually an economical way in which to present the information.

Many symbols have been given universal meanings. These meanings are useful as a guideline, as long as you remember that the symbols may mean something different to you. For example, drowning is said to symbolize a fear of being engulfed by an unexpressed need, but maybe you have a fear of water. It is often the feeling attached to it, rather than the symbol itself, that is significant.

controlling your dreams

You can remember and interpret your dreams, but can you control them? To a degree, and with time, practice and patience, you can. Dream incubation involves actively generating a desired dream and has been widely practised throughout history. There are various techniques that will help you to dream about a chosen subject, person or place, to generate ideas, make decisions or simply to have fun.

Psychic Suggestion

Consider carefully what it is you hope to achieve from a dream and write down what you would like to learn from it. Before going to bed, immerse yourself in the subject/person/place you wish to dream about. Look at photographs of the person, think about their character, try and remember times you have shared together, or look at photographs or objects from the place. If you have visited it, try to remember the time you spent there. To dream of a relationship, think about the other person, the times you have shared or the direction in which you want the relationship to go, or how you might change or improve it.

Positive Affirmation

Saying a short, upbeat sentence to yourself can help your mind work in a constructive way. It should be in the present tense and the first person; it should include your name and should be easy to remember. You can use positive affirmation to decide the subject matter of your dream, for example: "I, Jo, will dream tonight about surfing in Cornwall," or to help concentrate your mind on finding the solution to a particular problem. If you are using it for the latter, make sure you focus on the positive outcome and not negatively on the problem itself, for example: "I, Jo, will cope with my workload tomorrow," not "I, Jo, will not get stressed out and feel under pressure tomorrow."

Your affirmation sentence can be written down or spoken. Repeat it regularly during the day, and in bed repeat it to yourself to the rhythm of your breathing.

Looking at a photograph of someone can help you dream of them.

Study a photograph of a place you want to dream about.

Visualizing Dreams

Visualization is a form of daydreaming that can help bring about a desired mental state. Once you are in bed and feeling relaxed, empty your mind. Now, think as clearly as you can about the end result you wish to achieve from your dream, such as the solution to a practical problem or relationship dilemma. Now try to picture in your mind how you would behave and feel if the problem was resolved – relaxed, more confident and less anxious. Try to be as detailed as possible in your imaginings, then let your unconscious mind mull it over while you are asleep.

Dream Meetings

It is possible to share a dream experience with a friend or partner. Most people practised in the art of mutual dreaming, aspire actually to meet in their dreams. People who are emotionally close usually have the best results, as they often share many of their waking experiences, which can provide them with the dream's subject matter.

Choose a mutual destination that is familiar to both of you. Visualize the scene and describe it to your dream partner in as much detail as possible. Set a time to meet. Be very specific about the arrangements and rehearse them a few times before you go to sleep. In the morning, tell each other your dreams as soon as possible. Sometimes comparisons will not be immediately obvious, for example if you both dreamt in symbols, you will need to decipher the meanings first to see if they compare.

The most important thing is patience – if you don't succeed at first, try again. It is obviously easiest to compare notes if you share a bed with your dream partner.

Lucid Dreaming

A lucid dream is one in which the dreamer is aware that he or she is dreaming. Experienced lucid dreamers can consciously manipulate the dream's content – they can think and reason, make decisions and act on them. Not everybody can have lucid dreams easily, but it is possible to learn.

The term "lucid dreaming" was first coined by the Dutch physician Frederik Van Eeden, who began to study his own dreams in 1896. It has only been accepted and studied relatively recently, after dream researchers discovered solid evidence that lucid dreamers not only dream vividly but are also aware that they are dreaming.

Lucid dreamers are usually alerted to the fact that they are dreaming by an illogical or inaccurate trigger: for example, bumping into someone they know to be dead, or flying from a tall building. Sometimes it can be an emotional trigger such as fear or anxiety. Nightmares often lead to a period of lucidity: that fleeting sense of relief when you realize that the horrible scenario you are experiencing is just a dream.

Is there any point in being able to dream lucidly? Tibetan Buddhists believe that lucid dreams are a way of preparing for the afterlife, an environment similar to the dream world. Some masters of Tibetan yoga are said to be able to pass in and out of sleep without even losing consciousness.

A high proportion of ordinary dreams (some people have estimated it as high as two-thirds) have unpleasant elements. They may involve being attacked or chased, or falling from heights, and make you feel scared, anxious or miserable. Lucid dreams, however, rarely focus on unpleasant events. If a dream is frightening, lucid dreamers can detach themselves with the thought, "This is only a dream."

If you are aware that you are dreaming, you could, in theory, be able to change the course of the dream's events. You could decide where you wanted to go, what you wanted to do and who you wanted to meet. You could even decide to confront fears, for example to face the monster chasing you rather than run away from it. Or you could just decide to entertain yourself.

If you want to develop lucid dreaming, you first have to be able to recognize that you are dreaming. There are certain things you can do to help raise this awareness. First, ask yourself the question "Am I dreaming?" while you are awake during the day and just before you go to bed. This will make the question a constant presence in your thoughts. Check the physical reality around you. Is there anything strange or surreal about your surroundings? Can you float above the ground? Have you shrunk in size? The idea is that you make the same checks while you are asleep, and so come to realize when events are in a dream.

Try to maintain a level of mental alertness while falling asleep. Stephen LaBerge, the Director of the Lucidity Institute in California, suggests counting sheep or reciting the 12 times table. This should enable you to remain aware during the transition between wakefulness and sleep, with the aim that at some point you will become aware that you are dreaming. Repeat a positive affirmation before you go to sleep, such as "Tonight I will be consciously aware that I am dreaming."

There is an element of control with lucid dreaming, but you will still be restricted by your own expectations and limitations. You can direct the dream to a certain extent, but you cannot completely control it. For example, once you know you are dreaming, you might decide to visit a tropical island, but you won't know what it is like until you get there. On the whole, dreamers have to accept the basic scenario or concept of a dream, allowing it to evolve while exercising some control over their own actions or reactions. Exerting too much control could also wake you up.

Your ultimate aim could be to meet your partner in a dream.

nightmares

Bad dreams are, sadly, the ones everyone tends to remember the most. This may have something to do with the fact that most people have them so often. In one study it was found that one in 20 people has a nightmare at least once a week, although others go through their lives relatively unscathed, having very few nightmares. Dreams are more often negative than positive, and anxiety is reported to be the most common dream emotion.

Experiencing a Nightmare

Nightmares are laden with varying degrees of anxiety, from mild worry to blind panic. It is the feeling a nightmare evokes, rather than the dream itself, that is usually the most upsetting part of the experience, and even if you cannot recall the details, this is what informs you that you have just had an unpleasant dream experience. In extreme cases, you may even wake up with physical symptoms such as sweating or a pounding heart.

Causes of Nightmares

Certain physiological factors can trigger bad dreams. Eating rich food before going to bed can lead to indigestion and disturb the quality of your sleep; heavy drinkers who give up alcohol may suffer frightening dreams for a while afterwards; and certain drugs, such as BetaBlockers, can increase their frequency.

The strongest trigger, however, is psychological. If you are worried, concerned or miserable about something during the day, then these feelings will prey on your mind at night. They are reflected in common dream scenarios, which are not so much dramatic as mildly disturbing – sitting an examination; discovering a loved one in the arms of another; being inappropriately dressed at a social gathering, or ignored at a party; running but

A nightmare vision of Hell by Hieronymus Bosch.

not being able to move. More dramatic common nightmares include being chased by something or somebody; trying and failing to get somewhere; exams, tests or interviews that go horribly wrong, or for which you are unprepared; experiencing or witnessing violence; being strangled or suffocated; feeling paralysed and unable to move or escape.

Susceptibility to Nightmares

Why is it that some people suffer more often from nightmares than others? Dream studies have suggested that those who are more prone to nightmares are "thin-skinned" – they are sensitive, apprehensive and suffer a high level of tension in their waking lives which is carried over into their dreams.

There also appears to be a link between personality types and the types of nightmares people have. For example, ambitious high-achievers are said to have more fantastic, dramatic nightmares. Women have also been found to be more susceptible to nightmares than men. It is perhaps not surprising that feelings of helplessness, or of being threatened, tend to be rather more common in women's dreams.

Vivid nightmares often produce physical symptoms of anxiety.

Night Terrors

These frightening feelings are caused by a sleep transmission disorder which occurs when the brain switches over from slow-wave sleep but doesn't fully complete the process. They are not really dreams as they don't occur during REM sleep. Neither do they feature strong visual images, but they do provoke very physical reactions which can be alarming. The dreamer will not remember much about the cause of their terror – they will just have a fleeting image in their mind accompanied by feelings of guilt, anxiety or shame.

How to Deal with Nightmares

If stress and anxiety are the main causes of nightmares, it makes sense to try to reduce the stress levels in your life. This is easier said than done, of course, but even practising simple relaxation techniques before going to sleep could help.

The best way to cope with dream fears is to confront them. One method for achieving this is to think through your nightmare when you are awake, and rehearse it step by step. When you come to the nasty bit – when the monster appears, or a chase begins, or an attack looms – instead of running away, turn round and face it. Some therapists go even further and suggest that you not only stay put but actually fight back, either verbally or physically. The idea is that if you rehearse the confrontation in your waking life, you will prompt your memory so that you do the same when it happens in a dream. Another way to confront the fear would be to re-run it over and over again, recording a description of the dream on tape or writing it down, then listening to or re-reading your account. This works on the premise that by continually confronting your fear you will eventually become familiar with it and therefore weaken its power over you.

A dream guardian – real or imaginary – could protect you when you are having a nightmare.

Finally, you could appoint a dream guardian who can protect you. Think of a person or animal (it could be someone you know or simply imaginary), whom you could call upon to help you if you have a bad dream. Then imagine yourself back in the dream and call on your dream guardian for assistance. Tell yourself that the next time you have a bad dream your dream guardian will appear to help and protect you. As you fall asleep, remind yourself that your guardian will be there if needed. This is a particularly useful and comforting technique for children who suffer from nightmares.

Try fighting back instead of running away from the monsters in your dreams.

analysis of two dreams

Dreams are individually and uniquely personal, but there are certain themes and images common to everyone, irrespective of background or culture, which crop up again and again. Such common themes, however, can only really be understood in the context of individual lives. Psychoanalysts and dream therapists often explore the thoughts and feelings of their clients with reference to these archetypal images.

Dream Therapy

Whether you are experiencing troubled dreams which haunt your waking life, have a recurring dream that you would like to dispel, or just want to explore your dreams further, then dream therapy might be helpful to you.

Many schools of psychoanalysis use the study of dreams as part of their clinical practice. The therapy involves the patient talking about their dreams as a means of exploring their unconscious and the thoughts, feelings and issues contained within. The dream is then looked at in relation to the patient's life.

Water in a dream represents the unconscious mind.

On a less complex level, there are some therapists who work solely with dreams. There are also dream workshops, in which techniques for dream analysis are taught. Dream groups have also been set up, to which people bring their own dream material to be worked on by the group as a whole.

The following are accounts of two actual dreams which have been analysed by a psychoanalyst and a dream therapist. Both the therapist and the psychoanalyst were sent the narrative of the dream, together with some details about the dreamer and their situation at the time that they experienced the dream. The analyses draw on archetypal symbols present in the dreams as well as insights into the situations of the dreamers.

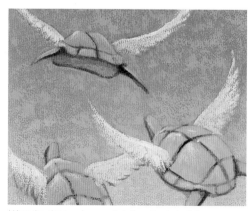

Winged turtles may be a symbol of creative potential.

"FLYING TURTLES"

At the time of her dream, Kate was 47 years old and working as an administrator. She was considering giving up her job and changing careers.

Kate is in a shallow pond with a lot of other people. They are in a race to row around the circumference of the pond. She begins the race in a boat, which then disappears and instead she is wading round, with water up to her knees. She feels very detached from the others. There are turtles of all different sizes swimming in the pond. The race has finished and everyone begins to leave the pond and walk up a path, the surface of which is covered with more turtles. Kate treads carefully, trying to avoid stepping on them, but she can feel some of the baby turtles getting crushed under her feet. She feels guilty about hurting them. Then suddenly they begin to grow wings, and fly away.

The Analysis

Water in dreams tends to signify the unconscious mind. Kate begins the race in a boat, which is a convenient way of travelling over water without being disturbed by it. It suggests something to do with her relationship with her unconscious, perhaps not being familiar with it, which is also indicated by the water's shallowness. The race is circular, with no beginning or end, which gives it a sense of futility and drudgery, and she is following the path of others. It is when Kate finds herself without a boat and wading through the water that she begins to feel detached from the other people.

The appearance of the turtles is a significant moment in the dream. As well as any personal significance or association they may have for Kate, turtles have a huge symbolic and mythological significance. In some cultures, they are believed to be divine. They often represent fertility and creativity, and turtles appear in numerous creation myths around the world.

Because of the creative significance of turtles, the dream is no doubt saying something about Kate's creativity, possibly a creative potential which hasn't yet been reached or realized. The turtles are also babies, so are symbolic of new life and potential. The fact that Kate walks on them potentially destroys the seeds of creativity, but they are not all destroyed and instead grow wings and fly away to safety, showing the potential for creative expression.

"THE YELLOW DOG"

Sally, in her late 30s, is a designer in the film industry. At the time of her dream, she was working hard, up against tight deadlines.

Sally is in a wide, tree-lined road with big, red-tiled houses set back from the street by long front gardens. There has been a flood and a fast-flowing torrent is running down the middle of the road. Sally is being swept along by the current. She tries to grab hold of a tree trunk and cling on to it. There are no other people around but there is no sense of her having lost anyone, nor is she trying to catch up with anyone. Suddenly, a large yellow labrador swims along. He holds his paw out in the air, leg out-stretched, and says to her, "Grab hold of me." He has managed to communicate without speaking. She holds on to the dog's paw (he is big, strong and solid) and he gets her to safety, but she doesn't remember how. Next, she is in a bar with people whom she doesn't know in real life but knows in her dream. The dog is still by her side, making sure that she is safe.

The Analysis

The setting represents affluence and stability, and could represent these aspects in Sally's life. The trees that line the road relate to family matters – trees are often linked to the family, hence the family tree. The road symbolizes direction in life. The flood shows that emotions are sweeping through any sense of stability. Sally may feel and are causing a huge upheaval. It is always better to go with the flow, but Sally is resisting being swept away and wants to be rescued. Grabbing the tree shows she is trying to feel grounded or "rooted".

The yellow dog represents faithfulness and loyalty, protection and rescue. He could be a real person and he may also repre-sent intellect, as the colour yellow symbolizes intelligence. Perhaps Sally relies on her intellect to rescue her from emotional issues because she doesn't want her feelings to get in the way. Even in a social setting – in the bar – the dog is still there to protect her, indicating that she feels she needs to use the ratio-nal part of her personality all the time.

The dreamer is resisting being swept along on a flood of emotion.

Common Dream Themes

Flying or floating: Flying dreams commonly bring a feeling of freedom and exhilaration; they are seldom frightening or unpleasant, and the dreamer often awakes with a sense of optimism. The actual process of flying is usually effortless and the body feels weightless.

Being chased: Being chased in a dream suggests that you are running away from a situation that is threatening or frightening, or simply in danger of dominating the rest of your life. Perhaps there are problems that you are not facing, or obligations that are waiting to be fulfilled.

Falling: Whether it is falling from a cliff, a building or a wall, falling is a universal dream theme with a number of meanings. It may signify feeling out of control or overwhelmed by a situation, such as the loss of a job or a divorce. Falling dreams also reflect a sense of having failed or "fallen down", so maybe you have tried to reach too high in your personal or professional life and fear that you are ready for a fall. Alternatively, the fall could symbolize a fear of "letting go".

Drowning: A dream about drowning could reflect an area in your life in which you are finding it difficult to "keep your head above water". Large bodies of water are generally seen to represent the unconscious, so drowning could symbolize feeling engulfed by repressed, unconscious issues.

Losing teeth: Whether they fall out in one go or slowly crumble, dreaming of losing teeth can be quite alarming, although it is very common. Such a dream may reflect fear of ageing (and loss of sexual attractiveness), fear of losing power and control, or fear of change. Biting or being bitten are obviously symbolic of aggression.

Being unable to move: Being rooted to the spot but desperate to escape is a fairly classic anxiety dream. The physical paralysis could be a reflection of an emotional paralysis – perhaps you feel unable or reluctant to make changes in your life, or to make a decision.

Being naked in public: Nakedness can represent the desire for freedom, or freedom of expression, reverting perhaps to childhood innocence. Being naked in public with others' disapproval could indicate fear of revealing your true self.

The faithful dog reaches out a rescuing paw to save the dreamer.

guide to dream symbols

Dreams use the language of metaphor and symbol to convey their meaning. Sometimes a symbol can be fairly straightforward, at other times it can be completely baffling and nonsensical. Some symbols are universal (for example, the dove as a symbol of peace and the cross as a sign of Christ), but within the context of a dream even these can mean different things to different people.

Interpreting Symbols

The most important factor to bear in mind when analysing the meaning of a dream symbol is the way it relates to your own personal experience. This list of symbols is intended as a springboard for your own specific interpretation. It is selective and by no means definitive – some symbols have just one possible interpretation, while others have a variety of meanings. The list should give guidance and spark off your own ideas. It is possible that, in time, you may even begin to develop your own list of dream symbols. Certain objects, people and situations may recur from time to time in your dreams and you will eventually be able to attach your own meaning or significance to them.

The important thing to remember is that the feeling, tone and setting of a dream, as well as its images and events, all have to be taken into consideration when you are exploring the possible meanings of symbols, and what they mean to you on a personal level.

Accident

Being involved in an accident or crash in a dream could be a straightforward fear of being physically harmed. It may also suggest that you are in a state of anxiety, or even fear, or that you are heading for an emotional "crash" or collision. If the general feeling of the dream is positive, although violent, it could symbolize a part of your life that you are letting go.

Actor/actress

Dreams in which you or other people appear as actors tend to represent the public, rather than private, self. If it is an unpleasant dream about acting, it could refer to a situation or situations in your waking life in which you feel that you are being forced to "put on an act".

Aeroplane

An aeroplane can be a positive symbol of liberation and freedom, particularly if you are the pilot and are able to "rise above" a situation or soar to new heights.

Angel

Traditionally seen as messengers of God, angels symbolize purity and goodness. They are also thought of as protectors and guides.

Avalanche

An avalanche signifies being overwhelmed or fearing disaster. If the avalanche is snow or ice, it may symbolize "frozen" emotions that could be expressed or experienced.

Baby

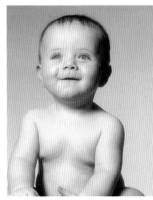

A baby may represent a new beginning, development or opportunity in your life. It can also represent your own "inner baby", the part of the adult you that is still craving to feel secure and looked after.

Bed

A bed can be a symbol of security, warmth and comfort, maybe even of escaping from the outside world. If a bed appears in a dream about marriage or a relationship, then the state of the bed could be seen as representing the state of the relationship.

Bird

Birds carry a variety of meanings. Their flight represents freedom, and they also have a variety of religious meanings as messengers of the divine or symbols of the soul. They represent the "higher self" in most cultures. Blackbirds, crows, ravens and vultures are traditionally interpreted as omens of death. The dove is a symbol of peace and reconciliation.

Birth

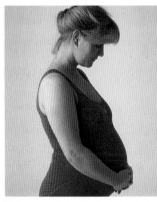

Birth can symbolize the beginning (actual or potential) of a new idea or project, or a sense of beginning a new stage in your life. Pregnant women often dream of difficult or strange births (for example, giving birth to kittens) which could reflect their anxiety about childbirth.

Book

Books represent knowledge and wisdom, or the historical record of the dreamer's life. A dusty old book could symbolize forgotten or neglected knowledge, or an earlier "chapter" of your life. The opening and closing of a book may represent the opening or closing chapter of your life.

Bride/Bridegroom

Weddings can symbolize the union of opposite yet complementary parts of yourself, the most obvious being the union of the masculine and feminine parts of your personality. In Jungian psychology, images of a bride or groom represent the *anima* (feminine traits repressed in the male) in men, and the *animus* (masculine traits repressed in the female) in women.

Car

A car usually represents yourself and, in particular, whether or not you feel in control of your life. If you are in the driver's seat, this may symbolize that you are taking charge of your life. If someone else is driving, you could feel over-dependent on others, or allow others control. You may be put in control of a car before you are ready, or even if you cannot drive.

Cat

Cats symbolize the feminine, sexuality, power and prosperity, and have both positive and negative connotations. They can be perceived as fertile and creative, but also "catty". In symbolism derived from folklore, a witch and a black cat generally stand for evil and bad luck.

Chased (being)

A dream about being chased can bring with it feelings of hopelessness and frustration because you feel you cannot escape. It may be worth looking at who is doing the chasing and what they represent. Is it a figure of authority, or something more threatening? Whatever is chasing you could be an aspect of yourself that you are afraid to confront.

Child

A child could symbolize your own "inner child", the part of you that is in need of reassurance or needs to grow up. Dreaming of children can also symbolize a desire to go back to a more innocent, less complicated time in life. Like a baby, a child can also represent the possibility of a new beginning or a new attitude to life.

City

The meaning of a city depends whether you enjoy or dislike the urban environment. In Jungian psychology, the city represents the community, and could represent your relationships with other people. If you are lost in the city, this would probably represent a loss of direction in life. A ruined city may indicate neglected relationships or aims in life.

Clock/Watch

As symbols, clocks often reflect anxiety about not being on top of things or being behind schedule.

Death

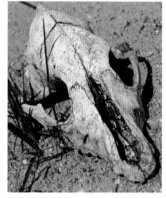

Dreams about death could express some anxiety about dying but, symbolically, death represents not so much an ending as a new beginning, so to dream of your own death could mean that you are preparing to start something new. If you dream of the death of a loved one, you may be rehearsing the actual event and unconsciously preparing for bereavement.

Dog

Animals signify the natural, instinctive and animal self. As domestic pets, dogs have a wide variety of symbolic meanings, including loyalty and companionship, going along with the pack and tamed wildness.

Door/Doorway

The meaning of a door or doorway depends entirely on how it appears in the dream. An open door could represent a new opportunity or phase in life, and going through the door would be to grasp that opportunity. Too many doors could suggest that a choice needs to be made. If the door is locked, it may indicate that something is being repressed or hidden.

Drowning

A dream about drowning could reflect an area in your life in which you are finding it difficult to keep your head above water. Water represents the unconscious and drowning could symbolize being engulfed. It is also a symbol for the emotions, and dreams about drowning can happen during an emotional crisis or if you are feeling overwhelmed by your feelings.

Falling

Psychologists have speculated that fearful falling dreams are rooted in early childhood, when you learn to take your first steps. Some scientists have offered a physiological explanation – that your muscles relax as you fall asleep and the falling sensation is the result of an involuntary muscle spasm, which becomes incorporated into a dream.

Fire

This element is a complex symbol meaning many different things, including passion, anger, illumination and danger. Fire can purge as well as consume, purify as well as destroy. An out-of-control fire in a dream could be a sign of unbridled passion or ambition.

Fish

Large areas of water represent the unconscious, so any creature living in water can represent a message or insight from the unconscious. Fish explore the depths of the ocean and are therefore positive symbols for anyone wanting to explore their own depths.

Flower

The flower is a natural symbol of beauty, fragility, harmlessness and the attraction of bees to nectar. In Asian yoga teachings, flowers represent the psychic centres, or chakras, on which to focus meditation.

Flying or Floating

One of the most common explanations of a flying dream is that it represents an ability to cope with life, rising above it and viewing it from an objective standpoint. It could also indicate a love of risk-taking and adventure. If you are flying in a bed or an armchair (or even on a carpet), this suggests a desire for adventure but within the confines of comfort and security.

Forest

A dark forest is a symbol of the unconscious, so venturing into a forest can be seen as an exploration of the unconscious mind. A forest can also represent a refuge from the demands of everyday life.

Giant

A giant can be a friendly or scary symbol, either helpful and protective or terrifying. Because of its size, a giant could represent something large or overwhelming in the dreamer's life, a gigantic obstacle that needs to be overcome.

Horse

This powerful animal represents noble actions. In general, it is a symbol of humankind's harnessing of the wild forces of nature. If you are riding a horse in your dream, it could indicate that you are in control of your life. It could also represent your own emotional state if the horse is running away with you, or if you are reining it in your dream.

Hospital

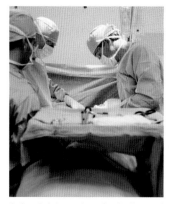

A hospital is a place for healing and getting back into the flow of life. It could also suggest that you may need to pay some attention to your health.

House

A house is usually interpreted as representing the dreamer. The living rooms of the house represent everyday life, the attic represents the higher self, and the cellar represents the unconscious. The state of the house is also relevant. Is it dark and cramped, or light and airy? Is it untidy? Do you get lost in it? Is it undergoing construction? Is it being decorated?

Interviews

Having to undergo an interview in a dream can induce the same feelings of anxiety as sitting an examination. The people on an interview panel could represent aspects of the dreamer, suggesting self-dissatisfaction or judgement.

Island

Finding yourself on an island in a dream may mean that you need peace and solitude. It could also suggest that you are afraid of venturing into your unconscious mind (represented by the surrounding water) and prefer to stay on firm ground.

Mirror

A classic identity crisis dream is one in which you look into a mirror and see someone else's face. The reflection may give you a clue to the nature of the identity problem. A cracked or clouded mirror reflects the distorted face (or image) you may be presenting to the world.

Monster

The appearance of a monster in a dream is usually caused by repressed emotions and fears. It could also represent a part of your personality that you consider unpleasant or ugly.

Mother

Symbolically, a mother represents giving life, love and nourishment. Being the mother in a dream denotes taking care of yourself or of a significant relationship in your life. The meaning of a dream about your own mother would depend entirely on your relationship with her, although the dream could be telling you something about that relationship.

Mountain

Climbing a mountain and reaching the top could be a symbol of achieving your goals in life. Surveying the landscape from the top of a mountain could represent looking at life objectively, or assessing it without emotional attachment. Descending a mountain could mean letting go of insurmountable issues.

Nakedness in Public

The meaning of your own nakedness in dreams depends very much on how it feels to you. If you experience feelings of embarrassment, shame and exposure, then this may reflect problems you have with feeling shy or socially inadequate. If, however, no-one seems to notice or care, it could mean that you are happy to reveal your "real self" to others.

Office

If you dream about your own office, this could simply be an indication that you are bringing work home with you and into your dreams. An office can also symbolize authority or your professional position in the world.

Paralyzed

Being rooted to the spot but feeling desperate to escape is a fairly classic anxiety dream. The physical paralysis could be a reflection of an emotional paralysis – perhaps you feel unable or reluctant to make changes in your life, or to make a decision, or maybe you are frustrated about a situation over which you feel you have no control.

River

As with the sea, a river is a large body of water and generally represents emotion. Watching a river flow passively may indicate that life is passing by without enough direction. If the river is bursting its banks, you may feel out of control. Crossing a river by a bridge may symbolize a change in life, or avoiding a flood of passion by observing the water from a safe position.

Road

In dreams, roads represent a direction or goal in life. If the road is straight and narrow, you may feel that you are on the right path. If it is winding or bumpy, your plans may be vague or you may be meeting with unexpected changes or obstacles. If you never get to your destination, something could be preventing you from reaching your goal.

School

A classroom typically represents learning but it can also mean competition or public esteem. Dreaming about being back in the classroom can indicate feelings of inadequacy, especially if the dream centres around unpleasant school experiences. School can also symbolize nostalgia, a desire to relive a feeling of ambition or joy from an earlier stage in life.

Sea

Large bodies of water generally represent the unconscious, so the sea could indicate your emotional state. Are you feeling lost in a small boat, or safe in a large one? Is the water calm or are you overwhelmed by huge waves? Are you afraid of monsters that lurk in the water? It is particularly important to take note of the emotional atmosphere of the dream.

Sex

This is a complex area with a broad range of meanings, depending entirely on the individual. Generally, having sex or seeing others having sex could be a straightforward expression of sexual desire, a desire to bond, or an indication of repressed desires for love. Dreaming about sex with someone "inappropriate" does not necessarily mean you harbour secret desires.

Slope

Trying to ascend a slippery slope is a common dream which suggests that you are failing to progress in a certain area. Stumbling or slipping down the slope may signify that you are forcing yourself to do things which go against your nature.

Station/Airport

Railway stations and airports represent a wide variety of possibilities – a new venture or idea ready to "take off", apprehension or excitement about the future, or a transition in life. They can also be confusing places, so their appearance in a dream may indicate that you need to sit down and sort through a particular problem or conflict.

Stranger

In Freudian terms, meeting a stranger in a dream may symbolize meeting a part of your own unconscious personality.

Teeth (losing)

Whether they fall out in one go or slowly crumble, dreaming of losing teeth is very common and slightly alarming. Such a dream may reflect fear of ageing (and loss of sexual attractiveness), fear of losing power and control, or fear of change.

Tests/Examinations

In dreams, examinations can stand for success or (fear of) failure in any area of your personal or professional life. Sitting an examination for which you have not prepared, or in a subject you haven't studied, is a classic fear-of-failure dream. Conversely, passing an exam or test could be seen as a metaphor for having succeeded in something.

Tower

A tower in your dream could be a symbol of caution and vigilance (symbolized by a watchtower) or imprisonment (a guard tower). It could also be an ivory tower, representing arrogance and aloofness.

Train

A missed train could symbolize missed opportunities in life, as could being on the wrong train or missing a stop. Travelling smoothly down the railway track may mean staying "on track" in life. According to Freudian interpretation, the train represents the penis and entering the tunnel (representing the vagina) is a symbol of sexual intercourse.

Violence

Horrifying scenes of violence or destruction may represent an overwhelming fear of loss of power or control. If you are the one being violent, this could represent a struggle for self-assertion, or a deep-rooted anger and resentment. Directed at you (rather than inflicted by you), violence often represents a sense of guilt and a desire for self-punishment.

mandalas

Mandalas are usually circular in form. In Sanskrit, *mandala* means both "circle" and "centre", denoting that it represents both the visible outer world (the circle) and the interior world of the mind and body (the centre). A mandala is a picture that tells the story of a journey that you can follow from the everyday world to the serene inner centre inside yourself, leading you to a deeper understanding of your relationship with the universe.

Everyone seeks happiness and the fulfilment of their dreams. Mandalas are a tool that can guide you straight to the heart of this search. In following the journey through a mandala you are seeking to find the wholeness that lies at your core, the stillness that always remains no matter what storms may surround you.

When you draw a mandala you can either create an image of your inner self or you can carefully draw out an image of a perfect world and aspire to its expression of harmony. In creating a mandala you open yourself to all the possibilities that exist both inside and outside yourself. You listen to the dreams of your heart, mind and soul and give them shape and colour inside the circle.

A mandala can take any form — seen rightly, any object can transport you from the mundane world to a world of beauty. Once you have begun working with mandalas you may start to perceive the seemingly random reality around you differently, turning what is everyday and commonplace into a journey to your deepest, innermost self.

ancient mandalas

The mandalas of different cultures and different times vary in their form and representation. However, although each may have used a different "language", the mandalas of all ages have described the same cosmos as our own. Irrespective of their historical and cultural origins, if you are able to tune in to their resonance deeply enough, the most ancient mandalas can help you on your journey to finding your own inner truth.

Patterns

Our ancient ancestors saw the pattern of the universe all around them, in the seasons, the waxing and waning moon, and the rising and setting sun. They marked these events with standing stones and circles, and these mandalas now form part of our landscape.

In England, the megalithic monument at Stonehenge heralds the passage of the summer solstice: the complex alignment of stones forms an annual calendar. Our ancestors' way of life was dependent on natural cycles. Stone circles such as Stonehenge are a symbol of their world. Human life is also a natural cycle, and our ancestors built elaborate burial mounds to honour it which also form physical mandalas. Newgrange, in Eire, is a good example. A single ceremonial chamber at the heart of the circular mound lies in darkness until the summer solstice, when at dawn the sun's rays penetrate the passageway, illuminating its dark walls.

The ancient Egyptians also understood the wheel of life. There is a theory that all their pyramids form part of a single pattern on the earth, mirroring the place in the sky where they believed the Pharaoh's spirit would be reborn. At the centre of this vast mandala is a coffin in the King's Chamber. This is the spiritual receptacle for the god's death and rebirth.

The symbolism from these burial places suggests that the centre of the mandala is a place of death and rebirth. We must let the past die in order for the future to open up before us.

The twists and turns of a maze are like a map of the path of life.

Labyrinths

The symbol of the maze occurs in every part of the world, as part of the quest for wisdom and self-knowledge. Each moment you must choose which direction to take, and every wrong decision will make the journey longer. But no matter how tortuous the path you must never lose sight of where you want to be – at the heart of your true self.

In Greek mythology, the story of Theseus and the Minotaur is centred on the legendary labyrinth at the palace of King Minos on Crete. Theseus has to find his way through the maze to confront and kill the monstrous Minotaur in order to claim his destiny as King.

Many simple grass-cut mazes survive from prehistory. They form a single narrow path, which weaves back and forth on itself. Monks and pilgrims would journey through the maze on their knees in deep meditation. These turf-cut mazes demonstrate the simplicity of life when its ever-changing patterns and directions can be accepted with pleasure and peace.

The Celtic triple-spiral maze has many different paths to its centre. Although it is possible to take a short cut through one leaf, in doing so the subtleties of the path are missed. It is only by changing the pattern of turns and not remaining fixed to any single rule that you can pass through the whole maze. It is a reminder that a rich life is one that is not fixated on the future, but relishes the twists and turns of every moment.

The mysterious pyramids were built as the final resting place on earth for the Pharaohs, who were regarded as reincarnations of a god.

Celtic Symbols

The ancient Celts were a diverse people whose influence spread across Europe and possibly as far as Asia. They shared a spiritual heritage of beliefs from the Iron Age to the dawn of Christianity. The Celts developed their understanding of the universe from their ancestors, having close affinities with nature, the seasons, and cycles of life, death and rebirth. Stones decorated with spiral designs and carved round figures, symbols of the earth, are found all across north-west Europe.

The pre-Christian, Celtic cross symbolizes the four seasons and the four directions – north, south, east and west – positioned over a circle of stone, which symbolizes the earth. With the advent of Christianity, the Celts took on elements of the new religion and their crosses became more elaborate. As their skill at stone-carving grew, they carved fantastic monuments with elaborate spirals, animals and mythical creatures from the stories of the saints. These Celtic crosses were inscribed with complete legends and stories which were typically Christian in flavour. A favourite theme, for example, showed the passage of a saint from this life to the next where he would reach enlightenment.

These richly decorated carvings gave rise to the first books – lavishly illustrated bibles which were filled with the symbology of the creatures known to the Celts. Snakes, wolves, fish, peacocks and eagles filled the pages of these illuminated manuscripts along with delicately drawn knotwork. In the Book of Kells, each evangelist was symbolized by his own animal and the decorated borders and letters of the gospels were a richly woven story of the wisdom written on each page. The book was not simply a script but a symbolic journey illuminating a path towards understanding the deeper meaning of the words at the centre.

A complex rose window symbolizes wholeness and universality.

Christian Symbols

Churches are traditionally built facing east, in the cross-shape of a mandala. East, where the sun rises, symbolizes the resurrection of the spirit of Jesus at Easter and his gift of new life. The altar is always placed at the eastern end of a church.

The ornate rose windows that adorn cathedrals and churches all over the world are also examples of Christian mandalas. The intricate patterns of stone arches, flowers and vivid colours fill the church with heavenly light and beauty. Sometimes this light spills on to a circular maze on the floor, symbolizing the pilgrim's journey to the spiritual centre of Christianity, Jerusalem.

During the Middle Ages, Hildegard of Bingen had a series of visions that she sought to communicate in music and illustration. She had had a gift for prophecy and vision from her childhood and went on to paint many images describing the world, with man and woman as the pinnacle of God's creation at the centre. In one of her visions she saw God enthroned at the centre of a vast mandala, radiating a circle of gold with a great wheel at his heart, expanding out to encircle the universe.

Hildegard also attempted to describe the harmony of the universe as a path to healing sickness. It was based on her vision of four principal human ailments and the four elements of earth, air, fire and water. She visualized her medicine as an image of the harmonious universe with the elements at the centre surrounded by the wind and the stars. Beyond this lay darkness and fire and the clear light of the sun. At the centre of our true selves, there is no sickness. There we are whole and healed, in harmony with God and the universe.

The intricately carved Celtic cross incorporates both the circle and the centre of a mandala.

native american mandalas

The Native American people traditionally see all life forms as an integral part of a single existence that surrounds them with its teachings. Every living creature, every rock or stone is part of the pattern of the universe. Everything contains a spirit, which is the essence of its connection with the world. To walk a path of beauty and truth is to walk in harmony with the spirits.

The Medicine Wheel

One of the most important Native American symbols of the universe is the mandala of the medicine wheel. This cross within a circle represents the four seasons (spring, summer, autumn, winter), the four directions (north, south, east, west) and the four elements (fire, water, earth, air), all of which are contained within the outer circle, which is representative of the world. In the two-dimensional wheel, the horizontal axis of the cross also represents the directions of below (Mother Earth) and above (Father Sky). The four seasons are symbolic of time, and the four compass points symbolize space. In addition to these basic concepts, particular animals, colours and qualities invest the medicine wheel with rich and never-ending layers of meaning within the circle that describes the cycle of life.

According to the symbology of the medicine wheel, when you are born you begin your journey on earth in the east at dawn, a place of light, vision and new beginnings. As you grow up and begin to learn about the world, you move to the south and a time of innocent self-expression and joy. As you grow further you develop your intuition and imagination and suffer the pain of growth in the west. Eventually you move for a time to rest in the north and intuition becomes wisdom. After replenishing your

A Navajo silversmith c. 1870.

strength, you are ready to begin your journey again in the east, and so the cycle rolls on and turns again, until, after many revolutions of the wheel, you pass into the sky as spirit.

The teaching of the medicine wheel is that you will keep moving around its circumference until you can reside in the centre. Here you become one with the wheel of life and are in harmony with its ever-changing patterns.

The Dream Catcher

The Native American "dream catcher" is a mandala of the dream world. This "wheel" is made from a single thread that is knotted into a spiral web and adorned with birds' feathers and decorative beads. It hangs above a person's head while they sleep and "catches" all the good dreams, whose teaching will remain on waking. The bad dreams, however, pass through the holes in the web and are released into the universe. At the centre of the catcher, the spirit can pass into the dream world.

In a similar manner, Native American shields are created to ensure protection from bad spirits and to act as a call to the person's spirit helpers. Each one of these shields is a unique, individually decorated circle made of skins, feathers, beads and threads. Each one is a weaving of the owner's own spiritual path and is a type of personalized mandala.

A beautiful and extraordinarily large medicine wheel in Sedona, Arizona.

navajo sand paintings

The Navajo believe that illness arises through disharmony with the world. When people do not respect their bodies or the earth, then they become sick. A medicine man (or woman) cures the sick by rebalancing their lives. The healer performs a ceremony, or Way, which is a carefully constructed pathway that brings the patient to a place of wholeness and releases him from his illness.

The Healing Mandala

The Way is centred on a mandala sand painting, the symbol of balance and harmony, and its story. The Navajo call the sand painting *iikááh* ("the place where the spirits come and go") as they believe that the painting is a doorway through which the spirits will pass as they are called upon in the story.

The healer diagnoses the nature of the patient's imbalance and chooses the most appropriate of hundreds of sand paintings and accompanying myths. The stories that are told are always deeply symbolic, speaking of the creation of the people and the earth and of how humanity has been taught by the spirits to live in harmony with all life.

The medicine man and his helpers begin the ceremony during the day in the hogan, a sacred lodge that has been specially blessed for the ceremony. The sand painting is created using string and other markers to plot the shapes and symbols accurately. The balance and positions of the spirit figures must be exact in order to create a place of harmony for the patient.

The base of the painting is built up using not only sand but ground corn and pollen or crushed petals, and above this, charcoal and ground stone are carefully poured to make the outlines of the figures, with shadows and colours. The figures of the characters in the story are created as solid shapes with the image of their whole bodies, back and front, poured into place to bring their complete presence symbolically into the circle.

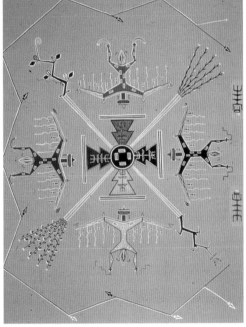

The Navajo healer uses entirely natural materials, including ground corn and petals as well as sand, in the design of the sand painting.

As night falls when the painting is drawn, the patient, who has not been present at the ceremony until now, comes to the hogan and sits in the centre of the mandala. The images of the spirits are thus in direct contact with the patient so that they may enter his or her body during the ceremony. The healer chants or sings the story of the pathway back to harmony, and while he listens to it, the patient focuses on understanding how he has deviated from his path and in which direction he must walk in future to remain happy, healthy and free.

When the story is told and the patient has heard the lessons and understands the changes he must make in his life, the spirits draw down the illness so that it falls into the mandala. The sand is now infected with the sickness and it is ritually disposed of so that the healed person is free to walk his new path of health.

A healing sand painting is created in a specially sanctified lodge.

indian and tibetan mandalas Traditional

mandalas are a visual meditation tool that helps guide the true seeker to a path of greater
understanding of themselves and the universe. Throughout Asia, both Hindus and Buddhists
focus on the attainment of wisdom and self-knowledge through meditation, gaining harmony
and achieving freedom from the cycle of mortality and the constraints of worldly desire.

Hindu Yantras

Devotees of the Hindu faith use circular
yantras in their meditations and ceremonies.
Each yantra contains a precisely drawn geometrical symbol of a divinity. Every divine being
has its own special symbol of interlocking
triangles, pointing up or down depending on
whether the deity is of the male or female sex.
Surrounding this are circles which symbolize
protection and a ring of petals signifying the
attendants of the deity. This is all contained
within a circular earth-city called *bhu-pura*,
enclosed by walls, from which all the guardians
of the eight directions sit in a perpetual state
of watchfulness.

A beautiful Buddhist mandala.

Yantras can be either a circle, drawn and used flat on the
earth, or a pyramid. A round receptacle is placed at the centre,
within which the deity will manifest. Yantras can be engraved only
on eight so-called tantric surfaces: gold, silver, copper, crystal,
birch, bone, hide (which includes paper) and a special stone
called *vishnu*. Only these materials, in combination with the use

of the correct colours in the design, will create
the balance and harmony of energies for the
deity to exist at the centre of the yantra.

Yantras are considered to be alive with the
spirit of the deity and must be "given breath"
in a ceremony. Scents are smeared over the
yantra, while a mantra is intoned over and over
again. In the Shri Yantra, letters are drawn
around the outside of the circle to symbolize
the sound of the creation goddess, Shakti, to
whom it is consecrated. When breath and life
are given to the yantra it is believed to gain
senses to perceive the world and a subtle or
spiritual body in which to live. Yantra are sacred
objects that can be used as the focus for meditation. In placing
themselves at the centre of the yantra devotees aim to become
centred in their whole being.

Buddhist Mandalas

Buddhists seek to attain enlightenment so that they can exist in
a place of perfect beauty in the universe in this lifetime or the
next. The mind and body are taught how to walk in harmony,
releasing the person from the constraints of ego and mundane
desires. Mandalas are drawn to strict rules to create perfect
balance and harmony from which to meditate. There are many
paths to enlightenment, and each has its own mandala and its
own Buddha to act as guide.

Tibetan Buddhists use the healing and teaching properties of
mandalas on a rolled cloth, called a *thang-ka*. These are usually
rectangular paintings showing the teachings of the Buddha, the
wheel of life, the cosmic tree, saints and other spiritual guides in
beautiful, richly coloured images. Tibetans also drawn circular
mandalas for meditation called *kyil-khor*. Each one contains a
wealth of symbols and meaning.

A monk meditates on the mandala by considering each
symbol in turn, moving from the edge inwards. The seeker must
first pass four outer barriers to enlightenment, which correspond
to purifying fire, intellectual strength, the eight states of complete
consciousness and the open, innocent heart. They then reach the
four gates of the Buddha's palace. In each of the four directions,
a protector spirit guards the doorway and must be faced before
the seeker can finally enter the palace and reach the mandala
centre and the Buddha within.

In a Hindu Yantra, every symbol represents a specific deity.

tibetan sand paintings

Tibetan Buddhists see mandalas all around them. They see themselves as mandalas, they see their country as a mandala and they see all beings, even themselves, as potential Buddhas. The pinnacle of Tibetan mandalas in the physical world is the form of sand painting called *dul-tson-kyil-khor*, or "mandala of coloured powders", and the most complex of these is the Wheel of Time, the Kalachakra.

The Wheel of Time

This path to enlightenment and its mandala describes all the wisdom of the cycles of the universe and the healing that comes from living in harmony with its unceasing rhythms. The Wheel of Time is a two-dimensional representation of a five-storey palace in which the Kalachakra Buddha lives, guarded by 722 divine male and female figures. Each pairing symbolizes one cyclic aspect of the world, and the whole mandala is a single picture of all the cycles in the universe.

The sand painting is seen as only a crude approximation of the true mandala, which as a three-dimensional concept can exist fully only in the mind's eye. The painted mandalas are created to act as aids to help the monks build the mental mandalas, which are necessary in order to follow the meditative ritual texts of Tibetan Buddhism. A monk will mentally walk through all the floors and rooms of the metaphysical palace and seek to pass each figure in turn as part of a meditation, until he reaches the Buddha at the centre and comes to an understanding of the universe moving around him.

The monks begin creating the sand painting with a ceremony to call on the goddess of creation and consecrate the site. They then draw the outline of the mandala on the floor, using white ink and following strict geometrical rules. The painting is created

Once completed, the mandala's role is finished and it is dismantled.

from the centre outwards, symbolizing the creation from a single egg into the universe that culminates in the conscious self. One monk works at each one of the four directions, pouring fine rivulets of coloured sand meticulously from a narrow metal funnel, called a *chak-pur*. For some sand paintings, powdered flowers, herbs, grains and even ground jewels are used to change the spiritual qualities of the mandala.

The palace at the centre of the Wheel of Time is built on the primal energies of the universe: earth, water, fire and wind. The ground floor of the palace contains the cycles of the earth, astronomy and human history. The next storey represents the Tibetan mind-body system of healing. On the third floor is the state of perfection for the human body and mind, which leads finally to the level for the perfect state of being. From this place the monk can truly understand the universe as seen by the Kalachakra Buddha and become one with his state of being.

Creating the Wheel of Time also brings great healing to its surroundings. Once the mandala is finished, its role is complete and a ceremony is performed to release that healing into the world. The sands are swept up from the outside to the centre of the circle and placed in an urn. This is carried ceremonially to a nearby river where it is emptied, carrying the healing sands out into the ocean and around the world to bring peace and harmony to the whole planet.

Coloured sand is poured through a metal funnel in a fine stream.

mandalas of man and nature

You use your senses to experience the world, a world that you are at the heart of. Around you is the air you breathe and the land you walk on. All the time you are awake you can sense the beauty of the whole universe around you. You do not need to go anywhere special to find it. It is always there, waiting for you. In every step you take, you are surrounded by the mandala of the world.

Contemporary Mandalas

In the 20th century, the Swiss psychologist Carl Gustav Jung (1875–1961) developed the use of mandalas as an aid to psychological understanding. He drew a mandala every day to express his innermost thoughts and feelings. Each time he noticed that within the circle he had drawn was a snapshot of his mental, emotional and spiritual state. It was as though the images were reflecting his inner self. He also realized that the expression of the circle was universal – children spontaneously draw them, as do adults when they doodle.

The psychiatrist C. G. Jung.

Jung came to see the mandala as a pathway to the self, and he began to use it in his work as a psychiatrist to help his patients make deeper connections with themselves. The circle or sphere of the mandala represents the psyche that holds within it, at the centre, the true self. He believed that the top of the mandala indicated emotions that were held in the conscious mind, while the base symbolized areas of feelings and thoughts that were deep in the unconscious.

Jung's influence has been far-reaching and today many people are interested in creating mandalas and using them as tools for self-expression. With the spread of many old magical traditions through Western civilization, new mandalas have appeared. The Order of the Golden Dawn is a group that combines Eastern traditions with Western magic. It has created a set of mandalas called Tattva Cards, as an aid to reaching the spiritual self. They contain simple symbols such as moons and circles that are meditated on to develop the vision and experience of the inner self.

Perhaps one of the most exciting forms of the mandala generated in recent times is that of computer art. Three-dimensional computer graphics can bring the realization of a mandala into another digital dimension. The information about the mandala on a computer is stored as a pattern of ones and zeros. This pattern is in itself another representation of the mandala that can be copied and communicated to any other computer throughout the world. Beyond this, all the words we speak into the telephone, all the faxes or e-mails that we send, become pulses of electricity or light radiating around the world in a never-ending stream, an invisible mandala of information, reaching us through television and radio and bouncing off satellites in space, or pulsing beneath the sea along vast cables of light.

The Human Body

Inside your body, your blood, your organs, your muscles, the electricity passing through your nervous system, each tiny part of you, moves and works in harmony with the whole, every single moment that you live, working in unceasing rhythm. When you stand on the earth and reach out with your arms, your silhouette forms a five-pointed star. It is extraordinary in its symmetry and regularity, and is part of the harmony of the universe.

The DNA strands at the centre of every single cell of your body combine to form a map, a blueprint in line with which you develop through life. You are the sum total of your parents and their parents and all their forebears stretching back before them. The genes in your body hold the history of every one of your ancestors, as well as the purity of your heart, mind, body and soul. Without guilt, fear, jealousy and all the other emotions that act as barriers to your true self, you can just be, exactly as your genes describe you. You hold the key to happiness in the centre of every cell of your body.

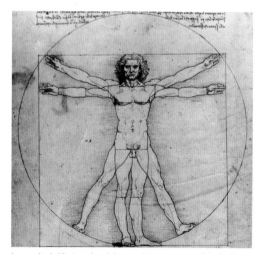

Leonardo da Vinci explored the exquisite geometry of the body.

Mandalas in the Sky

Whether by day or by night, the sky is a source of wonder and fascination. Throughout the year, clouds weave and spin above, forming intriguing patterns. They collect, swell and darken with rain, then part to reveal blue skies. Their patterns reflect the motion of the earth, the oceans and the wind. The flight of a butterfly on one side of the world may influence the weather on the other. Everything in the universe is connected, and the clouds are a reflection of every drop of water, everywhere.

Winter is the season for snow and ice. As moisture drops from the clouds, it freezes and captures in that instant all the motion of the wind and the earth to create a single, unique image – a snowflake. Each one is a picture of the winds and weather everywhere around you.

On a clear night you can see the movement of the stars as they slowly turn around the Pole Star, Polaris, sitting at the tail of the Little Bear constellation, unmoving in the northern sky. It has taken hundreds of years for the light of some and a few years for the light of other stars to reach the earth. In every moment you are looking into a myriad of histories. The canopy of stars spreads out in a vast mandala – a spinning image of space and time.

Mandalas on the Earth

Although it is not generally apparent, we are all living on a huge spinning sphere. As the earth spins, gravity connects you to the very core of the planet, keeping your feet firmly on the ground. You are at the centre of your own mandala. Rivers and oceans encircle you. Mountains, trees and tall buildings stretch above you. Urban or rural, your daily view is full of wonder that can enlighten your soul if you choose to notice.

A single stone is created by all the pressures and motions of the earth. It is formed over thousands of years from minerals and metals or boiled from the earth's crust and cooled over centuries. Water might pound its surface to smoothness or maybe grind it in the waves to form sand. Every stone carries within it an infinitely complex web of creation.

A tree, with its branches reaching out to the sky and roots spreading down into the earth, is a living mandala. Through its size, shape and texture it is a picture of its growing history. It

The constellations revolve around the Pole Star in a huge mandala.

embraces all the moments of its past, both recent and long ago. It indicates when the sun has shone on its branches, turning them upwards, and all the times when rain has soaked into the soil, encouraging its roots downwards. The trunk of a tree shows the same story, formed as a pattern of rings, built up year after year around the centre – the moment of its birth.

The Universal Pattern

There is beauty and truth throughout the cosmos. The food that you eat is full of complex molecules. The person you are today is built from the food you ate yesterday, last month, even last year. Each molecule is a beautiful arrangement of elements, held together in a pattern that your body can read and understand.

When you look at the elements – such as hydrogen and oxygen, which form water – you find that they too are a mandala of little electrons spinning in beautiful, harmonious waves around a centre, a nucleus. Inside the nucleus, you can see that the mandala of the universe is also there. Heavy protons dance a slow stately dance, a pattern from which all the energy of the sun is derived, while inside them little quarks buzz around each other, and so it goes on.

Switching from this intricately detailed, microscopic view of life and looking at the wider, bigger picture, you can see the earth rotating on its axis with humanity on its surface encircling that centre and the moon spinning around it. You can look out at the solar system and all the planets rotating about the sun in an ever-changing pattern. Beyond, you can see our galaxy, rotating as a beautiful spiral mandala about a bright central core. And even beyond this you see the expanding universe enfolding and spreading out into infinity. The universe never ceases. Everything is dancing in a pattern around you.

The symmetry of a spider's web typifies the harmony of nature.

ways of seeing

Looking deeply into the circle of a mandala means that you must look deeply into yourself. It sometimes takes courage to study the picture in front of you and see the storms and turmoil and yet also the peace and beauty that exists within the centre. By studying a mandala in sufficient depth and detail, you can connect with your inner self and look out at the world from the centre of your being.

Looking and Understanding

A mandala may be elegant and intricate, laden with symbols and vibrating with colour, or it may be simple and sparse. Either way it contains its own wisdom and truth. To unlock its secrets you must look below the superficial impression and understand the detail within each tiny aspect of the pattern. If you understand the message of each shape and colour it will help to change you and bring you closer to a place of peace.

This intricate way of seeing, of always looking more deeply into things, brings an original and fresh way of experiencing the world. Look more closely at a tree and you will see the patterns of moss over its bark. Study the moss and you will notice water droplets trapped in its rough surface. This is the way with mandalas. There is always more to see.

You can use this understanding to take action and make changes in your life. If you are in pain for example, you can look and see what is causing it. Perhaps you need to change something that you are doing, or maybe let go of some old hurts from the past. When you see what makes you happy you can alter your course in life to follow that path. Mandalas can tell you without sympathy or restraint, the truth of where you stand, and you can allow that honesty to permeate your life.

Colours

Through your cultural heritage you carry an understanding of the meanings for the colours that fill your life. Although every culture attaches its own meanings to various colours, they are often similar: after all, the sky is blue and the night is black no matter where you are in the world.

Each colour has its own meaning. Red is the colour of blood and life, and of the pain and passion which comes with the initiation of change. Orange signifies bright beginnings and the determination to move forwards into the light and away from the dark. Yellow conveys the need for motion, where you are almost there at the whirling centre, but have slipped and become stuck. Green stands for growth and harmony. It is the colour of innocence and joy when something new is beginning to form. Blue is a place of stillness and inner strength, from which you can express your dreams. Purple expresses the transformation of the past and faith and knowledge in your own inner centre.

The tiniest patch of moss holds thousands of water droplets.

The Rainbow

The rainbow is an especially beautiful colour symbol. Red, orange, yellow, green, blue, indigo and violet arranged in sequence, together make up the colour spectrum. It literally contains all the colours under the sun, without which there would be no life. It is created by the elements of fire and water – the rainwater in the air refracts the fire of the sun. It is a symbol of wholeness and hope, arching through the sky with the fabled pot of gold always at its end on the earth.

Chakras

In the East, Buddhists and Hindus believe that the body has seven energy centres, called chakras, that govern the health of the spiritual, mental and physical being. When healthy, these points are like spinning whirlpools of energy, circles of life. They are connected in a line that runs up from the base of the spine to the top of the head. Each chakra is responsible for a different area of life and is associated with a different colour.

Base chakra (blood red)
This centre is at the end of the spine. It is connected with passion and the primal energies for survival.
Navel chakra (orange)
This centre governs self-worth and self-belief.
Solar plexus chakra (yellow)
This symbolizes self-awareness and independence of being.
Heart chakra (green)
This is associated with taking responsibility for yourself and the ability to give and receive love unconditionally.
Throat chakra (light blue)
This centre represents honest self-expression and giving your talents to the world.
Third eye chakra (deep blue)
This is positioned between the eyes, where intuition, imagination and spiritual awareness sit.
Crown chakra (purple)
Positioned on top of the head, this represents your connection with the universe and the centre of your whole being.

Shapes

The everyday shapes that you see around you, or that you inscribe in a mandala, all have meaning and relevance if you choose to see it. When you look down at your drawing, trust your intuition about the shapes that you see. Always believe what your inner voice is saying and not what another person tells you. Basic shapes also have traditional meanings.

Circle: These are a symbol of wholeness and eternity. The inner circle of the mandala represents the most profound part of yourself. Its ring forms a barrier to what lies beyond, protecting something which is extremely precious and vulnerable.

Line: A single line can be straight and hard or curled and soft. It can be short and determined or long and sinuous. Hard lines often represent repression and pain. Softer lines may indicate indecision and lack of motion.

Cross: Two intersecting lines symbolize the crossing of two forces within you. They may be equally balanced if the cross is symmetrical or they may be antagonistic where one is dominating the other. The centre of the cross on the medicine wheel is the point of balance in a harmonious inner world.

Spiral: This is an ancient symbol of the womb. The spiral is a line that takes you from the broad sweeps of the outer life to an infinitely small centre where you cease to exist. It is therefore a symbol of change and rebirth into something new.

Crescent: This symbol is associated with the moon, which may be waxing and growing in strength or waning, symbolizing loss of power. It speaks of unconscious and instinctive powers.

Triangle: The three sides represent three aspects of yourself – mind, body and spirit. Together they interact and form a whole and may move you on to something new, in whichever direction they are pointing.

Square: The four sides of a square represent stability and security, the solid foundation of your personality and inner strength.

Star: These are brilliant signs of hope. Whether tiny specks or large brilliant objects, when times are dark they can remind you of the light within you and encourage you not to give up.

The changing moon reflects the rhythms and cycles of life on earth.

Numbers

The number of objects, the number of colours and the number of segments you use to divide up the mandala may all have significance, as numbers have their own symbolism.

One: The universe and eternity. One represents the uniqueness of every individual and every moment that you breathe. At any time, in any instant, you can change your life and be centred and at peace.

Two: Opposition and balance, equals and decisions. Night and day, sun and moon, each exists in harmony with the other. Two is the link between opposites where you must decide which path to take.

Three: The eternal balance between life, death and rebirth. It represents the whole self, physical, mental and spiritual.

Four: Change and cycles. It is shown on the medicine wheel by the four seasons and the four compass directions. You must always be moving with the wheel of life, letting the rhythm of its cycles flow through you and carry you on.

Five: The centre of the wheel, the fifth point in the circle of four directions. You have five fingers and five senses to interact with the world and when you stand, grounded with your legs apart, your body forms a five-pointed star. Five is the number of connection with the earth, the sky and the present moment.

Six: The four directions, north, south, east and west, plus the two opposites, earth and sky. Six is often connected with feminine energies and imagination, the "sixth sense".

Seven: The heavens, the sky, and the days of the week. There are seven colours of the rainbow, seven notes in the musical scale, seven chakras in the body, and seven visible planets. In a mandala it is the number of universal harmony.

Eight: Perfect balance. The eight-spoked Dharma wheel of consciousness in a traditional Buddhist mandala leads to a state of awareness which is perfectly balanced.

Nine: Deep wisdom and knowledge. A mystical number that represents the merging of the spiritual, mental and physical.

Ten: Completion. It is a sign of learning that allows you to be reborn into something new and different. It is often regarded as a number of perfection and balance.

The light and colour of nature can inspire new ways of seeing.

mandala meditation

A mandala is a picture of wholeness and harmony. It has been created from a place of wisdom and contains the essence of wisdom at its centre. Consequently, it is a powerful meditation tool which can help to restore a sense of inner strength and peace. You can use any mandala for your meditation – anything from a traditional Buddhist mandala to one created entirely by yourself.

An Inner Mandala

Place the mandala you have chosen for your meditation before you, preferably hanging on a wall in front of you rather than lying on the floor. Make sure it is well lit with natural or natural-coloured light so that you can see it clearly. Kneel with your back straight, your head up, and your hands resting comfortably in your lap. Close your mouth and breathe through your nose. Close your eyes. Count ten slow breaths and let your mind become still.

Now open your eyes and focus on the edge of the circle, noticing all the shapes and colours and what they mean to you. Move your eyes closer to the centre and look at all the intricate patterns of the mandala. Once you have looked at something, let it go from your mind and move on to the next pattern. Continue moving inwards, seeing and understanding all there is to see, until you reach the centre. Now focus on that smallest point at the centre of the mandala, and let your mind become still once more. Close your eyes and follow the entire journey again in your mind's eye,

Soft candlelight may help you to look more deeply.

starting at the outer wall of the mandala and moving in to the centre. See what you can remember of the experience, what you felt was important to you, and let the rest be forgotten. Don't struggle trying to remember every single detail. Paint the mandala as you recall it in your mind's eye and see its patterns and shapes inside you.

When you feel ready, mentally place your inner mandala in a special place. This could be somewhere inside you, such as in your heart, or in an imaginary place such as a golden casket, or in a favourite spot you know in nature. You can go back to this special place and reach that mandala whenever you want to meditate on it again or to be reminded of its beauty and peace.

Meditation for the Inner Self

First make the room into a meditation room by lighting candles, incense, playing soft and relaxing music and making sure that you have somewhere comfortable to sit.

To see into all the depth and subtlety of an inner mandala you must become quiet and still within yourself. Simple breathing and meditation exercises will quieten your mind and allow the voice at your centre to speak clearly. Place the mandala in front of you so that you can see it clearly. Kneel with your back straight and your head up. Relax, close your eyes, breathe slowly through your nose and take ten slow breaths to still your mind.

Open your eyes and gaze at the mandala. Let parts of it attract you and see what they remind you of. Notice shapes, patterns and colours. See what is at the edge and what is at the centre. Defocusing your eyes slightly may help you see more deeply into the mandala and allow it to "speak to you". Sit and gaze, letting thoughts triggered by the mandala rise and fall, all the time remaining focused on the painting. Spend five minutes or more on this meditation.

Once you feel you have seen everything, close your eyes and remember for a moment those parts of the mandala that held the strongest attraction for you. Did those parts have any particular messages for you about your life? If so, what can you do now to affect changes in your life in the light of that new knowledge? When you open your eyes have in mind one action that you will do in response to listening to your inner voice.

Burn incense in your room to prepare it for meditation.

healing with mandalas

Mandalas interact with the centre of your being and from this pivotal point you can affect great changes that will bring you to a place of health, happiness and harmony with the world. If you change the way you think, you can change the pattern of your whole life. If you follow the Navajo and Native American belief that all illness begins in the mind, by changing the way you think you can also remain healthy.

Acceptance

If you do fall sick, you can at least work to improve your mental attitude. Whether you are suffering from a mental, physical or spiritual illness, mandalas can help you focus on accepting the pain or sickness as a first step to letting it go and returning to health.

Find some quiet time to focus on your self. First lie down, with your hands by your sides, and breathe slowly. Focus on the pain or sickness inside you. Let it rise to the surface of your mind and body. Now sit and draw an inner mandala of that pain, expressing your inner self spontaneously on paper in any way you feel is right. Let every emotion and feeling that you have associated with the illness be expressed in the circle. Be true to your pain. If you feel despair try to give the feeling shape and colour in your drawing. If you have flu, for example, imagine what this "looks" like and express it wholeheartedly.

Listening

Sit quietly and focus on your mandala using the Meditation for the Inner Self described opposite. Consider carefully each symbol that you see and what it means to you. Think about your habits and what thoughts and actions may have helped to develop the

Use a natural object, such as a leaf, as a symbol of change.

illness. What can you do differently from now on? Pick a single change that you can make in your life which will lessen the chances of the sickness or pain recurring. For example, you may be able to think of a new way of behaving in your job that could reduce your stress levels and susceptibility to flu.

Releasing

Use meditation to contact a place of peace and hope inside yourself. Imagine a symbol that represents the change you have decided to try. This could be a tree, an egg or a rainbow for example, but it should have meaning and feel right for you. Paint or draw the symbol into a mandala, using all the positive intention you can muster. In this way you are physically working towards making the change in your life. Now meditate on the mandala and hold it in your mind's eye. Whenever you have an opportunity to make the change, remember the mandala and all the positive associations that it holds for you.

By making changes inside yourself, you not only affect your own life, but also the lives of the people around you. By bringing yourself to a place of healing you bring a little more health and happiness into the world, and the balance of the planet moves closer to a place of harmony too.

Focus on the beauty and harmony of the natural world to help you consider ways of changing your life for the better.

the centre of the mandala

Mandalas capture a moment in time, embodying it as a circular picture or object. The circle is a potent and universal symbol of wholeness and eternity, and its energy is focused at the centre. At the heart of the mandala is its deepest and most profound point. It is possible to pass this on to others as a gift or to use it to help bring you closer to your own centre of being.

Personal Mandalas

Creating a mandala for yourself allows you to give direct expression to your innermost thoughts and feelings, and to produce an aid to your meditations that will help you to understand yourself in new and deeper ways. A personalized mandala for someone else whom you know well is a very special gift honouring that person's qualities. Spend some time thinking about the person you want to give the mandala to. Meditate as you would for drawing your own inner mandala but think about the recipient rather than yourself. What are their joys and sorrows? Is there a special occasion that you want to honour? What is it about this person that you like? In the circle in your mind, think about the colours which most represent that person and what symbols you associate with your feelings. When you come to create the mandala consider the materials you could use and be creative in your expression of their inner essence.

Widening ripples on a pool are a natural mandala.

Understanding the Universe

You can also create a personal mandala to help bring more understanding and clarity of thought into difficult areas of your life. Is there someone with whom you find it hard to interact? Is there a creature that you fear? What things in life or in the world would you like to understand better?

Everything in the universe can be seen as a mandala, and you can therefore create a symbolic representation of anything that you like. Through making a personal mandala out of the universe around you, you can reach an understanding of any part of the cosmos.

Focus carefully during your meditation on the person, creature or part of the world that you want to understand. In the circle of your mind's eye, pull in patterns and colours that spontaneously come to mind. As you paint them, keep your attention focused on that person, creature or situation. Once you have finished, meditate on that inner circle and see what it tells you. You may see the world from the perspective of the other person or you may recognize some of your feelings about them. Listen to what the mandala says to you and the symbols will help guide you to a new place of understanding.

Changing your Life

By focusing your thoughts on changing an aspect of a mandala, you can focus your thoughts on changing your life. It is through your intent of purpose that you will change the way that you live in the world around you.

What do you dream of achieving? What changes do you need to make in your life to take you closer to your dream? Consider one change that you would like to make. Draw an inner mandala focused on that part of your life the way it is now. Express in your drawing of the mandala what it gives you, as well as what it denies you.

Now put it to one side and draw a second inner mandala. This time focus on your life after the change you are contemplating has occurred. Are you behaving differently? What does this change give you and what does it deny you? By painting the change and by holding the pattern of this second mandala in your mind you are actively seeking to make your new behaviour a reality in your life, and paving the way for it to happen.

Paint a personal mandala as a gift in honour of a close friend.

teachings of the mandala

The mandala teaches that in everyone there is a place of beauty. To live in this place is to be happy, healthy and free. This is the life of your dreams. Everyone has a different dream for their lives, and it is up to you to realize what is unfulfilled at your centre and begin to make the changes in your life that will enable you to be content and live at the centre of your dream.

Finding Truth

Mandalas are one of many tools that you can use to guide you to your centre and to find what burns at the heart of you. No matter which method you use, all require the deepest level of self-honesty. Speak your truth. Speak it loudly to yourself and louder still to everyone around you. It does not matter if no one else believes you. If you know in your heart that you are following your dream, you can then hold on to that belief and you will reach your goal. You can have anything you want, as long as you are true to your centre and your inner self. Paint a mandala of your dreams, of everything that you want in life. What is the one thing you want to achieve before you die? Paint it and hold it in your mind's eye as a talisman against your own doubts. As you reorient your life towards your centre, paint new mandalas which will reveal more and more about your dreams and perhaps show other new possibilities opening up.

The journey to the truth is not an easy one. In any mandala there are circles of fire to be crossed, and the tombs of old hurts to be unearthed and laid to rest. At the heart of each mandala, however, lies the centre, drawing you on and waiting for you to reach it. Take small steps along the path and slowly but surely you will find that you have crossed the mountain and come to rest in the life you always longed for.

The Buddhist Dharma Wheel, enshrined on a lotus flower and surrounded by sacred flames, represents the eight truths.

Living in Truth

On the road to your dream you will find obstacles. Buddhists use the eight-spoked Dharma Wheel to remind them of the eight precepts of the Buddha that guide them on the right path to fulfil their destiny.

Right Belief This is belief in yourself. You must be sure that you are listening to the true voice of your inner self and not to that of the ego.

Right Resolution This is the intent with which you take the steps on the road to your dream. This should always be approached with humility.

Right Speech These are the words that you speak on your journey to your centre. If you deny your truth, if you dishonour yourself, then you also deny that centre.

Right Action These are the deeds that you do in the pursuit of your dream. If you do not take the necessary action, you can never reach your goal.

Right Living This is a reminder that all your habits, good or bad, can take you closer to or further away from your centre. Right eating, sleeping and exercise can all take you closer to your dream.

Right Effort This is the energy that you use in your life. If the source of your inner energy is blocked, your actions will be half-hearted.

Right Thinking These are the thoughts that fuel your intent. If you think selfishly or with petty emotions then your intentions can never take you to your centre.

Right Peace This is the dream that you hold and the place where you can choose to be.

creating a mandala

creating a mandala

There are moments in life when you need to stop and look within. These are the times when you are feeling "out of touch" with yourself, when your inner voice has become muffled or simply lost in the business of your everyday life. At these times you need to reconnect with what you truly feel and to find out what it is you really need in order to become happy and healthy again.

The mandala traditions of the Buddhists provide a wealth of imagery and symbolism – beautiful circles containing palaces and diamonds, guardian spirits and lotus leaves. However, the essence of the mandala is translated into every language and culture, in sand paintings, medicine wheels, rose windows, stone circles and even computer-generated art. Regardless of time or place, every human being holds the key to unlock their unique path to happiness.

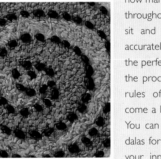

Creating a mandala can help you to find your still centre within. The art of creating a mandala involves turning your attention away from the outside world towards yourself and your inner universe. Every person is unique and each one of us has beautiful qualities. These may be evident or they may be hidden, but they are there all the same. By becoming quiet, by silencing all those loud voices in your head, shedding your endless worries, stilling your endless desires, you can recognize the peace and harmony that exists all around and inside you.

There are two paths that you can follow in creating your own mandala. The first is the more traditional way, which follows certain specific rules and procedures. This is how mandalas are traditionally created throughout the Buddhist world. If you sit and follow the elaborate steps accurately, you will create a picture of the perfect balance you are seeking. In the process of following the intricate rules of mandala-making, you can come a little closer to your inner self. You can keep these traditional mandalas for when you need to focus on your inner world, or destroy them when they have taken you to where you needed to be.

The second method is more spontaneous, free-flowing and less structured than the traditional approach. In this type the mandala is not planned. It is achieved by picking up a pen and simply drawing. This method is useful for giving you a window into your inner self. Through what you create, you can begin to see where you need to heal. The very act of drawing a mandala may be enough to bring you back to a place of peace and harmony with the world.

buddhist mandala

When you create a traditional mandala, you are working towards making a picture of perfect peace. It is important to start by creating the right space inside and outside yourself. Tibetan monks meditate and fast for three days before embarking on a painting. Although you need not go to such lengths, you can follow some simple steps to open yourself to the stillness and balance that you want to come into your life.

Preparation

Select a suitable place to draw the mandala, where you will be undisturbed and feel at peace. Fill the space with beautiful music or burn incense and candles to create a sense of peace.

Breathe in slowly through your nose. Start with your arms hanging loosely, fingertips touching, then raise your arms outwards and up above your head. Breathe out as you return to the relaxed position. Imagine that breath in as white light filling your lungs. As you breath out imagine that the air you are releasing contains all your worries and anxieties. Let your mind become quiet and still. Imagine that the music or incense is reaching into all the corners of the room and dissolving any dark areas into light. Picture your space bright and clear around you.

Shake your hands to loosen the wrists. Then clench them into a ball and release a few times, feeling the blood and life flow through your hands. Gently massage each finger right to the tip. You will feel your hands almost grow as they become energized.

Sit down and close your eyes. Keep your back straight and your body relaxed. Now you are ready to open your eyes and pick up the compass. Draw the outer circle. Now close your eyes and see it in your mind's eye. Look at the emptiness at its centre and imagine how it will be filled. Think about the journey you are describing, from the mundane world to the peace at the centre of the circle. Feel how close you are to the centre already.

Open your eyes, pick up your pencil and begin.

Focus on the feelings of harmony you want to bring into the space.

Drawing the Mandala

The following steps lead to a simplified Tibetan Buddhist mandala. The geometric rules follow similar patterns to those traditionally used by Buddhist monks, and some traditional symbols are used, although you may find it more helpful to use your own symbols. The mandala can be drawn to any scale.

You will need

- Pair of compasses
- Pencil
- Ruler
- Large sheet of paper
- Coloured pens or paints

1 Mark the mid-point of each of the four directions and then draw four circles from each of those points. Draw two diagonal lines to connect the intersections of these circles and the centre, to form the eight directions.

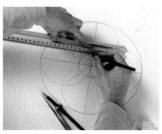

2 Mark the mid-point of each of the four directions of the second cross and draw a small circle to connect them together. This forms the walls of the central palace. Now draw the square to surround that circle.

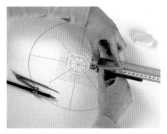

3 From the points where the diagonal lines cross the circumference, draw the square that fills the inner circle, then draw the circle that fills that. This final small circle is the seat of the Buddha at the centre of the mandala.

4 Along each arm of the first cross, mark the mid-point between the palace and the circle edge. Mark the mid-point between this on either side, repeating the subdivision four times. Draw four squares as the foundations of the palace.

5 Mark the mid-point of each half-side of the palace square. Subdivide again towards the centre. Connect the outer marks with the outer foundation of the palace and the inner marks with the next foundation. These are the palace gates.

6 Draw four circles with their centres at the middle of the outer foundation line and their width the distance to the palace. The outer semicircle, beyond the gates, is the area of the spirit that protects entry to the palace.

7 Finally, returning the point of the compass to the centre of the mandala, join the four marks within the circle edge to form four inner circles. These additional circles represent the four barriers to enlightenment.

8 When the drawing is complete, you can considering the colours and symbols you wish to use to fill the mandala. Each traditional colour has many layers of meaning, but use the ones you feel most express the symbolism of your mandala.

Colours and Symbols

The traditional colours used in Tibetan mandalas are white, yellow, red, green and blue, and sometimes gold is also added.

Within the Inner Palace at the centre sits the Buddha, who is both the representation of an enlightened being and of yourself when you are happy, healthy and free. The lotus flower with its eight petals is used by Buddhists to signify this state. The lotus grows in mud yet produces a beautiful flower. It symbolizes how it is possible to remain firmly rooted in the earth and yet reach for the sky.

The four directions within the palace signify the cycles of the earth and time. They are a reminder that the wheel of life is always turning and each step on the wheel can take you closer to the centre.

The foundations of the palace are the primal elements which make up the universe and from which we are all ultimately made. From the palace down, these four tiers are coloured with the yellow of earth, the white of water, the red of fire and the blue of wind.

Protective spirits, or doorkeepers, bar entry to the palace, one in each direction. Only those who approach with pure intent may pass through it. A traditional symbol that marks this space is the eight-spoked Dharma Wheel. Each one of the spokes represents one of the steps on the path to enlightenment, which are right belief, right resolution, right speech, right action, right living, right effort, right thinking and finally right peace.

Finally there are four outer barrier circles, indicating key stages through which you must pass. The outermost of these is a ring of fire, symbolizing the flames of purification which burn away ignorance. Moving in towards the centre of the mandala is a ring of diamonds, indicating light and illumination of the mind as well as the mental strength and endurance needed to reach the centre. Next there is a circle divided into eight burial grounds. These indicate the eight states of consciousness through which you must pass: seeing, hearing, tasting, smelling, body awareness, thinking, self-awareness and basic consciousness. The fourth barrier is a circle of lotus leaves. These symbolize the process of emotional rebirth that you have embarked upon.

native american mandala

The Navajo create sand paintings as part of a healing ceremony. This painting is based on one of a sequence used in a creation myth and ceremony called the Blessingway. The ceremony celebrates the coming into the world of abundance and life, represented by the four sacred crops, tobacco, squash, beans and corn. It is performed to celebrate or bring about a turning point in someone's life.

The Blessingway

The Navajo sand painting is traditionally made from sands or ground powders. However, these authentic ingredients are difficult to obtain. Instead, you can use paints or coloured pens, which will still allow you to capture the beauty of the painting. You may also add some natural materials if you like.

The Navajo follow strict measurements when creating the sand painting. Their exact rules are unknown, so you will have to use your intuition to create a mandala of balance and harmony.

You will need

- Pair of compasses
- Pencil
- Ruler
- Large sheet of paper
- Coloured pens or paints
- Natural materials, such as rice, leaves, stones and grasses

1 Begin by marking out a large circle with a radius of at least 15cm/6in. Draw a line across the centre, then draw a second line crossing it, using the compasses to bisect the 180° angle and establish the perpendicular. This cross in the circle forms the basic medicine wheel, with the four primary directions, east, south, west and north. Mark the mid-point between two directions and repeat this around the circle. You can now draw in the other four directions.

2 Replace the compass point in the centre and draw a small circle at the centre of the mandala, surrounded by a second one to represent the cosmic lake. Follow your instincts when deciding on the diameter of this circle. Now draw a large outer circle inside the circumference, again following your instincts as to how large you feel this needs to be. This circle represents the boundary of the earth, at the point where it meets the sky.

3 Draw a square a small distance outside the central circle and separate from it. Draw parallel lines close to either side of each of the four secondary directions. Draw short lines the same width apart to connect the inside of the square to the circle at each one of the primary four directions.

4 Rule a line across each corner of the square to join the intersections of the two parallel lines, creaing four small triangles. Using the same dimensions draw three more triangles along each direction towards the outer edge of the mandala. These represent the clouds of the sky which bring rain.

5 At the top of this line of small triangles draw a small circle with its centre on the direction line. Rule two perpendicular lines across the small circle to create a miniature medicine wheel. Repeat this small circle on all four secondary directions. These are the four mountains of the Navajo world.

6 Draw two guidelines down the centre of the mandala, the width of the inner circle apart. In the north, begin from the centre point of the square edge and draw a line to the intersection of one guideline with the outer circle. Do the same midway between this and the direction line and repeat on the other side so that you have a fan shape to represent tobacco. Repeat the process in the south to create the squash plant.

7 Draw in guidelines the width of the inner circle in the west direction. Starting from the centre of the square on that side, draw a zigzag line to the top to mark the bean plant. Finally, add leaves to the plant in the east, representing corn and three corn fruits. Tobacco and squash have their fruit on the circumference of the outer circle. The beans hang down from the leaves in the west and corn grows upwards in the east.

8 Finally, open the mandala in the east by removing a section of the circumference. You may want to invite some spirits or good thoughts to come into the centre of the mandala as you do so. The Navajo believe that only positive spirits may enter from the east direction. Draw a stylized head of the rainbow goddess at one end of the opening and a stylized body at the other end. The mandala is now ready to be coloured.

Colours and Symbols

Traditionally the Navajo use only living materials such as cornmeal, crushed flowers and pollen to create the Blessingway, so you may want to use grains such as rice or oats, or leaves, or stones, to build on the symbol of life. For colours the Navajo use one for each of the four directions: white for dawn in the east, blue for midday in the south, yellow for twilight in the west and black for night in the north.

As you paint the Blessingway mandala remember that it is a celebration of life and the precious and unique person that you are. The basic shapes of the mandala represent the unchanging elements of the natural world. The outer circle is the rainbow goddess who surrounds the universe. The cosmic lake is that from which all life emerged and whence it can be purified and reborn. Its boundary with the earth is represented by the square in the middle of the mandala. The small triangles and circles on the secondary directions stand for clouds and mountains, and the four crops, which are all sacred to the Navajo.

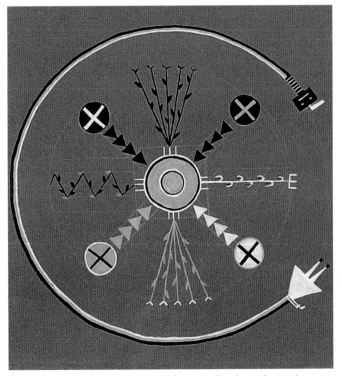

To fill the sand painting you can use paints, inks or any coloured natural materials.

creating new mandalas
There are many different ways to create interesting mandalas that you can put in special places to remind you of your connection with the world and its beauty. The drawing of a mandala can be a spontaneous act of expression from your inner self. However, first it is important to spend a few moments focusing on the part of yourself which you want to get in touch with and bring to the surface.

Using coloured paper can add an extra element of expression.

Drawing an Inner Mandala
First gather the materials you will need. Having a large pad of paper and pastels or crayons handy will save time when the moment to draw comes upon you. Other materials that are very expressive are watercolours, oil paints, and charcoal as these can allow soft and messy feelings to be drawn effectively.

Next, find a quiet place to be alone in peace for a while. Sit down in front of your paper and materials and use compasses or a plate to draw the outline of a circle in the centre of your paper. Close your eyes for a moment. Sit with your back straight and breathe slowly. Try not to think of anything in particular. When thoughts come to you don't follow them but just let them fade away. Count ten slow breaths and let your mind come to rest.

Now in your mind's eye imagine the circle you have drawn. Imagine what shapes you could fill it with and the colours you would choose. Open your eyes, pick up your brush or pencil. Allow yourself to put the pencil wherever you feel is the right spot on the paper. Pick up paints or pencils on a whim and draw whatever comes to mind. Remember that you can change the speed and pressure with which you move your hand. You can do anything, even tear holes in the paper.

As patterns begin to emerge you may find that you want to add layers of colours. Feel free to use your hands and parts of your body to smudge, imprint and outline shapes in the circle. Other parts of you may want to speak as much as your hands. Fill the circle completely. Remember that whatever you do it is right: there is no wrong inner mandala.

Medicine Wheel Picture
Another way to get at your deeper emotions is to create a medicine wheel or Celtic cross picture. Take a large piece of paper and draw a circle. Focus on the circle and use thick water-based paints to spread colour across the mandala. Use colours and shapes that express your feelings at that moment. Now fold the paper in half through the centre and press the two halves together firmly. Push the paint down and move it around inside the folded paper. Pull the two sides of the paper apart and then fold it again through the centre, making the second fold perpendicular to the last one to form a cross. Press down on the mandala wherever you feel the need. When you feel it is ready, open up the paper to reveal the circle of the mandala and the cross patterns and colours within it.

Living Mandalas
Using materials that sustain life can be very significant. Dried simple foods, such as rice grains, oats, seeds, lentils, beans, pasta and flour can all be added to a circle to create complex textured shapes. Find somewhere flat and smooth to work. Use chalk or a soft pencil to mark out the circle and any patterns or guidelines you want to express. Working from the centre of the circle outwards, pour in or place the food materials. Think about the depth of the patterns and the textures and shapes of the ingredients. For example, pasta shapes could be made into a spiral pattern, or oats could be piled into symbolic clouds and mountains.

Use candlelight and incense to create a relaxed atmosphere.

Rose Window

To bring a little illumination into your life you can create a translucent rose window using coloured tissue paper. Select three or four colours that you like and that mix attractively when you hold them up to the light together.

You will need
- Tissue paper in several colours
- Sheet of coloured paper
- Pair of compasses
- Pencil
- Scissors
- Glue stick (optional)
- Coloured thread and needle (optional)

A circle cut from a sheet of thicker, dark-coloured paper makes a frame for the window.

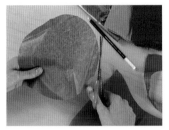

1 Start by cutting out identical-sized circles from coloured tissue papers and from a single sheet of thick paper. Fold the paper circle in half and in half again. Do this twice more until you have a thin folded segment. Now cut out patterns along all the edges, especially at the centre. The most effective patterns come from being bold and yet simple.

2 Put one circle of tissue paper aside: this will be left uncut to form the background to the design. Fold and cut the other pieces of tissue as before, making any shapes you want. Now unfold the paper and tissue circles. Each will be a different mandala, however, you can now layer them together to create the rose window.

3 Use the paper circle as the top layer to act as a mask and frame the different coloured patterns, then layer the tissue circles below it. Place the final uncut tissue circle at the bottom. To bind the layers together you can either use a very small amount of glue around the edges, or sew them with coloured thread at points around the circle.

Sand Mandala

The Navajo Indians have many mandalas, each of which is healing and relates to a highly symbolic myth. The medicine man would choose a mandala appropriate to the sick person's illness. The patient would sit inside the mandala and be healed by the spirits evoked by the mandala.

By using your own instinct, you can design, or choose a mandala that will help relieve you of your worries or ailment. The simple act of creation is itself very healing and the power of the mandala should not be underestimated. Centre yourself as well as you can with a short meditative routine and begin.

1 Use a pencil to draw a simple pattern on a white sheet of paper. Include shapes that are easy to fill with sand of different colours. Pour a small amount of coloured sand on to one area of your pattern. Start with the smaller and lighter areas.

2 Spread the sand around with your fingers until the picture is finished. Next, blow or brush the sand away to leave the paper clean again with all but your initial pencil drawing. Your mandala practice has now been completed.

ethereal

knowing

magic

craft

mysterious arts

All writing is the embodiment of knowledge, and therefore of power for those who can interpret it. Over the centuries the wisdom of the ancients came to be codified in complex systems of symbols. These arcane symbols of ancient shamans and mystics, whose meanings were known only to the initiated, possessed great power and became tools of psychological insight and prophecy. As the symbols were used by succeeding generations, the layers of meaning they acquired seemed to give them an intrinsic magic. By working with these symbols it is possible to tap into ancient wisdom to gain guidance and elicit knowledge of the future.

tarot

tarot

For hundreds of years, the Tarot has been a source of mystery and fascination, intriguing us with its compelling and enigmatic pictures and symbols. No one really knows where the Tarot originated, or how or why it works, but if we can "tune in" to the images we can gain access to a deeper understanding of ourselves and the people and events involved in our lives.

The Tarot deck is composed of 78 cards, which divide into two parts: the 22 cards of the Major Arcana and the 56 cards, in four suits, of the Minor Arcana, which closely parallels a normal pack of playing cards. The Major Arcana reflects the major turning points in our lives: our commitments, triumphs and tragedies, while the cards of the Minor Arcana deal with the more day-to-day aspects of life. Together, they constitute a guide to the incidents and issues that we have to handle.

This section provides a concise guide to the Tarot, with a general definition of each card. It also suggests different tarot spreads and ways in which you can use this ancient system of divination to give readings for yourself and others. Although there are general guidelines to the meaning of the cards, the ultimate aim is for you to develop your intuitive skills using the Tarot and to arrive at your own conclusions. In the end, each reader and their interpretation is as unique as a set of finger-prints. The Tarot still has the potential to be original and fresh and perhaps this is why it is as popular today as it was centuries ago.

aspects of the tarot

The Tarot is designed to relate, pictorially, what you are feeling inside. It reflects your psychological and emotional state as well as showing you the people and events involved in your life. You should use the images on the cards as a springboard, allowing their intuitive meaning to come through. However, while you are new to the Tarot, the following general guidelines can be applied to your reading of the cards.

Major Arcana

There are 21 numbered cards in the Major Arcana, plus the unnumbered Fool. The 21 cards represent states which affect everyone at some time. As the Major Arcana cards are so significant, they will always take special precedence in a Tarot spread.

The cards of the Major Arcana can be broken down into three groups, each consisting of seven cards. The first deals with the realm of the material world: material comforts, the choices that reflect and influence physical life, and higher education.

The second group deals with the realm of the intuitive mind. This covers aspects such as faith, free will, love and its transforming effect, and psychic understanding.

The third group is concerned with the combination of the first two and forms the realm of changing issues. It contains the most significant and powerful cards in the entire deck as they have the added bonus of challenging or altering the path of life you are actually on.

Astrology also plays a part in the composition of the Tarot deck. The sun, the moon, the twelve signs of the zodiac and the planets of the solar system are all reflected within the cards of the Major Arcana. The four suits of the Minor Arcana have astrological associations with the four classical elements of astrology: earth, air, fire and water.

Minor Arcana

Although it is possible to do Tarot readings using only the Major Arcana cards, the story would not really be complete without the 56 cards of the Minor Arcana. This group of cards completes the balance by showing the finer and more ordinary details of our lives, such as the people you know, places you frequent, particular events and day-to-day circumstances.

The Minor Arcana is broken down into four separate suits of 14 cards each. These are Cups, Wands, Pentacles and Swords, which correspond to Hearts, Clubs, Diamonds and Spades in an ordinary deck of playing cards. Their numerical order runs from ace to ten (pip cards), with four court cards – Page, Knight, Queen and King – to complete the sequence. Some modern tarot decks use cards called the Prince and Princess instead of the Page and Knight.

Each of the four suits deals with a different, yet equally significant, area or aspect of life. The suit of Cups deals with emotions and issues that are concerned with love and relationships. The suit of Wands deals with physical actions and activities and ambitions. The suit of Pentacles deals with all aspects of security, such as finance, your career, home and family. Finally, the suit of Swords deals with moral issues and the conflicts that can arise as a result.

While the cards of the Major Arcana reflect issues that have a dramatic impact, daily life is more likely to be made up of lots of little areas and incidents, some of which can seem quite boring or insignificant. These are shown by the Minor Arcana. It is by combining the two distinct parts of the Tarot deck that you can arrive at a more in-depth and realistic interpretation of your life and its circumstances.

Reading the Cards

The symbolism and meanings given here reflect a popular and traditional point of view. They represent an overview of the basic imagery that has been present in many forms in the cards during their history. Today there are hundreds of Tarot decks, each with their own vision and ideas about the Tarot. However, although a lot of decks will look very different to those shown here, in most cases these general descriptions will remain valid.

When you buy a new Tarot pack, all the cards will come in numerical and sequential order. For the purpose of learning each card's definition, it is probably useful to follow this order. Once the definitions have been mastered, however, there is no need to keep the cards in any particular order.

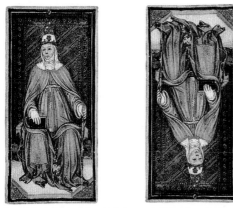

Some people like to distinguish between upright and reversed directions when the cards are laid out in a spread. The reversed direction can significantly alter the meaning of the card.

Aces

The Ace is the crowning card in any deck. Mathematically valued as either one or 11, it can be used to win card games because of its mathematical duality. This theme of winning or victory is also present in the Tarot, and Aces are usually seen as extremely positive cards and as the keystones of the Minor Arcana.

The Aces contain the powerful energy of the entire suit that they represent, the absolute truth of that particular element, whether it is fire, water, air or earth. They are of great help when approaching any new or difficult situation. The Ace cards are from the suits of Wands, Pentacles, Cups and Swords. The Major Arcana has no Ace card but the unnumbered Fool takes up its place in this grouping.

Eights

The Eights have a special role and are particularly important in a reading. This is because the figure 8 relates to the symbol of infinity, the never-ending cycle in which all lives spiral, always constant yet always changing. Any of the Eights will therefore highlight changes in your life, or the sense of moving forward. These cards are the eighth Major Arcana card, which will be called Strength or Justice depending on the pack, and the Eights in the suits of Wands, Pentacles, Cups and Swords in the Minor Arcana.

Fool

The only oddity of the Major Arcana is the Fool, whose number is zero. In medieval times, the Fool held a special place in society. For many people, he was an innocent in contact with the gods and was able to say and do more or less anything he liked. It is this idea that held sway and influenced the card imagery of the Fool when the Tarot was developed, and thus the Fool jumped into the Major Arcana in its own unique and individual way.

The Fool does not fit into any of the three sections of seven in the Major Arcana, so it can be placed either at the beginning or at the end of the Major group, in a similar way to the Aces of the Minor Suits. This decision is traditionally left to the individual, but for the purposes of this book and for learning the Major Arcana definitions, the Fool has been placed at the beginning.

Traditionally, the Fool is represented as a young, androgynous figure with a look of wonder in his eyes. In some decks he is sniffing a beautiful rose so intently that he does not notice he is just about to step over a dangerous cliff. The figure carries a staff with a bag attached to it, while at his heels a white animal snaps, almost as if it is trying to force the character over the edge of the precipice. The Fool is seen as an adventurous card and the feeling of change is often associated with it.

Pages

In former times, pages were young men and boys who worked in the royal courts, bringing messages, notices and letters and running errands. They served at table, helped the lords and ladies of the court to dress and did a multitude of other things. Being a page was the young person's education for a good position in life, and might eventually lead to a knighthood if they served well. In the Tarot deck, the Pages are not specifically male or female. They can represent some or all of the following elements: children, messages, communication (which may now include telephone calls, letters, e-mails or any other medium), information being given and passed on, studying, or apprenticeship.

Knights

In the days of chivalry, knights were men who served the king and his court. They were sent out on errands, to find new lands, make new discoveries, forge new ties and test their skills. In the Tarot, the Knights are figures of action; they take up quests – whether the goal is self-discovery and finding your purpose in life, or challenging misfortune and injustice on behalf of others. In today's society, where both men and women share the workplace and life's responsibilities, it is important to remember that Knights can be male or female.

Queen

The queen was considered to fulfill a role as the mature partner of the king, rather than as a ruler on her own account. In the Tarot deck, the Queen is a symbol of feminine power rather than imperious royalty. She can be both bride and mother. The Queen primarily represents women, and spheres of interest that have traditionally been associated with women: the home, relationships and emotional nurturing. A Queen can also represent a man who exhibits qualities or concerns in these areas.

King

The king was the ruler of the land, and his duty was to maintain law and order and preserve the safety of his kingdom. In the Tarot, the King is the symbol of masculine power, self-assertion and creative energy. Kings will primarily represent men and those spheres of interest that have traditionally been associated with men in a position of power and authority: ruling, responsibility and decision-making. A King can also represent a woman who exhibits qualities or concerns in these areas.

major arcana: the material world

The seven cards in the first group of the Major Arcana deal with situations that are connected to commitment through society's laws, such as marriage, success, higher education and the family. The Fool, numbered zero, begins this sequence, although he is sometimes placed last in the sequence of the Major Arcana, before or after the World.

0 the fool

planet Uranus

The fool is portrayed as a youthful figure dressed in particoloured clothes, sometimes with the cap and bells of the court jester. He carries a staff, representing his willpower, from which hangs a bag containing his worldly goods. A small animal, usually a dog, is often shown snapping aggressively at his heels. The animal is said to stand for the world of instinct. The fool is the agent of luck, always ready to change, and this is an adventurous card.

Upright

Spontaneity and a new beginning. New experiences will bring excitement, so accept the process of change. You will be taking a risk or an unknown step forwards.

Reversed

Venturing out without thinking results in frequent mistakes, so evaluate matters before going ahead. This could indicate a reluctance to accept responsibility.

1 the magician

planet Mercury

A man wearing long robes stands before a table as if he is about to perform a demonstration. His left hand is raised, pointing upwards towards the sky. In it he holds a wand. His right hand is holding a coin, but lowered, pointing towards the ground. Before him on the table lies a sword, a cup, a wand and a pentacle (or coin). Above his head there is an infinity symbol and surrounding him are flowers and other greenery.

Upright

This card warns you to bring all aspects of your life together: love, emotions, finances and morality. This is to prepare for changes and handle them well.

Reversed

An individual who conducts her/himself with great presence and perfectionism and who appears always to handle chaotic situations with ease.

11 the high priestess

the Moon

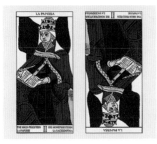

A woman in long, richly coloured, draped robes sits on a throne. Above her hangs a veil which sometimes has a flowing stream running behind it. The woman holds a book and often wears the symbol of the crescent moon, identifying her with the Egyptian goddess Isis. The High Priestess is also sometimes known as the Female Pope and symbolizes virginity.

Upright

Trust your intuition. Don't take things at face value. Look for answers to your questions within your heart. Use logic less to come to the right answer.

Reversed

Everything is out in the open, nothing is hidden and all the facts are obvious. You will now be able to make your decision, using both intuition and logic.

III the empress

The Empress is represented by a volup-tuous woman clothed in a long flowing dress and smiling serenely. She wears a crown and holds a sceptre and a protective shield with the symbol of an eagle. She is normally depicted in natural surroundings, with a stream flowing behind her. She represents security and motherhood.

planet Venus

Upright
The card to indicate fertility or pregnancy. For those beyond child-bearing years, it means domestic bliss.

Reversed
A woman who loves to care for others, though it can mean domestic disharmony.

IV the emperor

The Emperor is an older man sitting on an unseen throne. In his left hand he holds a sceptre and in his right he holds an imperial orb with a cross on it, which is a sign of authority. Sometimes he has a large eagle on his hat. He signifies a male influence, with confidence and worldly power, and a person well capable of using authority.

sign of Aries

Upright
Any established organization (bank, school, government office). It may mean you are trying to establish a company.

Reversed
Disarray or conflict with organizations. Take action and point out problems.

V the hierophant

Also known as the "High Priest", this figure is the male counterpart of the High Priestess. He also sits between two pillars, dressed like a churchman with a triple papal crown. He offers a benediction with his right hand and holds a sceptre with a cross on the top. Before him kneel two pleading supplicants.

sign of Taurus

Upright
The need for professional advice, or ritual, such as marriage, christening, or divorce.

Reversed
Someone who follows rules, perhaps an accountant or doctor. It also represents a stable and successful individual.

VI the lovers

A young man stands at a crossroads, and on each path a woman waits. The fair-haired woman stands on the right and the dark-haired on the left. Above the man flies Cupid or an angel, offering him the choice of either of these two paths. This card usually indicates love or possibly the beginning of a romance.

sign of Gemini

Upright
Instant chemistry in an intimate relation-ship formed by a chance meeting.

Reversed
Someone who challenges society's rules regarding gender roles, and will not fit a stereotype.

VII the chariot

A strong-looking male figure rides in a chariot pulled by two sphinxes or some-times two horses. In many decks the sphinx, or horse, on the right-hand side is light in colour and the one on the left is dark, representing good and evil. In the man's right hand there is a wand or sceptre. The canopy of the chariot is covered in stars.

sign of Cancer

Upright
A victory against the odds. There are many obstacles, but you feel that you are right.

Reversed
At this time, it would be unwise to apply any more pressure to the situation concerned. If you do, you risk pushing people or circumstances over the limit.

major arcana: the intuitive mind The

second group of seven Major Arcana cards focuses more on the individual than on society and worldly concerns. Decisions about the issues with which these cards are concerned are based more on how you feel rather than on what you think. This section deals with circumstances that really touch your heart, such as the search for personal faith, love and justice.

VIII justice

sign of Libra

A woman, who is identified with the Greek goddess of justice, sits on a throne. In her right hand she holds a set of scales and in her left a great double-edged sword. She is often blindfolded. This card indicates fairness and balance, the need to be logical and diplomatic and to argue in a balanced way. It can also refer to sustaining the balance of nature. In some decks, this card may appear as number 11, with Strength as number 8.

Upright

Justice will be served in the settling of an issue. A very favourable card in a karmic sense. Whatever the outcome of a particular situation, it will be a fair one.

Reversed

An injustice will take place. The outcome of a particular circumstance will be unfair. This reversed card can also indicate bias and a lack of balance in a situation.

IX the hermit

planet Jupiter

An old man with a dowager's hump who wears the dark robes of a monk. In one hand he holds a staff to support himself and in his other hand he holds a lighted lantern which he shines on the path before him. In some decks, the light from the lantern emits rays of light that resemble the beams of a star. The Hermit represents the wisdom of age, using his lantern to light the path towards self-enlightenment.

Upright

This is a preparation card, warning you to bring all the elements of your life together – emotions, action, finances and morality – to enable you to handle the changes ahead correctly.

Reversed

An individual who always appears to be "together". A person who handles difficult circumstances with ease.

X the wheel of fortune

sign of Virgo ♍

There is a wheel in the centre of the card with Fortune in the middle. In some decks the letters TARO are written upon the wheel in the position of the four cardinal points – north, south, east and west – as if the wheel were a compass. Sometimes figures or animals climb up the outside of the wheel. In this deck at the top of the wheel on a platform is a sphinx; in other decks it is often a man with ass's ears. The card indicates destiny and fate.

Upright

Fate will take a strong hand and redirect your path. The change may be good or bad. What you do after this redirection is in your own hands.

Reversed

Although you may have experienced a run of bad luck, this card indicates that things are changing and your life will be soon taking a turn for the better.

XI strength

In most decks, the strength or fortitude card is illustrated by a young man or woman controlling a lion in some manner. Some cards show Hercules killing the Nemean lion, whose skin he will wear to make himself invincible. The card indicates not only physical strength but also moral fortitude, self-discipline and courage. In some decks Strength appears as number 8 and Justice appears as number 11.

sign of Leo

Upright

There is no need to worry, or lose sight of your goals. Even if the road you are on is difficult, you will get there in the end. Be patient and persevere. Have confidence.

Reversed

You feel a need to seek reassurance from a trusted source to help you get back on the right track. Re-evaluate your position and consider where you are going.

XII the hanged man

A young man hangs from a tree by his left leg. His right leg is folded behind the left, making a shape like the number four. His arms are folded behind his back. The man's face does not look tortured but quite serene. The image represents a sacrifice of some kind which results in a transformation. It is identified with the Norse god Odin, who hanged himself from the World Tree in order to gain wisdom, and was reborn.

planet Neptune

Upright

Life is at a standstill. Although things may not be to your liking, it is not as bad as you think. Take life patiently until you see that the time is right to make the necessary improvements to your situation.

Reversed

A great contentment in life. You are feeling so happy with your present situation that you almost feel blissful.

XIII death

A skeletal figure wields either a bow or a large scythe. The ground he walks across is cracked, and in some decks he is walking through a field of bones and cutting off the heads of figures that have been buried up to their necks in the earth. Generally this card's meaning is not a negative one: it indicates getting rid of the old to make way for the new, or a time of change and renewal after a loss or an ordeal.

sign of Scorpio

Upright

Regeneration and rebirth, a new outlook on life. Sometimes this occurs after an unparalleled event has taken place, such as a near-death experience.

Reversed

A refusal to let change happen, or a situation end. This can lead to a deep depression which may create the need to seek advice from a doctor or counsellor.

XIV temperance

An angel-like figure holds a cup in each hand, from which she pours liquid, one into the other. Sometimes a pool of water is shown in which the angel has one foot placed in the pool and one foot placed on land. The card indicates moderation and the blending of opposites. The image of Temperance symbolizes balance, harmony and moderation, and another aspect of its meaning concerns the healing effects of time.

sign of Sagittarius

Upright

You need to test the waters first, not dive into the middle of a situation without thinking. Be patient and take things nice and slowly. Go carefully "where angels fear to tread". Exert some self-control.

Reversed

This indicates that it is time to re-evaluate the situation before you proceed so you do not make the same mistakes again.

major arcana: the realm of change

The seven cards of the final group of the Major Arcana are the most revered of all the Major cards because they go beyond the realm of society and the concern of the individual. They represent those universal laws and issues that have the power to bring about the kind of circumstances and events that can alter the course and path of all our lives.

XV the devil

sign of Capricorn

A large figure, half-human and half-beast in appearance, stands on a pedestal. He has a female torso and the legs of a goat, though they may be covered in scales. He also has horns and the wings of a bat or bird. Two other figures with horns, who may be a man and a woman or are sometimes lesser devils, are bound to the pedestal on which the devil is standing by heavy ropes around their necks, and stand on either side of him.

Upright

This challenging card indicates new-found passions, together with energy and enthusiasm. Rediscovering your innermost self and having the impetus to act on them.

Reversed

Obsessions, addictions, and compulsive behaviour. When passion is directed in a negative manner, seeing a given situation with clarity is almost impossible.

XVI the tower

planet Mars

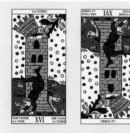

An apparently strongly built and impregnable high tower is being struck by a lightning bolt. This may be a dramatic and unforeseeable natural disaster, or the lightning may have been sent by an angry god as a punishment for the presumption of the tower's builders. As a result of the explosion, fire leaps from the tower and the top begins to crumble. One or more figures are falling to their doom at the base of the building.

Upright

Complete disruptions and disagreements in life that are sudden are difficult to deal with. It is necessary to abandon past ties. Coping with the disruption can eventually lead to enlightenment.

Reversed

The worst disruptions are over and it is time to put your life back together in a way that is more suitable and positive.

XVII the star

sign of Aquarius

A multitude of stars are shining in the night sky above a woman. This card shows a naked woman kneeling beside a pool or stream. She holds two cups in her hands. From one cup she pours water on to the land and from the other she pours it back into the pool. Resembling Venus, the goddess of beauty, she revives the land with the water from the pool, while the morning star heralds the beginning of a new dawn.

Upright

A wish come true, usually something you have hoped for since you were a child, such as meeting the perfect partner or the ideal career opportunity.

Reversed

What once seemed like a dream come true is no longer appealing. Now that you have your desire, you become filled with self-doubt and wonder if it was worth it.

XVIII the moon

Two dogs, one dark and one light in colour, bay up at a large shining moon. In other decks a woman holds a crescent moon. There may be a pool of water in the foreground, in which swims a crab. This is the emblem of Cancer, the astrological sign associated with the moon. The dogs suggest a connection with Anubis, the jackal-headed Egyptian god who presided over the dead and conducted souls into the afterlife.

sign of Pisces

Upright

Someone or something is not what it seems. There is a risk here that you are being lied to. Take another look at the situation and ask more questions.

Reversed

Lies or deceptions are being practised. It would be best to become detached from a particular person or situation at this time because neither is likely to change.

XIX the sun

In this very positive image, a large yellow sun shines down on a verdant garden of flowers in which two children or young people are playing or sitting talking together. The sun is a positive force of illumination, presaging good fortune, health, happiness and worldly success. It promotes growth and inspires vitality and confidence. However, if it is too bright it can also dazzle and blind you to the truth of a situation.

the Sun

Upright

A very positive card indicating growth and increased potential, such as progression in relationships, financial expansion, and physical growth (as in pregnancy).

Reversed

See your life for what it is and not what you think it is. Re-evaluate your situation to make better progress and have a clearer sense of purpose and direction.

XX judgement

An angel flies above the earth blowing a trumpet. On the earth below, people rise from a tomb with their arms and hands held open towards the sky. In some decks, a godly figure appears at the top of the picture. This card, portraying a vision of the Day of Judgement, symbolizes an end of a situation and then rejuvenation and regeneration. It may indicate that this is a good time to make a profound change in your life to free yourself from restrictions.

planet Pluto

Upright

An indication that what has been holding you up is ending. You are free to move forwards with a more positive attitude. The lifting of karmic restrictions.

Reversed

Poor judgement. This could keep you at a standstill or in a rut if you are not careful about the choices you make at this point. Take time to evaluate your direction.

XXI the world

A hermaphroditic figure dances lightly as if on air. In both hands she holds white wands, while around her there is a wreath or halo without a join. From all four corners of the card the same four beasts that are present on the Wheel of Fortune card look inwards towards the dancing figure. They are the creatures associated with the four fixed signs of the zodiac. In some decks, this card shows two children supporting a globe-like object.

planet Saturn

Upright

This is by far the most auspicious card in the deck. It indicates great success for the individual in all areas of life.

Reversed

A fear of your own success in life. It is as though the goal is within reach, but you hesitate to take it – perhaps through fear of it not being quite deserved or fear of being disappointed.

minor arcana: swords

When the Swords are present in a reading, the issues that are indicated by this suit concern any situations or actions to do with morality, moral conflict and conflicts in general. Think of an actual sword. It is sharply pointed, double-edged and made of strong metal, such as steel. The suit of Swords is related to the element of air. It equates to the suit of Spades in a pack of playing cards.

ace of swords

Upright
Victory and triumph after some difficulties and hard work. This time you have really achieved and it's been you alone who has done all the work. When the victory comes, it cannot be taken away. Well-deserved success.

Reversed
You must not put any more pressure on to a person or situation as you are in danger of pushing things over the edge. It would be best to sit back and allow the person or situation to calm down for a while, even though such a delay may be frustrating for you.

two of swords

Upright
Imposed self-protection, a wall is being put up between you and the outside world. This is usually due to your experience of upsetting situations which have caused you to build up your defences to guard against the pain.

Reversed
You are too overprotective and not allowing anyone to get close. Be more open-minded.

three of swords

Upright
You may experience heartache through a love triangle: for example you, your husband and your lover or you, your mother and your sister. Someone, if not all three people, will get hurt through choices that need to be made.

Reversed
Heartache through a love triangle as for the upright position, but on a less serious scale, such as disagreements, slight jealousies and insecurities, that can more easily be resolved.

four of swords

Upright
This card indicates that you need to take some time out to rest, recover and recuperate. This is in order to gather your energies for a difficult situation that has just arisen or lies ahead. You need to concentrate on pacing yourself.

Reversed
You may have been suffering from an illness or fatigue brought on by a difficult situation, but now you have rested you are ready to take on life and its challenges again. You are able to enter the rat-race once more.

five of swords

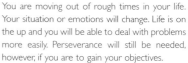

Upright
A rift or argument has happened and you must deal with this before your relationship can move forward. You have succeeded in proving an important point and your opinion has been noted.

Reversed
Now you have made your point successfully, there is no need to be petulant about the issue and rub salt into the wounds or you could be accused of being ruthless.

six of swords

Upright
You are moving out of rough times in your life. Your situation or emotions will change. Life is on the up and you will be able to deal with problems more easily. Perseverance will still be needed, however, if you are to gain your objectives.

Reversed
When it is reversed, this card could indicate a delay in your change of fortune, or that your situation is improving, but not quite so smoothly or as quickly as you would like it to.

seven of swords

Upright
Through your pride in your capabilities, or because you do not know how to say "no", you are taking on more than you can handle. Be vigilant and avoid becoming over-stressed.

Reversed
Certain pressures or problems that you have been experiencing in your life up to this point are beginning to ease up.

eight of swords

Upright
There are restrictions on your ability to get on with your life freely, such as living with a possessive partner, strict parents or being restricted through disability, pregnancy, culture or faith.

Reversed
The feelings of frustration or the restrictions that have been imposed on you are being lifted, enabling you to move on.

nine of swords

Upright
You are suffering from intense worries or stresses. You feel overwhelmed by these anxieties which you have been carrying alone. You need to explain your troubles to another person to make them more bearable.

Reversed
The stresses or worries have intensified, leading to anxiety and fear. This is quite a serious problem and you have reached a stage where it would be best to seek professional guidance.

ten of swords

Upright
Your feelings have already been deeply hurt as a result of a situation or person. This will have been a painful experience for you but you will bear it in the knowledge that it will come to an end and you will get it out of your system.

Reversed
This card has a very negative meaning when it is reversed, indicating a period of grief for you. Great pain or heartache will be inflicted on you intentionally by a person or situation.

page of swords

Upright
A wonderful feeling of enthusiasm, excitement and a desire to make a fresh start and take life head-on will come over you and make you feel as though it is New Year's Day again.

Reversed
A person you know is behaving frantically and impulsively, usually as a result of great excitement.

knight of swords

Upright
An individual with great determination, but also of great loyalty, conviction and strength of character. They will diligently pursue their aims while respecting and caring for others.

Reversed
A person whose zeal has led him or her to behave brashly, at times stepping on other people's feelings.

queen of swords

Upright
This woman is often a leader in her family or social group carrying the moral load. She can be stubborn but is deeply loyal to her loved ones. Her general demeanour is of someone strong and reliable, yet possibly a little aloof or distant.

Reversed
In outward appearance she is very similar to the upright Queen, but when reversed she can become extreme, judgemental and stubborn. She can come across as being cold and aloof.

king of swords

Upright
A man who will often have a fixed routine. He has a strong sense of responsibility and strong loyalties: he would rather suffer than let other people down. He is sensible, yet also emotional.

Reversed
A man who can be overly regimented and military in his routines. He is also rather harsh and cruel in his judgements, with a narrow outlook on life. Intolerance and narrow-mindedness are the key factors of this card.

minor arcana: wands
The issues that happen under this suit are connected with physical activity and action. Wands are concerned with the "here and now" and there is usually a lot of hubbub and activity surrounding them. Wands indicate a creative energy and an extrovert quality. They are also associated with intuition. The suit of Wands is related to the element of fire. It equates to the suit of Clubs in a pack of playing cards.

ace of wands

Upright
Put quite simply, the time to act on an idea is now! If you are planning any ventures or special tasks, now is the right time to get things moving. Karmically speaking, this time is most auspicious for the future of any given project or issue.

Reversed
Plans are currently put on hold or there is a lack of interest. Although it may be frustrating to wait, it is not the right time to proceed. It is better to wait until the timing feels right.

two of wands

Upright
Now is a good time to bring new people into your life and to share what you have to offer through friendship and lifestyle. This can increase your happiness and give meaning to your life.

Reversed
Someone who is living the life of a hermit and not finding happiness in that lifestyle. Now is the time to take drastic measures to become socially involved by taking up activities that have a varied group of people. The alternative is to face living life alone.

three of wands

Upright
It is time to pursue new directions in life. A new path is opening up and if you go down it, it will bring positive things into your life. This could indicate, for example, taking up higher learning or beginning to research a subject that interests you.

Reversed
You are being too passive, waiting for life to happen to you. It is time to formulate new ideas about the path that you can follow. Decide what it is you are interested in and take action.

four of wands

Upright
There is a warm and festive feeling in your life. Now is a good time to emphasize your feeling of goodwill by getting friends and family together to share in these positive vibrations. This could be through an informal get-together, such as a weekend away, a barbecue, a picnic, or a party.

Reversed
You feel fed up. You need to take physical action, such as changing your scenery by taking a holiday or redecorating your home.

five of wands

Upright
Discussions are taking place at the moment to clear the air on certain subjects. Usually these debates are beneficial and can lead to greater harmony between the parties involved.

Reversed
This card indicates that there is a degree of discord in current discussions or negotiations, which is causing all suggestions to hit a blank wall. Consequently, the matter that is under discussion will require time and patience before it is resolved.

six of wands

Upright
You will receive public recognition as a result of a job that is well done. Your peer group and those closest to you give you support for your actions. You feel satisfied with your efforts.

Reversed
This indicates that you will receive the recognition that has long been due to you for a good deed or achievement. Now you will be given adequate thanks for your efforts and will be able to look back on it with satisfaction.

seven of wands

Upright
You will need to protect and defend your current position. It is time to watch out for the competition in a personal or professional capacity, but you should have no problems.

Reversed
This card shows that you doubt yourself. You are in danger of being caught off-guard in a personal or professional capacity.

eight of wands

Upright
Life is moving in the fast lane. See which cards fall next to this card, as their course of action will be speeded up. For example, the World next to the Eight would mean that success is imminent.

Reversed
Things are grinding to a halt, or you feel misdirected. Re-evaluate your current position before pushing ahead with new ideas.

nine of wands

Upright
There is a chance that you are being overly defensive or suspicious, even paranoid about a person, event or situation that is currently important to you. It is best to examine your feelings carefully before you react.

Reversed
Your suspicions have been verified and it is time to move on in your life. The best advice is to look to the future and not to get too engrossed or involved in the problems of the past.

ten of wands

Upright
You are currently going through a lot of stresses and strains. You have many responsibilities at the moment, but you are quite capable of handling them, so don't worry too much about coming through this period successfully.

Reversed
The intense strains of recent times have started to subside and you are beginning to feel more relaxed and contented. This card reversed may also indicate the loss of someone close to you.

page of wands

Upright
The Page indicates news coming to you, for example, by post, telephone, or e-mail. It is information that will be of special interest and significance.

Reversed
Precisely the same as the definition for an upright position, except that the news or information you receive will be coming from someone who is younger than yourself.

knight of wands

Upright
A person who is soul-searching. Until they find the answers, do not try to pin them down. Wait and you will be rewarded with a life-long friend.

Reversed
A person chaotically looking for answers. Such chaos can lead to outbursts of temper from someone who is too extreme in their passions.

queen of wands

Upright
A woman who has a deep desire to be the centre of attention. She is charismatic and knows how to use her charms in order to better herself. She is often exotic in appearance and good with her hands as well as her mind.

Reversed
When reversed, the Queen becomes competitive and manipulative in order to be the centre of attention. She puts more value on what she can win for herself than on people.

king of wands

Upright
A man who is non-judgemental, with a welcoming and giving nature devoid of any competitive streak. He prefers to be close to nature in order to feel grounded in life. In appearance, he is as relaxed as his personality.

Reversed
When reversed, the king is rather eccentric. He does not have good "people skills" and he does not understand humanity and its blatant vulgarity. He can appear intolerant or narrow-minded.

minor arcana: pentacles
The pentacle is a gold disc that symbolizes money, and the issues that fall under this suit are to do with security and the material elements of life, such as career, investments, family, marriage, children, home, and any of those things that give us security or a sense of belonging. The suit of Pentacles is related to the element of earth. It equates to the suit of Diamonds in a pack of playing cards.

ace of pentacles

Upright
Great rewards or success concerning a security issue. This could be a sudden windfall or the feeling of finally achieving success in your career. This is also the card to indicate total success in a relationship, suggesting security and contentment.

Reversed
This card indicates a reversal of fortune that involves your financial situation or a relationship. This is a time of feeling "at your lowest point" and of experiencing the inner emptiness.

two of pentacles

Upright
You need to keep up your balancing act for a little while longer. Don't make any decision to drop any one aspect of your life just yet: you will need to wait for some more information before making that choice.

Reversed
You are in a situation that is difficult to control. A greater degree of flexibility may help. Assessing, then organizing your priorities would give you a considerable advantage at a time like this.

three of pentacles

Upright
The three of Pentacles represents a signature on contracts or some other important paperwork. This could mean that you will be signing a document such as a marriage certificate, an employment contract, mortgage, or divorce papers.

Reversed
There will be a delay in signing contracts or official documents at this time, and this could lead you to feel very frustrated. When this card is reversed, it can also be a sign of impending quarrels.

four of pentacles

Upright
You have some real fears about finances and feel the need to hold on to your money. Perhaps you have experienced financial stresses which have left you feeling insecure.

Reversed
You may feel deeply insecure in financial matters from a real cause in the past. It has left you fearful of spending money even when you are financially secure. Pay attention to emotional matters and do not lose sight of what is truly important .

five of pentacles

Upright
This card warns of a financial disaster or serious loss of security of some kind that has occurred recently or else is on the way. This insecurity may be as a result of losing your job, bankruptcy, or general money losses of some kind.

Reversed
The financial or security loss has already taken place and you may feel a sense of helplessness. The task of putting things back together should not be put off any longer.

six of pentacles

Upright
You will be looked after or treated fairly regarding a security issue. An indication of generosity in a financial way, such things as a pay rise, a profitable house sale, a generous divorce or court settlement, for example.

Reversed
You may receive unfair treatment around a security issue – such as a well-deserved pay rise, divorce, house sale or a legal settlement. You are not happy about the outcome.

seven of pentacles

Upright
Now is a good time to spoil yourself or make an investment and get the benefits of your hard work. This would not have any adverse effect on your finances at this time.

Reversed
It is time to stop "saving up for a rainy day". This attitude towards your finances is no longer appropriate: treat yourself.

eight of pentacles

Upright
You have a talent with your hands that could earn you financial rewards and could become a career. This card refers to any person who works with their hands.

Reversed
You have talent, but it needs fine tuning. Practise your skill, so that you become able enough to proceed with a proper career.

nine of pentacles

Upright
This card represents a woman whose natural demeanour attracts a good lifestyle. She looks competent and well groomed. If she has a partner, he is most likely to be successful.

Reversed
When the card is reversed, it indicates a woman who can employ ruthless methods in obtaining a satisfactory lifestyle for herself. She may marry a man for his money, or embark on an affair for the sake of the material rewards.

ten of pentacles

Upright
An established secure home, family or relationship. This card can also indicate the actual fabric of a home, which is usually an older property in pleasant surroundings, where several generations of the family have lived.

Reversed
This card indicates disharmony in a usually secure, established home, such as petty quarrels and potential disorganization. There could also be instability regarding the family and finances.

page of pentacles

Upright
News about security is coming your way. This may be a win of money, a birthday gift or a small inheritance. It may be that you hear of a job vacancy, and you get the job.

Reversed
This card indicates that a person younger than yourself is giving you news or information in relation to security.

knight of pentacles

Upright
This person is determined to get ahead in life. They plan strategically, knowing exactly how to succeed. This is a focused person.

Reversed
Similar to the upright Knight, but ruthless. These types will tend to burn their bridges as they continue to move up in the world, thereby making plenty of enemies along the way.

queen of pentacles

Upright
This card indicates a woman with strong maternal and material instincts. Her domestic life is important to her, and marriage and children are the path she often chooses. She will work hard to make her surroundings comfortable.

Reversed
This woman goes ruthlessly towards her goals. Often this reflects a very insecure or unstable childhood. She overcompensates for security and love by chasing financial success.

king of pentacles

Upright
A successful and powerful man with a great sense of responsibility towards his family, friends and career. He does not come across as overconfident. Usually he will make a sympathetic and caring partner for a woman.

Reversed
When reversed, this King is very insecure about his role. This may be due to a failed marriage, business or lack of interest from his children. He finds it hard to let go of the past.

minor arcana: cups

When the suit of Cups is present in a reading, the issues are connected with love, emotions and intuitive faculties. The symbol of the cup resembles a chalice or sacred drinking vessel and brings to mind the holy grail or the cup of life. Consequently, the issues of the Cups cards have a spiritual quality. The suit of Cups is related to the element of water. It equates to the suit of Hearts in the pack of playing cards.

ace of cups

Upright
This card is also known as the "Holy Grail" or "Cup of Life". Some consider it to be by far the most important card. It indicates a miracle or blessing. Any subject that the Ace of Cups is near will be blessed with good fortune.

Reversed
This card denotes disappointment or sadness. It can indicate a person with a large ego. This person tends to fall quite hard and they need to accept other people's views and feelings.

four of cups

Upright
This card indicates a new friendship. It can also warn that an offer of an emotional nature will be put to you, but with strings attached. It would be wise to find out what these strings are before accepting the offer.

Reversed
You may be the victim of feeling that "the grass is greener on the other side" and have now got yourself emotionally involved in a situation that is not as good as it first seemed.

two of cups

Upright
This card represents the forming of an important relationship built on common interests, friendship and a higher understanding of adult love and companionship. Usually it will be sustainable over a long period of time and grow and develop.

Reversed
A disagreement has taken place between two parties that is really quite petty. One person needs to break the ice and make the important first move towards reconciliation.

five of cups

Upright
You are in a situation in which an emotional sacrifice will need to be made, such as deciding between your husband and children, and your lover. In this case the lover would be sacrificed because of the commitment to your family.

Reversed
A similar type of sacrifice would have to be made as in the upright card, but in this instance it is less heart-rending. For example, it might be between your hobby and your career.

three of cups

Upright
This card denotes rejoicing, optimism and growth. It indicates formal celebrations of events such as weddings, anniversaries, christenings, or a promotion.

Reversed
Formal celebrations of happy events will meet with some discord. This may arise through personality conflicts, or bad timing in communications when things would have been better dealt with at another time in another place.

six of cups

Upright
This card shows that you are currently dealing with memories of your past. These may be connected with a person, with issues that were important in your childhood, or they may be concerned with children themselves.

Reversed
The reversed card indicates memories from the recent past. You will be dealing with a memory of a person or an event from roughly within the last five years.

seven of cups

Upright
This card indicates that you have plenty of opportunities and may be unsure of which one to choose. Whichever one you take will prove very rewarding and emotionally fulfilling.

Reversed
Emotionally it seems that there is no one interesting or nothing that fascinates you. This barren time will quickly pass.

page of cups

Upright
This card is always present when a person is trying to gain your affection or attention. It is known as the "Courtship Card".

Reversed
The reversed card is similar to the upright definition, except that the attention will come from a person younger than yourself.

eight of cups

Upright
All that has been familiar to you emotionally, such as a secure relationship, has now gone past its "sell-by date". It may be time to venture out into the world alone.

Reversed
You are able to re-evaluate yourself and the past. This enables you to abandon old ties and move forwards to the future.

knight of cups

Upright
The Knight of Cups can indicate a lover or a more abstract affair of the heart such as artistic self-expression. Perhaps a new partner is putting on their best behaviour to court you.

Reversed
This card denotes a person will be flirtatious, wanting affection due to their own lack of self-worth.

nine of cups

Upright
You are feeling a sense of emotional abundance, sensuality and fulfilment, and that "all is right with the world".

Reversed
This card denotes complacency. Emotionally you are quite spoilt, and you may be in danger of taking for granted the love and attention you receive from others with whom you have relationships. There may also be the feeling that you are never satisfied with your life.

queen of cups

Upright
This woman has an ability to listen to others and to be interested in what they have to say. She is captivating and has a sensual, understated look that attracts others. The Queen of Cups makes a wonderful partner, friend, mother and colleague.

Reversed
Similar to the upright Queen, but plagued by deeply-rooted insecurity, doubting herself. This means that she may stay in relationships where her good nature is taken for granted.

ten of cups

Upright
This card represents a fresh, new start in the home. This can be an actual new home, or introducing a new aspect to the existing one – such as a child, a new partner, or even making structural changes to the property.

Reversed
You will experience stress on the domestic front due to a disruption or a new introduction into the home. These stresses will usually work themselves through given some time and patience.

king of cups

Upright
This man enjoys socializing, entertaining and people in general. He is at his best when he has an appreciative audience. He is creative and is drawn to the world of art, theatre and music.

Reversed
This man suffers from deep insecurities and has a tendency to get involved with people who are not good for him. Owing to his need to be noticed, he will go to great lengths to get attention. He needs to watch out for depression.

reading the tarot

reading the tarot

The Tarot is a user-friendly form of divination because of the highly visual prompt that each of the 78 cards contains. For thousands of years, people have communicated through the use of creative thought and story-telling. By learning to interpret the Tarot with discretion and kindness for your friends and family, you can continue this age-old practice of learning from the spoken word and picture.

Almost as much energy needs to be put in before interpreting the Tarot cards as into the actual reading itself. It is important to create a calm environment, preferably with soft lighting, as the setting for a reading. Too much background noise or too many bright lights can disturb your concentration. Privacy is also vitally important because quite personal and adult sub-

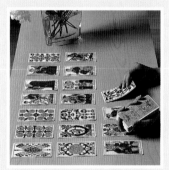

jects may be discussed while doing a reading for another person (who is known as the "querent"). Eye contact and a caring smile always help the querent to feel at ease when you are reading their cards.

At the beginning of the reading, the querent should concentrate on the subject or issue of their reading. At the same time, they should handle the cards, shuffling them in some way. As soon as the querent feels they have concen-trated and handled the cards for long enough, they can stop. This process will be different for each individual. Some people will take only a short time to get issues clear in their minds, while others will take longer to focus. However, it must be left up to the querent to decide when they are ready. They should pass you the deck when they finish. It is during the shuffling process that some of the cards become reversed. This is caused by the querent either deliberately turning the cards around, or by dropping a few in the handling process and putting them back in the deck reversed. Either way, it is the individual's unique handling of the cards that will determine how they fall when they are passed over to you to be interpreted.

When you finish a reading, always ask the querent if they understand and accept the information you have given them. It is with this final step that you will be able to monitor your skill as a reader, and gradually increase your skill in reading the cards effectively. For instance, perhaps everything that you said was true – then great! That will give you a real boost of confidence. Or maybe some things were incorrect – the person will let you know either way. Even if the whole reading was incorrect, you should not let this put you off, but remember that you are still learning and we all learn through our mistakes.

how to read the tarot

When you are giving or receiving a reading, the best way to look at this beautiful deck of cards is that it is like going to a good friend for advice. Remember that it does not control fate, or tell you how to live your life: but it can raise issues and help to give you a clearer picture of where you stand. If you are just starting to practise reading the Tarot, let the querent know that you are a beginner.

1 Gently clear and focus your mind. Try to let go of your own personal problems or issues. This will get easier with time, although if you have difficulty doing this now, try focusing your mind on one thing, such as a rainbow or a sunrise.

2 Clear the pack of cards by making sure all the cards are upright before giving them to the querent. To give the querent reversed cards is unfair, as their reading would be influenced by the actions of the previous person who handled the cards.

3 Next, shuffle the cards. It is vital to do this as it gives the cards a fresh start. The tarot cards are larger than normal playing cards and this may take practice. Make sure you focus on keeping your mind clear while doing this.

4 Ask the querent to concentrate as clearly as possible on the issues or areas of life that she is currently concerned about and that she wishes the cards to comment on. These will be the ones you will be interpreting for her.

5 Hand the querent the pack of cards and ask her to shuffle it. She should still be concentrating on the issues she wants the Tarot to look into. Only when she feels that she has shuffled the cards for long enough should she hand the complete pack back to you.

6 Choose whichever spread you are most comfortable with, draw the cards from the top of the pack and lay them down in the correct sequence, face up. As you gain more practice, you will learn other sequences, which may be more or less complicated, and adapt them to your reading.

7 Now read the cards. Remember that you are starting to learn and understand the Tarot. If what you are interpreting does not make sense or is too delicate a subject to take up, it is best to use discretion and plead ignorance in order to take the pressure off.

8 When you have ascertained and interpreted all you can from the cards, let the querent know that you have finished the reading by drawing to a conclusion. Ask if she has understood and accepted the information you have given her.

quick guides

This one-page guide to the meanings of the Tarot cards may be useful while you are learning to interpret them. The brief notes on the Major Arcana will help you to remember their meanings in general terms. For the cards of the Minor Arcana, take the general background definition of the particular suit and cross-reference it with the general numerical meaning for the number given below.

MAJOR ARCANA

FOOL *Spontaneity, change, risk*

MAGICIAN *Preparation, flexibility*

HIGH PRIESTESS *Intuition, premonition*

EMPRESS *Fertility, domestic bliss*

EMPEROR *Organization, authority*

HIEROPHANT *Professional advice, ritual*

LOVERS *Instant chemistry*

CHARIOT *Competition, victory*

JUSTICE *Fairness, balance*

HERMIT *Self-awareness, renewal*

WHEEL OF FORTUNE *Fate, redirection*

STRENGTH *Fortitude, self-belief*

HANGED MAN *Stagnation, renewal*

DEATH *Regeneration, transformation*

TEMPERANCE *Circumspection, self-control*

DEVIL *New passion, energy*

TOWER *Disruption of past ties*

STAR *Wish come true*

MOON *Deception, insincerity*

SUN *Progress, growth*

JUDGEMENT *Lifting of restriction*

WORLD *Success, contentment*

MINOR ARCANA

ACE *Potential, new, beginnings*

TWO *Affirmation, choice, pledge, commitment*

THREE *Clarification, plans made public, appreciation*

FOUR *Manifestion, creation of a plan, stoicism*

FIVE *Adjustment, challenge, possible conflict*

SIX *Poise, contentment, victory*

SEVEN *Imagination, options, variety*

EIGHT *Organization, evaluation, experience, commitments*

NINE *Integration, contentment*

TEN *Hesitation, resistance to change*

PAGE *Information*

KNIGHT *Focus, single-minded*

QUEEN *Fulfilment, deep satisfaction, skill, maturity*

KING *Competition, realization*

the celtic cross spread

The Celtic Cross is the best Tarot spread to use when you have a specific question on your mind that can be answered with a "yes" or "no", such as "I have just had a job interview – will I get the job?" This is because it deals with one issue at a time. Lay the cards out following the order of the sequence shown. The position of each card refers to a different issue as listed below.

POSITION

1	Person in question
2	Possibilities or problems
3	Best course of action
4	Influences from the past
5	Current atmosphere
6	Short-term future
7	The present state of the situation
8	Outside influences
9	Home environment
10	The querent's subconscious feelings
11	Long-term future

THE CELTIC CROSS EXPLAINED

1 Person in question: The card in this position indicates the querent.

2 Possibilities or problems: This will indicate either possibilities for a solution and a positive way forwards, or problems that may occur along the way.

3 Best course of action: This shows the road to follow in order to achieve the desired outcome.

4 Influences from the past: This card is about a person or something from the querent's past that is present now or affecting the current situation.

5 Current atmosphere: This represents the mood of the situation. This may be light and positive or heavy and serious.

6 Short-term future: This represents how the situation will develop over the next three months.

7 The present state of the situation: This tells us whether the current situation is precarious or stable. It indicates where it is now in relation to the future outcome.

8 Outside influences: This represents other people or issues that may have an effect on the desired outcome or that need to be taken into consideration.

9 Home environment: This tells us something about the querent's home environment at the present time.

10 The querent's subconscious feelings: This indicates whether the querent feels positive or negative about the situation and its outcome.

11 Long-term future: The final card of the spread represents the likely long-term outcome of the situation, forecasting over the next six to twelve months.

SAMPLE READING

1 Person in question: Death: This woman has formulated a whole new outlook on her life, and has recently discovered new energy, both mentally and physically.

2 Possibilities or problems: Five of Swords: She may feel the need to prove herself morally in the right over the issue that is concerning her, or to show that she is correct to have her new energetic feelings.

3 Best course of action: The Hermit: Now she should take "time out" for herself so she can gather all her thoughts and feelings towards her new-found direction.

4 Influences from the past: King of Cups: A very people-oriented man associated with the recent past might be the cause for her new thoughts, feelings and inspiration.

5 Current atmosphere: Two of Pentacles: Now it may be best to carry on juggling two important aspects of her life in order to keep things in balance for the moment.

6 Short-term future: Eight of Cups: Over the next three months, this woman will be making an emotional departure from her old lifestyle and going in a new direction.

7 The present state of the situation: Page of Cups: She will be very popular and sought after as she moves in her new direction.

8 Outside influences: Four of Swords: It would be best to keep her thoughts or opinions about her future direction, right or wrong, to herself. This is so that she can maintain some sort of control over her thoughts about her new direction.

9 Home environment: Six of Cups: The woman is looking at the home she lives in at the moment as a past-tense situation. A new home is likely in the near future.

10 The querent's subconscious feelings: The Hanged Man: Sub-consciously she feels that she is in a rut, and she is looking forward to making even bigger changes in her life when the time is right.

11 Long-term future: The High Priestess: The woman is right to put her trust in her instincts and gut feelings about her life. It is by following her intuition that she has been able to make the choices that she is now acting upon.

the romany spread

In the past, this spread was used most widely by travelling fortune-tellers. It is also known as the Gypsy spread. Many Tarot readers find it useful because it can look at a person's past, present and future together. It is best used when the querent has various issues that they are dealing with and they want to see how these things will turn out. The querent is simply seeking some general insights into their current situation.

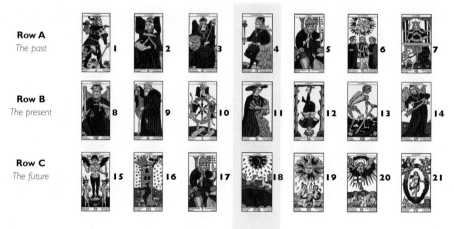

Row A
The past
1 2 3 4 5 6 7

Row B
The present
8 9 10 11 12 13 14

Row C
The future
15 16 17 18 19 20 21

Column D
Pinpointing the person

THE ROMANY SPREAD EXPLAINED

ROW A The Past
The first set of seven cards deals with the querent's past. Cards 1, 2 and 3 represent the more distant past, while cards 5, 6 and 7 represent the more recent past.

ROW B The Present
The second set of seven cards engages with present-time issues that are going on for the querent. "What is going on right now?"

ROW C The Future
The final set of seven cards looks to the future of a person's life and what is likely to take place in this time. The future is taken to mean the span of time over the next eight months.

COLUMN D Pinpointing the Person
Cards 4, 11 and 18 form a central vertical column. By interpreting this small group of three cards, the reader can gain an insight into what the querent is really curious or concerned about.

Reading the Cards

The Romany spread consists of three rows of seven cards. These three rows correspond to the past, present and future. The middle card of each row is also read as a separate vertical column, and relates to the querent. Begin reading with Column D, then read the rows A, B, and C from left to right.

SAMPLE READING FOR A MAN

Column D: By looking first at column D (cards in positions 4, 11 and 18) you can deduce that this man is feeling emotionally balanced with a positive and focused attitude. There is also a nurturing and caring woman in his life.

Row A: In the past, some information about a financial issue (possibly his career) led this man in a new direction, moving away from his past associations. This direction, which gave him a great feeling of excitement, turned into his way of life. Now, however, he needs to put his trust in a new direction.

Row B: As the querent has balance in his home life, he can take on new routines and improve his present situation. This can be best accomplished by being careful with finances and staying well-organized.

Row C: A blessing in disguise will take place for this man, but it means that a three-way emotional involvement will not work out. He should focus on the friendship of the strong, nurturing female in his life. By doing so, his creative endeavours will bear fruit.

Row A *The past*

Row B *The present*

Row C *The future*

Column D
Pinpointing the person

SAMPLE READING FOR A WOMAN

Column D: By looking first at column D (cards in positions 4, 11 and 18), you deduce that this woman has specific goals relating to her career. She is looking for more money and greater opportunities to support her interests.

Row A : This woman has high moral standards and was stressed in the past due to her sense of fair play. Recently, she has embarked on a particular professional goal by taking new steps and a calculated risk at her own expense, leaving her feeling a bit isolated, like the Hermit.

Row B: The woman is seeking professional advice about her situation, as she feels betrayed professionally by something that has jeopardized her plans. She seems to have the support of a philosophical partner, who encourages her to make positive choices.

Row C: She will soon receive news about a professional goal which will leave her feeling more emotionally balanced. The final outcome is one of total success in all areas of her life.

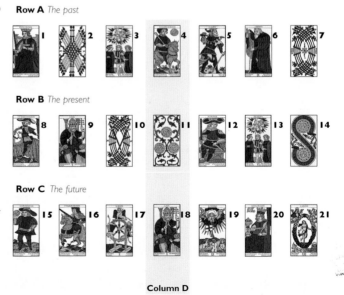

Row A *The past*

Row B *The present*

Row C *The future*

Column D
Pinpointing the person

I Ching

Ching

People have always sought answers to what might be. Will I be wealthy? Will I achieve my goal? Will I marry? Will I be happy? It seems to be an intrinsic part of human nature to want to know what the future holds. This is understandable: the future can be a frightening proposition, but there are no absolutes. Paradoxically, the only certainty in life is change: things are always in a state of flux, day slips into night and night into day. Inorganic elements are transmuted into organic life that progresses through a series of changes, and when that life ends the elements are released and another change is initiated. Spring progresses to summer, summer to autumn, autumn to winter and winter to spring.

In all change, however, there are certain patterns, and it is this predictability that the shamans of ancient China referred to when they were called upon to give advice and divinations on forth-coming events. These "bamboo shamans" of 4,000 years ago burnt the shoulder blade of an ox, inscribed with the particular question, and divined the answer from the patterns of the cracks that appeared. Later they used tortoise shells in the same manner, the tortoise being revered as a symbol of wisdom and longevity.

This was the origin of the I Ching, which translates as "The Book of Changes". As it developed, it became more than just an oracular device for fortune-telling. The ancient sages began to see that this body of wisdom could be used as a blueprint for understanding the workings of the universe.

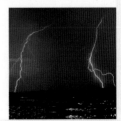

the origins of the i ching

The i ching has survived invasions, wars and other tumultuous cultural upheavals. It was first devised from observing the natural world, the ebb and flow of its cycles. The counsel the I Ching offers is based upon adopting a more harmonious approach to life, having an awareness and a respect for the influences acting upon every part of the universe, including humanity.

Yin and Yang

According to ancient Chinese philosophy, the time before the universe and the earth were created was known as Wu Chi, which means "ultimate nothingness". Out of this formless chaos was born the principle of yin and yang, the fundamental law underlying all of creation. Yin and yang are represented by the Tai Chi, the well-known symbol comprised of a circle divided into two equal segments, one black, one white. These are the complementary opposites apparent in everything; one cannot exist without the

Yin and yang lines can be combined in pairs to give four different variations.

other, although they are characterized by extremities that make them seem poles apart. Where yin is dark, yang is light; where yin is weak, yang is firm; where yin is feminine, yang is masculine; where yin is receptive, yang is active, and so on.

The Unifying Principle

The Tai Chi symbolizes the polarity of the two forces but it also shows a germinative quality: each holds within itself the seed of the other, and each is in constant flux: yang starts from a small point, grows and at its peak transforms into yin, which starts from a small point, transmuting to yang at its zenith, and so the cycle continues. Yin and yang are transient states of being, and the interplay of these two elemental energies, or forces, gives rise to creation. A good example is a pan of boiling water. As heat is applied and it begins to simmer, the water near the bottom expands and rises, exhibiting yang qualities; this allows the cooler water, the yin component, to sink. The polarity has now been reversed and what was yin becomes yang, and vice versa.

The Pa Kua

Both the trigrams and the hexagrams of the I Ching are known as *kua*, and the customary arrangement of the eight trigrams (*pa kua*) is often used together with the Tai Chi as a charm or talisman to ward off harm. The Pa Kua appears on flags and plaques, and around geomantic mirrors. Two layouts are used: the Early Heaven Arrangement, attributed to the legendary emperor Fu Hsi, and the Later Heaven Arrangement, shown here, which is attributed to Wen, first emperor of the Chou dynasty, who expanded and refined the I Ching by creating the 64 hexagrams.

YIN YANG

YIN	YANG
Moon	Sun
Winter	Summer
Dark	Light
Feminine	Masculine
Interior	Exterior
Low	High
Stillness	Movement
Silence	Noise
Passive	Active
Odd numbers	Even numbers
Earth	Heaven
Shade	Sunshine
Cold	Heat
Soft	Hard
Valleys	Hills
Still water	Mountains
Gardens	Houses
Sleep	Wakefulness

Gradations of Yin and Yang

It is not known how long ago the philosophy of yin and yang first appeared in written form but the symbols have been in use for millennia. Yang is represented by a single unbroken line and yin by a single broken line:

——— yang (positive)

— — yin (negative)

In this basic form, these symbols can be used in a simple "yes/no" fashion and a question can be answered with the toss of a coin. Yang is "yes", the "heads" side of the coin and yin is "no", the "tails" side. However, this system gives no depth or insight into the nature of a situation, no gradation showing what areas can change to give a satisfactory outcome.

Yin and yang are very definite – black and white, hard and soft, and so on – and there are an infinite number of points between the two extremes. This polarity of opposites was only the beginning of a philosophical system that could be used to study the workings of the universe and to apply it to aligning humans with the creative principle. There are also relative values of yin and yang: a person or thing can be yang in relation to A but yin in relation to B. For example, water is yang compared to wind but yin compared to wood, while wood is yang compared to water but yin compared to rock. Rock is yang when compared to wood but yin in comparison with fire.

Creation results from a synergy of the two forces working together and combining to form different structures. The ancient Chinese sages realized that to give a more tonal quality, to produce the gradation or "shading", further refinement was necessary. To this end, a second line was added to each yin or yang line. The pairs could be combined to produce four different variations which could be used to represent intermediate states of being: yang-yang is yang at its fullest; yin-yin is yin at its fullest; yang-yin is "rising" yang; and yin-yang is "rising" yin.

The Cardinal Directions

These four new symbols gave different strengths to the two basic ones. They were seen to fit with the natural order of the world, and each was associated with one of the four cardinal directions. In this way they came to be arrayed in a square form. They were also seen to be representative of the four seasons and times of day, and the gradation was thus perceived to progress in a natural and symmetrical way.

Yang-yin was aligned with the east, the spring and the sunrise; yang-yang, with the positive energy at its fullest, with the south, the summer and with noon, the brightest time of the day. Yin-yang was associated with the west, the autumn and the sunset, and yin-yin with the north, the winter, and with midnight.

The Pa Kua

Further refinement came with the addition of a third line to produce the eight basic trigrams which came to form the basis of the I Ching. The eight symbols were given specific names and arranged in the Pa Kua, an eight-sided figure derived from the previous square form, showing the opposing pairs of forces. The Tai Chi symbol of yin and yang frequently appears in the centre of the diagram. The trigrams are read from the bottom upwards or from the centre of the Pa Kua outwards.

The venerated sage and philosopher, Confucius, who valued the I Ching highly and extended its use and popularity.

development of the I Ching

The I Ching, itself very ancient, was the crystallization in written form of an even older tradition of divination, in which the patterns seen in nature were used as indicators of the likely outcome of immediate conditions. These patterns were formalized in the symbols of the I Ching, with commentaries to interpret the patterns and offer insights into the forces, or changes, occurring at a given time.

A Blueprint for the Universe

The early stages of the I Ching are shrouded in ancient myth and legend, but the original rendition of the work into written form is credited to the legendary first Emperor of China, Fu Hsi. Fu Hsi was said to have been a great sage and scholar. He was also credited with the invention of weaving and the making of fishing nets, and was seen as a great benefactor of his people. After many years observing and contemplating the natural world and himself, he came to an understanding of the basic patterns underlying everything. Using this wisdom, he composed the eight three-lined diagrams (the trigrams) which are the basis of the I Ching. According to one legend, the emperor saw the trigrams in the patterns on the back of a tortoise. The story relates to the tradition of using tortoise shells in divination by heating them in a fire until they cracked, then interpreting the patterns of the cracks. The eight trigrams represented the eight fundamental forces of nature which embody and exemplify the creation that surrounds us.

The original Pa Kua was called the "Early Heaven Arrangement" but it was revised at a later date to give a clearer definition of the dynamic interplay of the complementary opposites which work together to produce the changes in creation.

A portrait of the legendary first Emperor, the learned Fu Hsi.

The Development of the Trigrams

During the next millennium the trigrams were largely untouched, the next transformation being attributed to King Wen, a feudal lord from the province of Chou in western China. According to tradition, King Wen was imprisoned in 1143 BC by the Emperor Chou Hsin. While he languished in prison, King Wen passed the time by working with the trigrams. He found that by arranging them in all possible paired combinations they produced 64 six-lined diagrams (hexagrams). He also wrote a commentary on the hexagrams that refined the interplay of the energies that each of them symbolized, explaining them and giving advice on what needed to be looked at in relation to the question that had been asked during a consultation. After his release from prison, King Wen waged war against Chou Hsin, eventually overthrowing him and founding the Chou dynasty.

King Wen's son, the Duke of Chou, added another dimension to the 64 hexagrams of the I Ching by giving each line a specific meaning for a deeper insight. The individual lines are highlighted by transforming yin and yang, when each force at its extreme is changed to its opposite.

Later History of the I Ching

Some 500 years later the venerable Chinese sage and philosopher Confucius, who valued the I Ching highly, added more observations and commentaries to the treatise. This gave further weight to an already significant work and extended its popularity as an oracle to be consulted in order to determine a course of action to effect a beneficial change in a situation. In AD 175, the texts of the "Five Confucian Classics", including the I Ching, were engraved on stone.

The I Ching became an integral part of Chinese culture, but did not become widely known in the West until it was translated in the late 19th century by the German missionary and Sinologist, Richard Wilhelm. This initial translation into German was readily embraced by the renowned psychiatrist Carl Jung, who saw it as confirmation of his theories of synchronicity and the subconscious. An English translation soon followed and numerous other translations and interpretations have ensured its widespread appeal, giving people from all walks of life advice on problems and self-development.

A carved stone tortoise, symbolizing wisdom, commemorates the story of the beginnings of the I Ching.

the eight trigrams

The trigrams were given attributes and characteristics that helped to define them symbolically in terms of the natural world, human social arrangements, colours, animal totems and body parts, to name just a few. In an I Ching consultation, these images are used metaphorically to give depth and refinement to the hexagrams that are constructed by arranging the trigrams in pairs.

 Ch'ien represents heaven, the power of the universe, and the creative. In the family it is the father, and in the body it is associated with the head. It is strong and active, the three yang lines representing vitality, limitless potential and endurance. Its colour is blinding white and its animal is the horse. It also symbolizes ice and the fruit of a tree.

 K'un represents earth, the receptive. The family member is the mother and the body part is the belly. It is gentle and passive, the three yin lines representing endless nurturing and devotion. Its colour is black and its animal is the cow. It also symbolizes the supportive tree trunk and a large cloth or cart, carrying all things without distinction.

 Chen represents thunder, the arousing. In the family it is the eldest son, and in the body it is the foot. It is violent and determined, filled with spontaneity and excitement. Its colour is bright red and its animal is the dragon, the symbol of speed and power. It also represents the fast-growing reed, volcanoes and earthquakes.
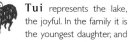

 Sun represents wind, the gentle and penetrating. In the family it is the eldest daughter, and in the body the thighs. It is soothing yet persevering and just, characterizing flexibility and strength, and permeating all things like the wind. Its colour is lush green and its animal is the cat or tiger. It also symbolizes tall, graceful trees such as the willow, that can bend before the wind and spring back easily.

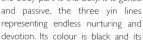 **K'an** represents water, the abysmal. In the family it is the middle son, and the body part is the ear. It is dangerous and fearless, full of hidden perils and swirling, erosive forces. Its colour is deep blue and its animal the pig or boar. It is also symbolic of marrowy wood, soft and spongy, able to soak up water but lacking great strength.

 Li represents fire, the clinging. In the family it is the middle daughter, and in the body the eyes. It is bright, warm and clear, corresponding to beauty and intelligence. The lives of others benefit from its radiance. Its colour is warm orange, the colour of fire and the sun, and its animal is the peacock. Li also represents dry, brittle trees.

 **Ken** represents the mountain, the stillness. The family member is the youngest son and the body part is the hand. It is calm, meditative and earnest, able to withdraw yet to grasp things firmly. Its colour is imperial purple and its animal is the dog. It is also seen as a hermit and as a strong, gnarled tree, twisted from its position on a mountain.

Tui represents the lake, the joyful. In the family it is the youngest daughter, and in the body it is associated with the mouth and lips, always ready to smile in friendliness. It is tender and sensual on the outside, making it attractive and inviting, yet it possesses a hard, iron core. Its colour is yellow and its animal is the sheep. It also evokes the spirit of a witch or sorceress, and represents mist and harvests.

consulting the oracle

The I Ching does not tell you what to do. It counsels on the nature of a problem and the best way to deal with it. It is the Sage that is aware of all possibilities and the insights it offers are pertinent to you and your situation. The onus of effecting the change is on you accepting the advice and acting on it. For a consultation several things are needed, physical and metaphysical, but principally a reflective state of mind.

Ritual

The most important factors to bring to an I Ching consultation are an open mind and humility. It is not necessary to prostrate yourself, but you do need to leave your ego at the door to show proper respect to a wise and venerated Sage. In fact, the humility has already begun because you have taken the first steps in approaching the oracle for advice, recognizing that you have a need for assistance and that there is a higher power you can call upon.

As an aid to achieving a calm and receptive state of mind when approaching the I Ching, it is useful to perform a small ritual to help you relax and focus your intent. Light a candle and contemplate the flame. A living

Hold the coins for a moment in your hand before you throw them, as you would throw dice.

flame is beautiful and as you give it your attention imagine it illuminating you inside. Burn some incense: its calming effects have been used for thousands of years and the smoke also has cleans-

ing properties. As you watch the smoke, imagine it pervading your aura, purifying it of any negative energies that you have accumulated. Pass the coins through the incense smoke to purify them. The effects of the smoke will also cleanse the auras of objects and places. Breathe deeply and slowly from your diaphragm for a few breaths. This helps to relax you and focus your attention.

When consulting the I Ching you are circumventing the conscious mind, and all the hormones and emotions that have such a large effect on it, and contacting the higher self. This is the part of you which is in direct communication with the rest of creation, the part of you through which intuition flows and which wants only what is best for you. With time and practice it will become easier to reach a calm state of mind and it may be that after a while a ritual is unnecessary, although it does serve to differentiate the consultation from the day-to-day life you are seeking help with.

Formulating a Question

What are you consulting the I Ching about? What are you seeking guidance on? It is necessary to determine the subject first so that you can pose the question in a way that is not at all ambiguous. It is necessary to approach the subject with the seriousness it deserves. The I Ching is not a party game and will not respond if you ask frivolous questions or are indifferent to the counsel it offers.

Some people consult the I Ching on a daily basis concerning the best way to act on that day, others consult it only at times of crisis or when at a crossroads in life. The frequency is not important, but if you ask too often it is a sign that you are probably not relaxed. Don't repeat questions because that indicates that you have no faith in the answer you first received; this may lead to the Sage withdrawing assistance and further answers you receive will be confused or garbled.

Try to maintain an objective, detached attitude. If you are emotionally involved in the question, if it is of great importance to you when you ask it, the charged nature of your physical state will interfere with the clarity of the process. In an emotional state you will also be less receptive to the answer you receive because it may not be the one you were hoping for.

Write your question down to clarify it and help you focus on it.

Constructing a Hexagram

The usual way to construct a hexagram is to cast three coins. They can be of any denomination but it is best if they are all of the same size and value. Old Chinese coins are satisfying to use.

Use the same coins each time and do not let anyone else touch them because their auras can be influenced by energies from another source. Treat them with respect because they are an important link to the Sage. Traditionally the coins were blessed and purified then stored with the I Ching on a shelf above shoulder height, only to be moved for purposes of a consultation.

The faces of the coins are assigned a value, which when added together determines whether a line of a hexagram will be yin or yang. The "heads" side (the more heavily inscribed side on a Chinese coin) is considered yang and is valued at three, while the "tails" side is yin and is given a value of two. When the coins are thrown, a total of six, seven, eight or nine is obtained, giving lines that are either yin (even numbers) or yang (odd numbers).

Hold the coins while you focus on what you seek guidance on, then shake them gently in your cupped hands while concentrating on the question. Drop the coins on to a hard surface such as a table or the floor and add up their values. Repeat five times until you have six totals. The first line is at the bottom and the hexagram is constructed upwards, following the path of organic growth. In the following example, x denotes "heads" (3) and – denotes "tails" (2):

```
Sixth throw:   x  x  –  = 8
Fifth throw:   x  x  –  = 8      K'un    ==
Fourth throw:  x  x  –  = 8              ==

Third throw:   x  –  –  = 7
Second throw:  x  –  –  = 7      Ch'ien  ==
First throw:   x  –  –  = 7              ==
```

If, when you cast the coins, you throw only sevens and eights it indicates that the answer is very clear and you need only read the interpretation of the relevant hexagram.

Old Chinese coins have a symbolic connection with the I Ching.

Use candles to help you in your meditation while you are concentrating on the situation you wish to ask a question about.

Changing Lines

The totals of the coins' faces can produce two odd numbers and two even numbers. The seven and the eight stay the same. The six and the nine, however, represent old yin and old yang which means that they are at their extremes, so each changes to its opposite, altering the result and giving you a second hexagram to interpret as part of the consultation.

Six is old yin, written —x— and becomes young yang.
Seven is young yang, written ——— and stays the same.
Eight is young yin, written — — and stays the same.
Nine is old yang, written —•— and changes to young yin.

The changing lines give deeper insights into a reading. The initial hexagram relates to present conditions; the changing lines produce a second hexagram which relates to the future outcome of a situation or helps to clarify the original question. If you receive a hexagram with changing lines, read the interpretation of the first hexagram and the lines that are changing, then go to the second hexagram and read the interpretation only. The following example shows changing lines:

```
Sixth throw:   x  x  x  = 9
Fifth throw:   x  –  –  = 7      Sun becomes K'an
Fourth throw:  x  x  –  = 8

Third throw:   x  x  –  = 8
Second throw:  –  –  –  = 6      Chen becomes Tui
First throw:   x  –  –  = 7
```

The first throw produced hexagram number 42, I (Increase), with lines two and six changing, which then gave hexagram number 60, Chieh (Limitation). Going to the relevant page, you would read the interpretation and lines two and six of I, then you would go to Chieh and read the interpretation only.

table of trigrams

Once the hexagram is obtained, it can be identified using this table. The left-hand side shows the lower trigrams, and the top shows the upper trigrams. Find the component trigrams of the hexagram you have constructed and the square where they meet will give the number of the hexagram. When you have that number, turn to the relevant page and read the interpretation of it.

Upper Trigrams

Lower Trigrams	CH'IEN	CHEN	K'AN	KEN	TUI	LI	SUN	K'UN
CH'IEN	1	34	5	26	43	14	9	11
CHEN	25	51	3	27	17	21	42	24
K'AN	6	40	29	4	47	64	59	7
KEN	33	62	39	52	31	56	53	15
TUI	10	54	60	41	58	38	61	19
LI	13	55	63	22	49	30	37	36
SUN	44	32	48	18	28	50	57	46
K'UN	12	16	8	23	45	35	20	2

table of hexagrams

This table shows the 64 hexagrams, arranged according to the trigrams which make them up. Hexagrams are always constructed from the bottom up, which is also the traditional method of writing Chinese characters. This follows the patterns and structures of nature, since everything grows from the ground upwards. Like the trigrams, each hexagram has a name and a basic meaning.

	CH'IEN	CHEN	K'AN	KEN	TUI	LI	SUN	K'UN
CH'IEN								
CHEN								
K'AN								
KEN								
TUI								
LI								
SUN								
K'UN								

the hexagrams

the hexagrams

The 64 hexagrams of the I Ching are all the possible combinations of the eight trigrams of the Pa Kua. Although two
trigrams form a complete hexagram, they maintain their
individuality in the structure by virtue of their relative positions. The lower trigram represents the basis or foundation
of the situation, and the upper trigram reflects the manner

in which the circumstances can unfold
or develop. In addition to this distinction, each of the six lines has its own
significance in terms of its position in
the hexagram, which is read from the
bottom upwards.

The first line (at the bottom) is
related to the early beginnings of a situation and can be seen as someone of
low social standing. The second line is
where the subject resides: this is the
core of the lower trigram. The third line is the transition
from the lower trigram to the upper and is associated with
the pitfalls that lie in wait for someone rising above their
station without due care.

The fourth line is seen as the officer, the intermediary
between the ruler and the masses. As the first line of the
upper trigram it also signifies a successful rise from the
lower trigram to the upper.

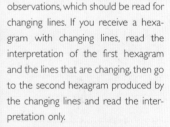

The fifth line represents the ruler, and is the core of the
upper trigram. It can also symbolize good fortune. The sixth
line indicates that there are things beyond even rulers and
is a caution against reaching too high.

The commentaries on the 64 hexagrams are set out on
the following pages, with the Duke of Chou's additional
observations, which should be read for
changing lines. If you receive a hexagram with changing lines, read the
interpretation of the first hexagram
and the lines that are changing, then go
to the second hexagram produced by
the changing lines and read the interpretation only.

To benefit from reading the interpretation you need to keep the same
open, detached frame of mind with
which you formulated your question and constructed the
hexagram. Read the text carefully. It may be useful to note
down your immediate responses or thoughts relating to
the interpretation. If you feel that the answers you have
received are unclear, it could mean that you did not phrase
your question with sufficient clarity, or that you are not in a
sufficiently receptive state on this occasion. Leave it and
come back to it later.

乾 1 CH'IEN – The creative *Masculine, dynamic, inspiring, overbearing*

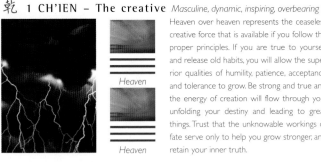

Heaven

Heaven

Heaven over heaven represents the ceaseless creative force that is available if you follow the proper principles. If you are true to yourself and release old habits, you will allow the superior qualities of humility, patience, acceptance and tolerance to grow. Be strong and true and the energy of creation will flow through you, unfolding your destiny and leading to great things. Trust that the unknowable workings of fate serve only to help you grow stronger, and retain your inner truth.

Line readings
6 Retain your humility and acceptance, or you will suffer a great fall.
5 Join with other like-minded people and work together for mutual benefit.
4 Trust in your inner truth to guide you and do not hesitate in coming to a decision when you have to make a choice.
3 Do not let adulation go to your head.
2 The best way to exert an influence is to lead by example.
1 Be patient and listen to your heart to tell you when to act.

坤 2 K'UN – The receptive *Feminine, yielding, gentle, providing, bountiful*

Earth

Earth

This is the complement to the first hexagram. For the creative to take root and flourish, it needs receptive ground to provide nourishment. Cultivate the receptive nature that will provide the appropriate ground for wisdom to grow. The earth is the endless provider, giving without seeking recognition. This is the time to follow because there is not enough experience to lead or initiate change. Concentrate on developing inner strength: what you receive now will produce bountiful results in future.

Line readings
6 Remain passive and receptive to ideas and be guided by the Sage.
5 Concentrate upon what you know to be true and right for you.
4 Keep yourself to yourself and be reserved in your actions and words.
3 Be inspired by others but do not trumpet your own achievements.
2 Respond to circumstances as they arise with suppleness and adaptability.
1 Use this time to consolidate what you learn and to develop your inner truth.

屯 3 CHUN – Difficult beginnings *Immaturity, perseverance*

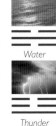

Water

Thunder

This is a time of potential growth, but like any new venture there is often initial adversity. As the seedling perseveres and grows, so will you overcome difficult beginnings if you persevere in holding on to proper principles. A new situation can develop in any direction; by being aware of this possibility you can correct harmful growth before it goes too far. Accept help that is offered and remain steadfast during this chaotic time, allowing it to resolve itself, and your progress will be successful.

Line readings
6 Trust in the guidance of the I Ching and you will win through eventually.
5 Trying to force a resolution will inevitably result in failure.
4 Sincerely ally yourself to others who are also true and sincere, and all will go well.
3 Be cautious and trust your instincts to alert you to hidden hazards.
2 Wait patiently for a solution that is correct in all respects.
1 Progress is difficult but be patient and the way ahead will become apparent.

蒙 4 MÊNG – Youthful folly *Inexperience, guidance, enthusiasm, tuition*

Mountain

Water

Youth is a time of inexperience but it is possible to be old yet inexperienced in a certain area. Youth is also a time of boundless enthusiasm which can lead to folly, but enthusiasm can see you through the setbacks that inexperience can cause. Beginner's luck will eventually run out, however, and to continue to grow it is necessary to seek guidance from an experienced teacher and to learn from your mistakes. The I Ching offers this guidance and its wisdom can help you to learn as you grow.

Line readings
6 Do not dwell on mistakes, but accept the lesson and move on.
5 Be free of arrogance and set ideas and you will benefit accordingly.
4 Experience is learning and the harder the lesson, the greater the benefit.
3 Beware of turning respect and admiration for another into idolatry.
2 Listen to all; it is possible to learn even from those who are inexperienced.
1 Accept criticism and advice that is well founded but maintain your enthusiasm.

需 5 HSU – Waiting *Correctness, patience, perseverance, nourishment*

Water

Heaven

There is a time for advancement and a time for patient non-action. Now is the time to wait and have faith in the order of things. This image is of clouds gathering before rain can fall. They are the creative potential which will bring nourishment to the land when the time is right. To gather creative energy you must wait with calm patience, maintaining the inner truth that will allow the universe to work. Use this time to observe yourself and to correct any inferior feelings that cause imbalance.

Line readings

6 The situation is coming to a resolution, although perhaps not as you had hoped for.
5 There is always calm in a storm but beware, the situation is not yet resolved.
4 Remain calm and confident that things are as they should be.
3 Do not give in to inner doubts but wait with calmness and discipline.
2 Keep your self-discipline and do not respond to attacks from others.
1 An outside influence is approaching. Prepare yourself by remaining calm and focused.

訟 6 SUNG – Conflict *Opposition, disengagement, communication*

Heaven

Water

Conflict arises from within and the strong connection to heaven is being eroded by the swirling confusion of water. By trying to impose your view instead of accepting what comes, your conflict with the universe attracts external opposition. This clash cannot be overcome by force as confrontation only feeds the ego. Disengage from doubts, fears and impatience, and communicate with others to help resolve conflict. Accept and respect the advice of someone wiser than you in this situation.

Line readings

6 Conflict gives rise to more conflict. In the long run it is better just to let it go.
5 Accept the wisdom of an objective third party and things will work out well.
4 Stay calm and resolved and recognize the pointlessness of conflict.
3 By retaining your integrity and humility you can achieve great things.
2 Calmly pulling back from conflict will bring benefits to all involved.
1 Defuse a situation before it has a chance to get out of hand.

師 7 SHIH – The army *Unity, harmony, acting in concert, strength, division*

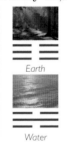

Earth

Water

Dissent in the ranks causes unrest and instability because the leader is overbearing, unjust or weak-willed. An army needs a strong leader who commands respect with compassion, strength and wisdom. You are a divided army because your general is not leading by example. Lack of inner harmony brings disunity to other relationships. Be firm in your purpose and exemplary in your actions and you will be an inspiration to others, gaining their support and achieving a worthy goal.

Line readings

6 Success is yours but you should reflect honestly on how it was gained.
5 Retaliation against disruptive elements should be restrained and understanding.
4 Unless you are working coherently there can be no advancement.
3 Maintain your honesty and integrity and a realistic sense of authority.
2 It is the mutual support between the leader and followers that carries the day.
1 Retain your understanding of justice and correct behaviour.

比 8 PI – Holding together *Union, bonding, co-operation*

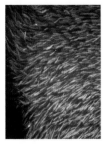

Water

Earth

Harmony – the water soaking into the earth – produces a good harvest. A union needs to be harmonious for the best results, whether the relationship is with yourself or with others. Strengthen bonds by reviewing your actions and demeanour. Are you being truthful? Your position of power doesn't mean that you can do what you like. However, it does require steadiness of principle in the face of challenges and temptations. Maintain your inner truth and sincerity and you will achieve much.

Line readings

6 Proceed cautiously but do not hesitate to enter a beneficial union.
5 Don't sink to coercion or flattery to hold on to someone who wants to go.
4 Be yourself and feel free to express your thoughts and feelings more.
3 Be wary of joining with people who may lead you astray.
2 Do not be swayed by inferior principles just to keep the image of harmony.
1 Lack of truth, in yourself or with others, leads to disunity.

小畜 9 HSIAO CH'U – Taming by the small *Patience, strength*

Wind

Heaven

Others recognize who you are and what you stand for, but not sufficiently to allow trouble-free advancement. Forcing your way is beneath you and will only bring misfortune. The only way to progress is to remain focused and seek to remove obstacles with gentle actions. Look to the long term rather than to immediate satisfaction; by planting seeds now you will reap a rich harvest in future. Cultivate patience, adaptability and detachment, and accept that all you can do is change yourself.

Line readings

6 Success is imminent. Keep to the correct principles to ensure its arrival.
5 If you share your good fortune with others it will be increased.
4 Retreat from confrontations, even if you are misunderstood, and things will work out well.
3 Do not let doubts or over-confidence tempt you to force an issue.
2 Remain firm and devoted to your inner truth and all will come right.
1 Impatience causes despair and hasty actions, which will not benefit you.

履 10 LU – Conduct *Caution, courtesy, simplicity, innocence*

Heaven

Lake

The allusion is to stepping on a tiger's tail: overstepping the mark and causing offence. Be aware of caution and restraint. If you conduct yourself with humility and good humour, it is possible to walk on the most dangerous ground with a degree of safety. By maintaining simplicity of thought and deed, and innocent expression of your inner truth, others will accept you for who you are. Do not be sub-servient to those above nor domineering to those below and you will meet with success.

Line readings

6 True achievement is measured in the manner of attainment as well as in the rewards gained.
5 Be resolute and determined with yourself but not hard and judgemental with others.
4 Do not be tempted to avert or interfere with a difficult situation; just leave it alone.
3 Don't over-estimate yourself or your abilities, allow things to develop as they will.
2 You know what is correct; doubts and questions will only bring trouble.
1 Step lightly with quiet confidence and without ambition to ensure smooth progress.

泰 11 TAI – Peace *Balance, harmony, new growth, prosperity*

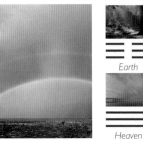

Earth

Heaven

Your inner harmony is reflected in the peace around you. Earth above indicates an open attitude to events, and heaven below suggests a time of burgeoning potential. In such fertile ground it is possible to grow to great heights but you need to maintain your inner balance. Most spiritual growth comes through challenging times: do not relax into complacency just because times are good. To develop new growth potential you need to remain devoted to the correct principles of the I Ching.

Line readings

6 Good fortune fades, to be replaced by a time of learning. Accept what comes calmly.
5 Maintain your inner calmness and patience; things are progressing as they should.
4 Do not boast to others or try to manipulate them as this will lead to your downfall.
3 Keep your equanimity in difficult times because they will change.
2 Be generous and forbearing and do not allow good fortune to cloud your judgement.
1 Others are attracted by your positivity. Welcome them and act together.

否 12 P'I – Standstill *Lack of progress, barriers, stagnation*

Heaven

Earth

P'i is the reverse of Tai (11), indicating that the creative is leaving and the receptive is rising. The run of good fortune has waned and now comes a time of stagnation. This lack of progress does not mean that you cannot develop your inner truth. Be receptive to the lessons and don't struggle against those who hold the upper hand because that will only serve to make them stronger. Retreat into yourself and have faith that things will improve faster if you persevere in the correct manner.

Line readings

6 By acting with a pure heart and honest intent you will meet with good fortune.
5 Adhere to your higher principles to strengthen your inner truth.
4 Acting in a pure and simple manner will bring benefits and support from others.
3 Make no judgements of others but do what you know to be right.
2 Times are hard but the best way to proceed is by enduring.
1 Withdraw from an adverse situation and wait patiently for better times.

13 T'UNG JÊN – Fellowship with others *Co-operation*

Heaven

Fire

A union of equals comes together to work towards a mutual goal, with no reservations or hidden agendas. To function coherently requires openness, honesty and a sense of fairness felt by all. If there are reservations within the group it will not work. These need to be addressed if you are to continue or a state of chaos will prevail. This hexagram also refers to joining with the Sage, being sincerely committed to seeking the wisdom and truth without regard to having it proven to yourself.

Line readings

6 Good fortune will come if you whole-heartedly embrace the wisdom of the Sage.
5 Bonds based on love and respect are unbreakable and reconciliation will come.
4 Misunderstandings lead to trouble. It is better to disengage than to continue fighting.
3 Feelings of mistrust will grow and break the union unless dealt with quickly.
2 Creation of factions within the group will lead to failure.
I For a union to endure there needs to be openness between the parties involved.

14 TA YU – Possessing plenty *Wealth, abundance, honour*

Fire

Heaven

By following true and honest intentions you are entering a period of great abundance, from which you can shine like a fire in the heavens. You have reached this point by retaining your humility and integrity. Carry on in this manner and you will continue to rise and prosper, becoming a guiding light for others. It is important to guard against unworthy thoughts and actions or seeking to use your influence to further your own ends. If you abuse your strength it will be lost to you.

Line readings

6 Continue with modesty and humility and great abundance will come.
5 Do not be effusive or stand-offish but accept people with a quiet dignity.
4 Rise above petty competition and you will continue on your ascent.
3 Do not hoard your wealth, spiritual or material, because that leads to stagnation.
2 Remain free of attachments because possessions can become fetters.
I Do not be waylaid by feelings of arrogance or superiority as your good fortune continues.

15 CH'IEN – Modesty *Quietly progressing, steadfast, developing*

Earth

Mountain

Strive to remain modest in your dealings. The image of the mountain below the earth is one of curtailing ostentatious behaviour to deepen and develop the inner self. Modesty is about perceiving what is good and right, and being steadfast in acting upon it and following those actions through. If you maintain awareness and follow the correct path, deeper contact with the Sage and with your inner truth is forged, strengthening you and enabling you to face any obstacles with calm confidence.

Line readings

6 A truly modest person knows what is right and has the strength to follow it.
5 You may have to assert yourself but do so without resorting to aggression.
4 Do what needs to be done quietly, efficiently and with respect.
3 Modesty brings success and attention. Do not become complacent or conceited.
2 Others recognize a deep modesty in you and react accordingly.
I True modesty brings its own rewards. Do not expect recognition for your actions.

16 YU – Enthusiasm *Energy, opportunity, support*

Thunder

Earth

This is a good time to start a new undertaking. Your boundless enthusiasm provides the energy and strength to see it through and your vigour will communicate to others, who will join with you and lend their support. However, the enthusiasm needs to be derived from a strong inner clarity of what is right and what needs to be done. If it springs from an egotistical desire to be seen to be successful, you will become unbalanced and the energy will not be sufficient to carry you through.

Line readings

6 Enthusiasm springing from the desires of the ego will lead to misfortune.
5 Look within to determine if you carry the seeds of doubt.
4 Maintaining a correct enthusiasm for your endeavours will lead to success.
3 You know what is best so you can rely on your own judgement.
2 Retain a sense of propriety and a realistic view of what can be done.
I An arrogant manner towards others will prove to be your undoing.

隨 17 SUI – Following *Acceptance, following, joy*

Lake

Thunder

A fundamental principle of the I Ching is an acceptance of what is, while maintaining equanimity in response to events. This hexagram relates to following and being followed. The principles of the I Ching arouse the interest of a follower and adherence to the principles of humility, inner truth and acceptance, lead to joy. Other people see the joy in a true follower and their interest is aroused. To show them the way to true joy you must remain steadfast to the principles of the Sage, the I Ching.

Line readings

6 Being receptive to the principles of the Sage brings what is needed at the right time.
5 By being true to yourself you ensure great success because the universe assists you.
4 Do not let flattery go to your head or your clarity will become clouded.
3 It may be time to part from people or ideas that conflict with your inner knowledge.
2 Inferior attitudes will prevent you hearing wisdom from truly wise people and the Sage.
1 Wisdom can come from unexpected sources. Be respectful and listen to all.

蠱 18 KU – Work on corruption *Disruption, decay, spoiled, repairing*

Mountain

Wind

The ideogram represents decay and corruption. The hexagram portrays wind blowing around the base of the mountain, a deep-rooted disorder. However, there is a chance to redeem the situation by correcting improper attitudes and ideas. This will take strength of character and decisive action but first it is necessary to ascertain the root cause, which requires a period of meditation and introspection. Once established, work quickly to repair the damage and guard against its return.

Line readings

6 Following the path of inner truth may isolate you but this will not be permanent.
5 Your efforts at repair have been noticed by others, who may be inspired to aid you.
4 Deal with the corruption now to avoid further disruption.
3 An excessive approach has led to a minor upset but no great harm has been done.
2 Use gentle persistence to address the decay. Excessive vigour will increase disruption.
1 Decay in this case is coming from a pattern learned rather than from an inner voice.

臨 19 LIN – Approach *Advance, waxing power, strength, benevolence*

Earth

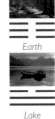

Lake

This hexagram refers to what is approaching you and how you approach life. There are good times coming imminently and any undertaking you begin will be successful. This is because you have cultivated the correct internal equanimity and the higher powers approach you to give assistance. Just because times are good you should not relax the inner discipline that has brought about your success. If you do, the progress that has begun will halt and your good fortune will melt away.

Line readings

6 You have reached a point of development where you are able to help others.
5 Don't interfere or have doubts about the abilities of those helping you.
4 An open-minded attitude towards others will ensure success.
3 Keep your attitudes to yourself and others under control to ensure continued progress.
2 The correct approach will help you through the bad times that follow the good times.
1 Fortunate circumstances make your progress seem effortless; maintain discipline.

觀 20 KUAN – Contemplation *Meditation, understanding, example*

Wind

Earth

By contemplating or meditating upon the principles of the I Ching, those attributes become a part of your make-up and you become a guiding light for all to see. The creative power of the universe also works in unseen ways, influencing situations and people without conscious intent. This position of strength has been attained by perseverance in adhering to inner correctness. It allows the universal energy to transmute petty aspects of the self into tolerance, patience and understanding.

Line readings

6 Your contemplation has achieved the desired results in yourself.
5 Contemplation furthers your understanding but only becomes wisdom in practice.
4 Your wisdom can have a positive influence on others but do not force it on them.
3 You have enough self-awareness to recognize when improper responses to life arise.
2 Do not expect to make great leaps forward. Gradual progress is inexorable and lasts.
1 Just because you follow the teachings of the Sage you cannot expect others to do so.

21 SHIH HO – Biting through *Clarity, decisiveness, obstacle, unity*

Fire

Thunder

An obstruction is preventing a mouth from closing properly to allow nourishment. There is an obstacle, which could be an incorrect attitude that needs to be dealt with now. You need clarity to see the problem and decisiveness of action to "bite" through it. This does not mean using aggressive force because an overly robust response will bring misfortune. Return to the principles of correctness laid out in the I Ching. Use your inner strength to withdraw and embrace the Sage.

Line readings
6 Severe misfortune will be the result of persisting stubbornly.
5 Stay impartial and objective in order to respond correctly to others.
4 You begin to see progress in dealing with the problem. Maintain your balance.
3 You are faced with an old problem. The correct way to deal with it is to withdraw.
2 In responding to an obstacle you may have gone too far but there is no great harm done.
1 This is a new obstacle, a first offence. Be lenient in how you deal with it.

22 PI – Grace *Adornment, beauty, simplicity*

Mountain

Fire

Grace is perfect poise, beauty and balance. True grace comes from a firm inner truth, humility and acceptance, whereas false grace relies on external appearances to beautify the self for the appeasement of the ego. Grace is the embodiment of nature and possesses a beauty that is effortless. Similarly, a person who does not try to be alluring but cultivates devotion to the simplicity of the inner truth of the Sage possesses a grace and beauty that shines through the dowdiest of coverings.

Line readings
6 The external trappings of success are false. True power and grace shine from within.
5 Concentrate on simplicity and sincerity and don't be tempted to seek material wealth.
4 Do not try to impress others with an outward show of brilliance.
3 All seems well but don't fall into complacency and arrogance.
2 Cultivate an ability to see through surface adornment to perceive underlying integrity.
1 Let modesty be your guide to inner truth.

23 PO – Splitting apart *Strong, enduring, patient, non-action*

Mountain

Earth

Everything seems to be going horribly wrong, but nothing can be done about it except to weather the storm. To attempt to influence the situation will only prolong it because such a desire is driven by the ego, which seeks to dominate and control. By withdrawing from unfavourable circumstances and engaging in patient non-action the creative power can settle the situation favourably. Be like the mountain, strong and immovable, resting solidly on the earth of your proper principles.

Line readings
6 Do not dwell on what has passed but step forward with optimism into better times.
5 By accepting what comes conditions become more favourable.
4 The storm has reached its peak. Cling to correct principles and endure it.
3 Anchor yourself to the Sage's principles. Don't worry about opposition from others.
2 Resist the urge to interfere and have patience. This situation won't last indefinitely.
1 Acting in response to fear and doubt will end in disaster. Things are as they should be.

24 FU – Return *Change, turning point, improvement*

Earth

Thunder

Just as the winter solstice presages the returning power of the sun, this hexagram, which is related to that time of year, tells of a time of increasing fortune. It is also a reminder to look for the light of inner truth to guide your path. In the same way that the seasons progress in an inexorable cycle, so too do the ebb and flow of fortune and misfortune. Watch and wait as things progress and develop at their own rate, and draw in your strength for the time of growth that is approaching.

Line readings
6 Now is the time for careful self-evaluation and for correcting improper attitudes.
5 If you are moved to excuse your behaviour, you are aware that you are in the wrong.
4 In going your own way you may have to offend others. True friends will understand.
3 Change can be frightening but there is no gain if you keep returning to bad habits.
2 Be careful of allowing your pride to stop you from learning from others.
1 Be aware when you stray from a true and honest path and return before you go too far.

无妄 25 WU WANG – Innocence *Purity, present moment, sincerity, intuition*

Heaven

Thunder

Innocence is living purely in the present, as a child does, with no thought of tomorrow or yesterday. The innocent child accepts the guidance of the wiser adult and trusts that all will be well. Develop innocence so that there is no anticipation of events and no holding on to what has passed, good or bad. The pure spirit, the higher self, is directly connected to the rest of creation. If you nurture it, intuition flows and it is possible to follow the guidance of the wiser adult, the Sage, as it leads us through life.

Line readings

6 Do not try to force an issue but step back and let the truth unfold.
5 Remain innocent and detached and a problem will quickly pass on its own.
4 Stay true to yourself and be guided by the teachings of the Sage.
3 Stay calm and strengthen your innocence in the face of a misfortune.
2 Do not dwell on past mistakes or anticipate future goals.
1 Trust your first instincts because intuition flows from the cosmos.

大畜 26 TA CH'U – Taming by the great *Keeping still, practice*

Mountain

Heaven

It is a time to put into practice the teachings of the I Ching. To remain calm and detached in the face of hostile provocations is a great test of the strength of your character. Hold firmly to the sense of inner truth – the power of the great – and use the difficulties as opportunities to increase your understanding by purifying your thoughts and actions. These attacks may come from people who are jealous and fearful of your spiritual progress, or from inner aspects of yourself that clamour for attention.

Line readings

6 Creative energy released and guided by your correct behaviour will bring success.
5 Acting out of desire causes great disruption to your equanimity. Stay calm and detached.
4 Curb actions that arise from strong emotions and you will know the time to act.
3 Proceed with determination and caution because there are still problems ahead.
2 By staying calm you conserve your energy for greater advantage when the time is right.
1 Staying patient in a difficult situation will bring a quicker resolution.

頤 27 I – The corners of the mouth *Discipline, meditation*

Mountain

Thunder

The image of the hexagram is a mouth, open and ready to receive nourishment. As healthy food nourishes the body, healthy thoughts and actions nourish the spirit. By feeding on the desires of the ego you promote the growth of inferior spiritual qualities. Meditation is a way to cultivate a tranquil, receptive state that allows wisdom to flow from the universe, nourishing your higher self and influencing others positively as the peace and tranquillity it instils radiates outwards.

Line readings

6 Others turn to you for guidance. Remain humble and sincere in your dealings.
5 Strengthen your discipline and follow the Sage before you try to help others.
4 You will receive help by seeking to nourish yourself in the proper manner.
3 Feeding on desires is never fulfilling because there is always something else to be had.
2 Seeking nourishment from others will weaken you and bring misfortune.
1 You have everything you need, so you should be content with it.

大過 28 TA KUO – Preponderance of the great *Pressure, growth*

Lake

Wind

This hexagram indicates a situation of almost unbearable pressure and it seems likely that you will give way beneath the weight. There is an understandable temptation to escape and seek a refuge, but that only delays the inevitable. To keep running only weakens your resolve. Now is the time to stand firm. You are equal to the task and by relying on your inner truth and integrity you will emerge stronger. This may require a sacrifice on your part to bring a wider benefit to others.

Line readings

6 You are in over your head because of over-confidence. Return to patience and humility.
5 To progress in a renewed relationship the problems undermining it must be resolved.
4 Do not exploit the respect that others have for you or there will be cause for regret.
3 Stop your headlong rush, which is propelling you towards disaster.
2 This is a time of renewal. Things will go well if you stay alert and proceed cautiously.
1 Be cautious as you advance and test each step. Do not fear to pull back from danger.

坎 29 K'AN – The abysmal *Depths, despair, danger, alertness*

Water

Water

Flowing water follows the path of least resistance on its journey from the heavens to the sea. The doubling of water indicates depths of despair, dangerous chasms created by giving in to strong emotions that urge you to seek an easy solution. Other depths within yourself, if plumbed, can provide the strength to see you through difficulties. Flow with the current of change instead of struggling against it. Open your heart and be receptive to allow the universe to work out the best solution.

Line readings

6 Your predicament comes from ignoring what you know is right. Listen to your heart.
5 A thing will come to fruition when it is ready. Stop striving and go with the flow.
4 Be sincere in all your thoughts and actions and help will come to you.
3 Any movement is dangerous. Retreat into stillness until a solution presents itself.
2 Slowly and cautiously is the way to find your path through the abyss that faces you.
1 Be alert to danger or bad habits and return to the path of peaceful acceptance.

離 30 LI – The clinging *Dependence, passion, brilliance, intensity*

Fire

Fire

Fire gives warmth, illumination and simple beauty burning with a captivating intensity. But fire depends upon wood to give it form, and clings to it with passion. You depend on external things for your survival, but there is another dimension that gives you a passion for life, and that is a spiritual connection to the rest of creation. Clinging to correct principles gives us the strength to live a joyful and fulfilling life, able to face difficulties with equanimity and paradoxically to gain independence.

Line readings

6 The ego still holds sway and needs to be silenced before progress can be made.
5 Be humble and accepting in the face of adversity and good fortune will be yours.
4 Perseverance will bring its rewards.
3 Accepting that things come in their own time allows their healthy development.
2 Do not succumb to despair or over-exuberance. Moderation in all things will bring good fortune.
1 Listening to desires and inferior attitudes leads to misfortune.

咸 31 HSIEN – Influence *Harmony, mutual benefit, unifying, courtship*

Lake

Mountain

This hexagram indicates the approach of an influence. The constituent trigrams represent the third son and the third daughter, suggesting courtship. This involves following the correct procedure to bring about a joyful and mutually beneficial union. To be able to receive benefits from external influences you must be open-minded and gentle. To have a beneficial influence on others we need to maintain our inner independence and integrity, acting from a position of quiet inner truth and humility.

Line readings

6 Let your knowledge become deeds and they will have more influence than words alone.
5 You need a strong will to hold firm to your inner truth but beware of being too rigid.
4 By always speaking and acting with integrity you will have a positive influence on others.
3 Desire can cause you to act rashly or to seek to use your influence for selfish gains.
2 Have patience. Correct progress takes time and to act now will lead to misfortune.
1 Maintain a firm discipline in the early stages of an influence and success will be easier.

恆 32 HÊNG – Duration *Persistence, progress, endurance, stamina*

Thunder

Wind

This is a time of endurance, which requires persistence and stamina. By calling upon the enduring principles of calmness, humility and sincerity, you will achieve success. You may be going through a change, but the counsel of this hexagram is to hold your equanimity. Do not wish or hope for something to be better or fear that things will get worse, but remain constant and unwavering in your actions as you deal with the situation, doing what needs to be done with calmness, detachment and integrity.

Line readings

6 Stay calm and in the present to allow the creative energy of the universe to work.
5 Allow others to make their own way, learning through their own experiences.
4 What you seek will not be found if you look in the wrong places or in the wrong way.
3 Do not measure yourself against others but remain strong and certain in your path.
2 Your intuition flows through your higher self. Trust in it to guide you.
1 Expecting too much too soon leads to disappointment. Stay focused on the present.

遯 33 TUN – Retreat *Withdrawal, conserving strength, stillness, order, safety*

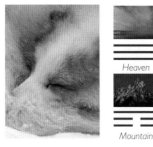

Heaven

Mountain

There is a natural ebb and flow of energy, which the discerning person recognizes and accepts. Faced with the onset of winter, a tree does not put forth new growth but draws in its strength and waits for spring. When there are superior forces marshalled against you, it is best to retreat into calm stillness and to conserve and organize your strength. Retreat is acceptance of unfavourable odds, performing a strategic withdrawal in order to make preparations for a more favourable time to advance.

Line readings

6 You are correct in retreating and your path will open up before you.
5 You have seen the wisdom of retreating now and must act decisively.
4 A correct retreat will only strengthen you.
3 Don't allow others to interfere with your priority to withdraw.
2 A fair and proper resolution cannot come about if you demand it or interfere to try to change the situation.
1 Withdraw from a negative situation now and take no further action.

大壯 34 TA CHUANG – Power of the great *Strength, heaven*

Thunder

Heaven

This is a time of increasing strength, but you must guard against complacency. You reach this position with the help of the Sage. In following the correct principles of patience, humility, gentleness and detachment, you align yourself with the creative forces of the universe and can achieve great things. Remember the other counsels: reticence, timeliness and balance. If, through a misguided belief in your power, you seek to use this influence to benefit your own ends, the resulting misfortune will be great.

Line readings

6 Pressing forward without due consideration can lead to entanglements that will hinder you.
5 It is sometimes necessary to be harsh but do not carry the punishment too far.
4 Remain true to your principles: resistance will crumble and good fortune is assured.
3 Use your strength wisely, not as a battering ram. Advance when there is no resistance.
2 Gentle persistence will lead to further progress so maintain discipline in easy times.
1 Don't be tempted to use your power to force issues to a conclusion.

晉 35 CHIN – Progress *Advancement, dawning, rising*

Fire

Earth

Fire over earth represents sunrise and indicates great progress. The sun climbs effortlessly in the sky because it follows the natural laws of the universe. The growth of your understanding and influence will also be easy if you remember where the light of your brilliance comes from and follow the guidance of the Sage. Clouds can obscure the sun and your judgement can become clouded if you do not work for progress for its own sake rather than in the pursuit of selfish goals.

Line readings

6 Treating others harshly to teach them a lesson is an abuse of your power.
5 Progress is not always obvious but by remaining detached you have made great gains.
4 Using your power for selfish gains or material possessions will lead to misfortune.
3 It is not weak to receive help. Keep to your path truly and accept aid gratefully.
2 Don't compromise your principles for the sake of a union.
1 Progress seems slow in coming but keep your faith and gains will accrue.

明夷 36 MING I – Darkening of the light *Oppression, inner light*

Earth

Fire

Earth over fire represents sunset, a time of approaching darkness, when the only light left is inner brightness. When you are engulfed by difficult circumstances, it is necessary to keep that inner light bright to guide you. Giving in to weakness or indulging in feelings of despair dims the brightness within. Now, more than ever, is a time for detachment and perseverance at maintaining an inner truth. Things progress slowly but progress they do, so have faith in the creative power of the universe.

Line readings

6 Hold fast to your true path and firm your resolve, and you will win through.
5 There is no shame in hiding your true self from those who may wish you harm.
4 Realizing you are on the wrong path enables you to leave it. To stay is foolish.
3 Identifying the problem is only half the job. Persevere in dismantling the blockage.
2 Accept aid that is offered and, in turn, be unstinting in your efforts to help others.
1 Detach yourself from a desire for progress and continue with patient perseverance.

家人 37 CHIA JÊN – The family *Harmony, loyalty, health, balance, structure*

For a family to be successful it needs a firm structure with a strong, honest leader and harmonious relationships. This togetherness stems from mutual love, respect and loyalty, so that there is a willingness to put the welfare of the whole above individual desires. This firm foundation is essential for the health of all human communities and needs to start with the individual. By cultivating the correct principles of acceptance, humility, modesty and gentleness you attract and develop healthy relationships.

Wind

Fire

Line readings

6 Good fortune will be yours if you keep your actions and thoughts correct.
5 Your influence will be greater if you act out of truth rather than by trying to force issues.
4 Ensure your actions are for the right reasons, not based upon inferior emotions.
3 Be fair but firm when dealing with others. Weakness or aggression will bring misfortune.
2 Do not resort to bullying or aggression to get your own way.
1 Set clear boundaries; if people know their limits they can act more freely within them.

睽 38 K'UEI – Opposition *Misunderstanding, resistance, adversity*

Opposition arises through misunderstandings and this is because people, events or situations are judged by their external appearances. If you feel that life is not fair because it is not what you desire, you misunderstand the way the universe works. Resisting the flow of creative energy only increases the power of such inferior attitudes. Everything that comes to you is appropriate for your learning and spiritual growth, but this can only be discerned by looking for the lessons within.

Fire

Lake

Line readings

6 You feel threatened by others or by life but your paranoia is unfounded.
5 Openness and understanding will allow a firm relationship to grow.
4 Trust in the universe and keep an open heart and you will meet like-minded people.
3 Circumstances seem against you but all is as it should be, so look for the lesson.
2 Understanding can be overlooked unless you receive everyone and everything openly.
1 Accept what comes. Do not chase dreams or people as that will only drive them away.

蹇 39 CHIEN – Obstruction *Obstacles, barriers, blockage, stuck*

When faced with obstacles, you may indulge in self-pity or seek to overcome them forcibly. These attitudes only make the obstruction seem even more insurmountable. If you give in to these emotions, you block the assistance of the higher self. There is no point in blaming others for the predicament, the answers will come from looking within. It is best to retreat from the problem and examine the self for attitudes that need correcting, and to seek advice from a wise friend or counsellor.

Water

Mountain

Line readings

6 Others may need your help. Do not forsake them even if the difficulties seem too great.
5 The current situation is hard work but by persevering you will receive help.
4 If you wait correctly, you will gain what is needed to make advance easier.
3 Take time to consider the matter carefully before acting.
2 Don't waste yourself blaming others for an obstruction that is not of your making.
1 Forging ahead will make things worse. Easy advancement will come when the time is right.

解 40 HSIEH – Deliverance *Relief, release, growth, progression*

Thunder and water together suggest a great thunderstorm that purges and refreshes. Look within when faced with obstacles and seek to correct improper attitudes. Because of the work you have done on yourself, you are being released and the way is clear for steady progression. Now is a time to step forward with confidence and balance. Don't brood on what has gone but forgive and forget any past harms that have been done, accepting them as lessons needed to reach this point.

Thunder

Water

Line readings

6 There is a last vestige of ego preventing complete deliverance. Let it go and be free.
5 Deliverance comes from firm rejection of old habits and inferior influences.
4 Don't cling to old ideas or acquaintances that may halt your progress.
3 Do not succumb to pride and arrogance lest you undo all your good work.
2 Use your wisdom to see through false praise, which will halt your progress.
1 An obstacle has been overcome. Take time to reflect on it and ensure it does not return.

損 41 SUN – Decrease *Discipline, simplicity, limited, drawing in, restriction*

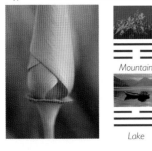

Mountain

Lake

Decrease is not necessarily a bad time, it is simply another state in the constant flux of life. Everyone reaches a point where energies need to be garnered to avoid depleting them further. A period is coming which requires a return to simplicity. It is a time for restricting the demands of the ego to strive for success or the attainment of goals. Power is limited but, by drawing in and exercising firm discipline, it is possible to rely on the inner strength available to get through the lean period.

Line readings
6 Persevering on the path of honesty and sincerity will bring success.
5 Good fortune will come by following what is true and correct in yourself.
4 If you adopt a humble and sincere attitude you will attract others to you.
3 Releasing inferior elements will allow beneficial aid to come.
2 Do not compromise yourself to help others; to do so will be to the detriment of all.
1 If others seek your aid, give it with love and humility but do not over-extend yourself.

益 42 I – Increase *Improvement, gain, progress, assistance*

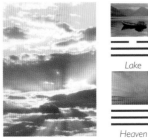

Wind

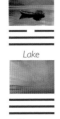

Thunder

Like decrease, increase is an inevitable state in the endless cycle of changes. Now is a time when great progress can be made. When you persevere on a path of correctness, the creative power invigorates you. Beware of complacency and remember the source of your good fortune. Be generous and sincere in sharing it with others. This will draw out what is good in them and they will support you. Strengthen your inner resolve and be firm in eliminating inferior elements in your character.

Line readings
6 It is beneficial to give assistance when it is requested of you.
5 Kindness brings its own respect and recognition without being sought.
4 If your guidance as a mediator is sought, be gracious and sincere in the role.
3 Even mistakes turn out well, but learn from them so that they are not repeated.
2 An open acceptance of the workings of fate means that no obstacles can stand before you.
1 By remaining selfless you will bring the success that you seek.

夬 43 KUAI – Breakthrough *Resoluteness, determination, resistance*

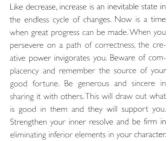

Lake

Heaven

A breakthrough comes if you are resolute in dealing with the inferior influences of the ego. By resisting emotional responses, it is possible to defuse them before they become too great. This allows the creative higher powers to flow, unfolding destiny propitiously. Once the breakthrough has occurred, you must remain resolute, and not resort to other inferior expressions such as pride, arrogance or complacency. If these enter, the Sage will withdraw and other obstructions will be experienced.

Line readings
6 The breakthrough has come about and success seems assured. Maintain your discipline to carry it on.
5 Do not judge those who behave incorrectly; they must make their own mistakes.
4 There is a danger that resoluteness will turn to hardness and intolerance.
3 Do not be provoked into action.
2 By remaining cautious and watchful, you will see dangers approaching.
1 Be aware of your own limitations and don't be over-confident.

姤 44 KOU – Coming to meet *Caution, temptation, tolerance*

Heaven

Wind

Be non-judgemental, sincere and humble when meeting the Sage or other people. This gives you the ability to deal with any mishaps calmly and efficiently. There is also a warning here not to meet inferior elements halfway and thus allow them to develop from a weak position to one of growing strength. It is a time for self-examination to test the correctness of ideas, situations and potential allies. If your suspicions are aroused, listen to them because they come from the higher self, which knows what is best.

Line readings
6 Withdraw from the challenges of inferior elements in others who are hostile.
5 Trust in your inner truth and don't use your understanding to berate or impress others.
4 Don't dismiss others out of hand, no matter how offensive they may be.
3 If you feel under attack, retreat into stillness to avoid extending the conflict.
2 Aggressive resistance of inferior emotions will only make them stronger.
1 Negative influences should be nipped in the bud while they are still weak.

萃 45 TS'UI – Gathering together *Peace, prosperity, leadership*

Lake

Earth

When a group acts together towards a well-defined goal, the whole is greater than the sum of the parts. For such a union to prosper, however, requires a strong leader. To be such a leader means gathering within oneself the principles of correctness in order to deal with the outside world calmly. Acting from a stable base, he or she will transmit their strengths to their followers without words or coercion, but if their inner truth is not sincere that will be sensed and the support will fade away.

Line readings

6 If you are sincere in your devotion to the correct principles success will be yours.
5 Remain firm in your goals and don't be afraid to go on alone if necessary.
4 Success is assured if you work selflessly for the general good.
3 Be tolerant of outsiders and do not hold grudges against someone who has strayed.
2 Join with people you feel naturally drawn to and trust in the creative higher powers.
1 Make sure your goals are of the highest order and not just self-serving aims.

升 46 SHÊNG – Pushing upwards *Direction, ascending, growth*

Earth

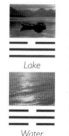

Wind

The hexagram suggests a sapling growing stronger and great progress can be made by persisting in what is right. A growing tree draws strength from its roots, which indicates that by maintaining a connection with the Sage, the origin of this success, you will remain strong and firmly rooted. Do not be afraid, simply trust and follow the guidance of the Sage, asking for help from those able and willing to give it. Nothing can stand in your way if you push steadily towards the light.

Line readings

6 How a goal is achieved has as much importance, if not more, than the goal itself.
5 Progress may seem slow but have patience, growth is sure and steady.
4 New opportunities approach and success is assured if you maintain your discipline.
3 How far you go depends on how closely you follow the Sage.
2 By sacrificing petty concerns of the ego you will further your growth greatly.
1 The teaching of the I Ching draws you on and by reaching for it you invoke its aid.

困 47 K'UN – Oppression *Exhaustion, stretched, adversity, endurance*

Lake

Water

The water is below the lake and therefore the lake is dried up. These are testing times with little or no progress. Be steadfast in the principles laid out in the I Ching. Facing this adverse time with equanimity will allow the lake to refill, plugging the leaks that drain away the precious reserves. A great drain on energy and resources, leading to fatigue, is often caused by harbouring untruths, so this is a time for self-assessment. Look within to see if you are being true to your spirit, your path and the Sage.

Line readings

6 The time of oppression is almost over and it is only negative attitudes that hold you back.
5 The oppression is great but have faith in the workings of fate to see you through.
4 A closed mind is the greatest oppression so dispel fixed ideas about yourself or others.
3 The obstacles are within so look to your attitudes and see what may need correcting.
2 Do not wish for more but be grateful for what you have and draw strength from it.
1 Resist the feelings of despondency and look within for inner reserves of strength.

井 48 CHING – The well *Spiritual nourishment, counsel, guidance, wisdom*

Water

Wind

Water is a fundamental requirement for survival and must be treated with respect. The image of the well in this hexagram refers to the I Ching as a source of spiritual sustenance that is freely available to any who wish to draw from it. But Ching also serves as a reminder to treat that deep wisdom with respect and not to muddy its waters with frivolous queries or indifference. To gain the full benefits, you need to draw from it with sincerity and to accept its guidance wholeheartedly.

Line readings

6 Give of yourself to others and your fortune will be multiplied.
5 Knowledge becomes wisdom only when it is used. Apply your wisdom for the benefit of all.
4 Keep to the principles of the Sage to maintain the quality of your inner truth.
3 You are avoiding what is right for you. Unused talents are wasted.
2 Focus your energy and intent on something worthwhile instead of misusing it.
1 If you neglect yourself, you must not be surprised if others also neglect you.

革 49 KO – Revolution *Change, advance, devotion*

Lake

Fire

The ideogram represents an animal's pelt undergoing its seasonal change. Ko signifies that changes are afoot or that attitudes need to be revolutionized to effect progress. Whichever is the case, now is the time to consider yourself deeply, to analyse your motives and instil the necessary change of heart that will set things in motion. Success is assured if you act from a position of selflessness, because this will bring the support needed and give an awareness of the right time to act.

Line readings

6 The major change is done. Now is a time for fine-tuning in order to carry the change on.
5 Actions based on proper principles make you stand out and others will follow.
4 For change to be long-lasting your motives need to be pure.
3 Don't act too hastily or be too hesitant, but remain balanced and follow your intuition.
2 Prepare yourself carefully before making any radical changes.
1 Develop your inner strength carefully before making your move.

鼎 50 TING – The cauldron *Growth, sacrifice, nourishment*

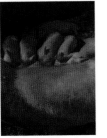

Fire

Wind

Ting derives its name from the image created by the hexagram. The bottom line is the legs of the cauldron, the next three the belly, the fifth the handles, and the top line the lid. The cauldron was the heart of a household: if it was full of food there was sufficient for everyone. This hexagram is related to Ching (48) because it is about providing nourishment, but whereas the Well is about individual spiritual growth, Ting is more about developing what is good within you for the benefit of society at large.

Line readings

6 Lead others by your own example in being open, honest and gentle.
5 Remain modest and sincere and you will receive help in difficult times.
4 Stay alert to potential dangers and don't take on more than you can manage.
3 Don't look for recognition but be patient; just reward comes in its own time.
2 Others may be envious of your success but that cannot harm you.
1 By acting with honesty and purity of intent, success is assured.

震 51 CHÊN – The arousing *Shock, movement, stimulation, excitement*

Thunder

Thunder

Thunder piled on thunder represents the incredible power of nature. Is it terrifying? Does that initial jolt give way to excitement or are you unperturbed by momentous events? If you are shocked it indicates that areas or attitudes need looking at. The bigger the shock, the bigger the imbalance. The truly powerful person is unmoved by such occurrences, being in complete harmony with the universal laws. Now is a time to look within and determine where self-correction needs to be made.

Line readings

6 The shock marks the end of the old. Contemplate ways of making a fresh beginning.
5 Shock after shock threatens to unbalance you. Retain your equanimity, all will be well.
4 All movement is blocked; it is a time for stillness and self-evaluation.
3 Use the shock to open your mind and look for possible avenues of action.
2 Let go of possessions and fear. What is really important will be returned.
1 The shock has come as a lesson. Do not be afraid but accept it gratefully.

艮 52 KÊN – Keeping still *Stillness, observing, quietness, clarity, readiness*

Mountain

Mountain

Mountain after mountain stretching away into the distance is the very image of stillness. Stillness means not allowing the mind to be ruled by strong emotions because it is not possible to be still with a clamouring mind. What is needed is a calm detachment, observing the emotions but not acting on them, gaining clarity that confers a state of alert readiness. Being alert allows you to see what needs to be done and readiness empowers you to do it, acting when action is needed.

Line readings

6 You are at the peak of the mountain, allowing perfect stillness and clarity.
5 Excessive talking is a sign of a restless mind. Calm your thoughts and speech.
4 If you keep calm and still inside, external influences will have no effect.
3 Don't allow your stillness to be transformed into inflexibility.
2 Don't be pulled along by someone else if it doesn't feel right for you.
1 It is easier to keep still before you move. Be cautious and don't act impulsively.

漸 **53 CHIEN – Development** *Gradual progress, patience, steady growth*

Wind

Mountain

Wood over mountain represents a tree on a mountainside. In such an exposed environment it needs to have firm roots and to grow gradually, but once it is established it will live long, have an unparalleled view and be visible from a long way off. It is the same for us: to enjoy the benefits of a fine position it is necessary to grow gradually, progressing step by step and learning all the lessons that life brings. The goal may seem a long way off but with patience and diligence it will be arrived at.

Line readings

6 Your progress is visible from afar, serving as an inspiration to others.
5 Your progress may isolate you but it also brings freedom as you continue.
4 Where you are is only temporary but take time to relax before you go on.
3 Rash actions will bring regret. Allow things to develop gradually.
2 Your advance is steady and you can feel secure in sharing your self-development.
1 At the beginning of a journey there is often anxiety. Keep your goal in mind to progress.

歸妹 **54 KUEI MEI – Marrying maiden** *Impulsiveness, discipline*

Thunder

Lake

The image called up by this hexagram is that of thunder creating waves on a lake, indicating how desires can lead to the disturbance of equanimity and to impulsive actions. To act on desires is not to follow the principles of the I Ching. There will always be desires and problems in relationships, but Kuei counsels that by following proper conduct they will be minimized. Proper conduct means maintaining detachment, accepting and being wary of compromising principles by following desires.

Line readings

6 You need to be sincere in word and action in your relationships.
5 Be prepared to stand back and let others come to the fore.
4 Be patient and persevere towards your goal.
3 Don't expect too much progress too soon. There is no disgrace in starting out from a lowly position.
2 You may be let down by someone but keep your faith in those you love.
1 With the proper attitude progress is possible, whatever your position.

豐 **55 FÊNG – Abundance** *Fullness, power, wise actions, plenty*

Thunder

Fire

Thunder and fire represent movement and clarity. They also indicate developing an inner awareness to see your position and to move when the time is right, to take full advantage of these cycles of waxing and waning power. While a thunderstorm fills the sky it is full of power and its influence is felt universally but, like all things, it will pass. Do not look to such a time but live for the present moment, making the most of this period of abundance and influence to achieve great gains.

Line readings

6 Arrogance and conceit will only bring you alienation and misfortune.
5 You can achieve great things with the help of others. Listen to them with respect.
4 Don't get lost in confusion but be guided by your inner clarity.
3 Hold to your inner truth and nothing can stand in your way.
2 Your influence will shine through. There is no need to pretend to greatness.
1 Your inner clarity will know the time to advance and your energy will see you through.

旅 **56 LU – The wanderer** *Moving, restless, temporary, transient*

Fire

Mountain

The idea of transience comes from the component trigrams which represent a bush fire on a mountain, always seeking more fuel. This can relate to physical travel but it also refers to progressing through life: the best way to proceed on that journey is as if passing through a strange land. When travelling in unfamiliar territory it is wise to be cautious, reserved and respectful, to follow your instincts about places and situations, to carry only what is necessary, with no attachments.

Line readings

6 Be careful of taking your good fortune for granted or it may be lost.
5 Your talents will be recognized more fully if you behave correctly.
4 You are settled for now but you know in your heart that you are not satisfied.
3 Don't involve yourself in something that is really no concern of yours.
2 With the right attitude you will always find a resting place and friends.
1 Remain free of attachments and trivialities and your journey will be much easier.

巽 57 SUN – The gentle *Gentle, penetrating, wind, persistence*

Wind

Wind

To effect any long-lasting change it is necessary to be like a constant gentle wind. When faced with problems it is tempting to take vigorous action, but violent storms wreak havoc and only stir up the local environment. This hexagram advises gentle penetration to dispel any blockages that may stand in your way. To be consistent requires a well-defined goal to focus on, one that can be aimed at with persistent effort. In this way changes will have far-reaching effects and be of a long-term nature.

Line readings

6 To search too hard for inferior elements will cause disruption.
5 Things may have started badly but, if you are duly cautious, they will turn out well.
4 By adhering to your principles and your integrity you will reap great rewards.
3 Dwelling on negative influences gives them more strength. Correct them and move on.
2 Search inside yourself to discover any negative influences.
1 Gentleness does not mean softness. Be sure in your goal and firm in your intent.

兌 58 TUI – The joyous *Inner strength, fulfilment, harmony, joy*

Lake

Lake

You are surrounded by imperatives – to make life better you must have this or must do that – but material gains do not bring lasting joy because there will always be something else to desire. To be fulfilled and live in harmony you need to devote yourself to humility, detachment, modesty and acceptance. By doing this you achieve an independence based on an inner strength which means that, whatever the situation you find yourself in, it can be faced with calm equanimity. That is true joy.

Line readings

6 Following pleasure for its own sake will escalate out of control.
5 You are surrounded by inferior attitudes in yourself and others: do not give in to them.
4 Pursuit of inferior aims brings misfortune. Turn to what is higher for lasting joy.
3 Don't be tempted by material gains, they will soon fade away.
2 If you remain sincere in seeking joy, good fortune will be yours.
1 Release your attachments and experience the joy of freedom.

渙 59 HUAN – Dispersion *Division, dissolution, rigidity, stubbornness*

Wind

Water

Stubborn attitudes lead to harshness and rigidity, blocking the acceptance of people and situations in a free and open manner. This in turn leads to divisions and a lack of unity both within the self and with others. To try and break these fixed ideas forcefully will do no good because they are strong and deep-rooted. The best way to deal with them is to be like the warm spring wind which blows persistently over the winter ice, dissolving it gently and allowing the river to flow freely again.

Line readings

6 Don't focus on negative influences or a dangerous situation will develop.
5 A fresh idea can unite people and dispel negativity and misunderstandings.
4 It may be necessary to sacrifice a short-term goal for a long-term benefit.
3 The best way to deal with your problems is to help someone else.
2 Do not judge others harshly. Understanding them will help you understand yourself.
1 Resolve misunderstandings quickly before alienation sets in.

節 60 CHIEH – Limitation *Restraint, moderation, guidelines, boundaries*

Water

Lake

Limitation is not the same as restriction, rather it means being prudent with resources. In order to be able to use what is available to its fullest potential, you need guidelines. If you know your boundaries you will have a greater freedom of expression within them, because you will know how far you can go with your expenditure. On a physical level you cannot live beyond your means, and similarly on a spiritual level it is wise to restrain desires and fears that are the cause of troubled thinking.

Line readings

6 Severe limitations become restrictive and lead to resentment.
5 Don't enforce limitations on others that you don't follow yourself.
4 Accept natural limitations. Move when you can, stay still when you can't.
3 Be careful of over-extending yourself. You must recognize that you are responsible for knowing your own limits.
2 Do not hesitate, the way is clear.
1 Know your limitations. To press forward now will bring misfortune.

61 CHUNG FU – Inner truth *Prejudice, understanding, acceptance*

Wind

Lake

Prejudices colour the way you relate to life. You cannot reach understanding if you indulge in pride, anger or self-pity. Chung Fu refers to the universal truth, the invisible force that manifests visible effects in life, and the inner truth which also has an invisible influence, good or bad. The I Ching counsels you to leave emotional responses behind and to try to understand the truth of a situation. By doing so your inner truth is emulating the universal inner truth and has a positive influence.

Line readings
6 Trying to persuade others of the right course will do no good. Lead by example and let them make their own way.
5 Inner truth will unite you with others.
4 Do not forget the source of your power when things are going well.
3 To maintain your independence and balance, do not rely on others.
2 Your inner truth, strong or weak, will be felt by others and they will react accordingly.
1 Do not be distracted by others from your inner truth.

62 HSIAO KUO – Preponderance of the small *Non-action*

Thunder

Mountain

This hexagram refers to the dominating presence of inferior attitudes (the small) which makes correct advance impossible. When faced with difficult circumstances it is tempting to be assertive and seek solutions, but this will only make things worse. The best course is patient non-action, relying on the principles of humility, modesty and acceptance to help you. Difficult times always reappear and should be seen for what they are: a test of commitment to the higher principles laid out in the I Ching.

Line readings
6 Pressing forward with something beyond you will bring disaster.
5 Seek help with your problem from someone who is wise and sincere.
4 Be patient and trust that the higher powers are working things out.
3 Show proper caution and don't expose yourself to risks.
2 You have made a small advance; be content with it for now.
1 To act now will bring misfortune. Bide your time and wait for a better opportunity.

63 CHI CHI – After completion *Order, balance, awareness*

Water

Fire

All the lines in this hexagram are perfectly balanced; out of chaos comes order, but this can change in an instant. Although this hexagram indicates hard work culminating in a time of order, there is a warning not to relax the discipline that has got you this far. Maintain an awareness of inferior elements that may arise and tumble the order into chaos again. If these are not recognized and dealt with before they manifest themselves, they will quickly swamp you and undo all your good work.

Line readings
6 Don't look back over past achievements but keep your eye to the future and move on.
5 Simplicity, both in thought and action, is the best way forward.
4 Minor setbacks are warnings of indiscipline, so pay heed to them.
3 To revert to inferior attitudes now will undo all your good work.
2 Remain modest and humble and what you seek will come to you.
1 Keep your discipline and awareness and progress is assured.

64 WEI CHI – Before completion *Caution, potential, clarity*

Fire

Water

This hexagram is the reverse of Chi Chi (63). Here, water is below, moving down, and fire is above, moving up, so the two energies cannot meet and combine. However, they just need to be repositioned so that fire (which represents clarity) can serve as a base for water (which represents action). During regenerative times such as these there is intense pressure to succeed but, to get anywhere worthwhile, you need to proceed cautiously and with firm dedication to higher principles.

Line readings
6 You have gained much but maintain your clarity and don't let things go to your head.
5 Maintain your integrity and perseverance and you will meet with success.
4 The endeavour has begun but there is much to do. You need dedication to reap rewards.
3 It is safe to act but seek help if you don't feel strong enough to do it alone.
2 Do not wait idly for change but prepare yourself for the time to act.
1 You cannot move forward safely without clarity. Impulsive actions bring disaster.

runes
runes

Part of the purpose of life is to learn lessons and gain knowledge and wisdom. Since the dawn of time, humankind has found signs and symbols fascinating and powerful. The power of the runes comes in what they have to teach us. The runes present lessons to us and, if used wisely, can facilitate the learning of those lessons quickly and efficiently.

The runes do not provide the answers to all of life's problems. Neither do they imbue their user with magical powers. They do, however, present signposts for the journey through life. The runes represent certain images, and by working with these, their guidance and teaching becomes accessible to all. The lore of rune-casting was once the domain of a chosen few, when only a minority sought spiritual enlightenment. Today, many people seek answers to questions, and these "seekers of wisdom" should have access to clear instruction regarding this ancient oracle.

This section gives guidance on making and using your own rune set. The imagery and meaning of each rune is featured in an easy reference guide and there are ideas for using and working with runes that go beyond simple divination.

The way of the runes is subtle but powerful and can have a profound effect on many levels. They are used not only for divination, but for protection, healing, empowerment and learning. The mystery of the runes is not a mystery at all, it is simply a path towards greater learning that anyone can tread.

using the runes
To learn from the runes, you need to "tune in" to their vibrations. Each rune has a corresponding tree, colour, herb and crystal which are keys to unlock its lessons. Working with these, you can set up a vibrational field that allows the subconscious mind to learn the vibration and teach its lesson to the conscious mind. Instead of using the conscious mind to try to find the lesson of each rune, you can allow the lesson to find you.

The History of the Runes
The runes were a sacred writing system used throughout the Germanic tribes of northern Europe, especially in Britain, Scandinavia and Iceland. Their origin is uncertain, but runic inscriptions have been found dating from AD 3. The script appears on memorial stones, weapons and tools and its angular style points to the fact that the runes were intended for carving, not writing.

The word "rune" comes from *runa*, meaning "a whisper" or "a secret", which implies a magical use. Throughout northern Europe, shamans existed who evolved a complex and deep spiritual tradition of which the runes were an intrinsic part, and runemasters were held in high esteem. They knew how to practise divination with the runes, and how to use them in magical and healing work.

Learn the lessons of balance and harmony from nature.

balance and harmony. The runes present symbols whose vibrations help us to become more balanced. They are like a series of lost chords that we need to find. The vibrations of the natural objects associated with them can help us to understand their lessons. They each hold some of the notes of the lost chords.

The ancient Celts and Vikings believed that everything in nature has a "spirit", an energy that can be communicated with and learnt from. This included trees, herbs, crystals, stones and even runes. Through meditation, they were able to "tune in" to their vibrations and learn from them. By meditating with gifts from nature, you will experience their vibrations. The first step is simply to touch, feel, hold, smell and meditate with them. The images and sensations that they offer will become easier to understand as you work with the runes.

Learning from the Runes
Everything in the universe is vibrating; nothing is still. Anything that is balanced and "healthy" has a harmonious vibration. Anything that is unbalanced and "unhealthy" has a discordant vibration. All natural things, such as plants, animals and crystals, have harmonious vibrations. Ultimately human beings are seeking

Meditating with angelica flowers will help you to unlock the meaning of the corresponding power rune, Elhaz.

Finding your Personal Rune
Hold the bag containing all your runes and empty your mind of all mundane thoughts. Ask the runes to show you your personal power rune which will be your guide. Pick out a single rune from the bag, hold it in your hand and meditate for a while, noting any images and thoughts that enter your mind.

You may wish to wear the corresponding colour and meditate beside the tree while holding the herb and crystal. If you have no access to these, picture them in your mind before you begin to meditate. Ask to be shown some of the lessons that your power rune has to teach you. These will often appear as images that enter your mind and should be noted down. Consider what they may mean, but do not worry if you cannot interpret them all as some of the lessons may only reveal themselves with time and patience. You cannot force understanding.

When you have worked with your power rune for a while, you may wish to research the corresponding tree, colour, herb and crystal – each has healing properties that may give you clues to the areas of your life that need healing and the lessons you need to learn. For example, the oak teaches strength but warns against inflexibility, as it is easily felled in a storm. The willow, on the other hand, teaches this flexibility as it bends in the wind. Even if a piece of it is broken off, that piece will root and grow into a new tree; so it also teaches the power of regeneration.

CONSULTING THE RUNES

Whenever you have a problem for which you can find no solution, a question for which you can find no answer or a decision you cannot make, you can consult the runes. They will not tell you precisely what to do or how to act. But what they will do is comment on a situation, giving you a new perspective from which to view things. This in turn will give you greater objectivity, which will then help you in your decision-making. The wisdom of the runes is more subtle than a simple "yes" or "no" answer. If this is what you want, you will have to flip a coin!

How Divination Works

If you have a problem or an issue for which you need guidance, you can focus your thoughts on that problem while holding your rune bag. This will send a vibration into the runes. The rune or runes that can provide guidance about the issue will resonate and you will unconsciously be attracted to pick out these runes. The more focused your thinking is, the clearer the answer will be. When focusing on the problem, ask the runes to comment on the issue rather than asking them a "yes" or "no" question.

If, for instance, you are undecided about whether to move into a new house, rather than asking the runes, "Should I move into a new house?", you should say, "I would like the runes to comment on the issue of whether or not I should move into a new house." Likewise, if you are asking about a possible partner in love, you should ask the runes to comment on your relationship rather than just asking, "Is this the right person for me?"

Drawing the Runes

Once you have focused on the question you want to ask, you can draw runes in one of two ways. You can pick individual runes out of the bag and lay them on your casting cloth in front of you. Alternatively, you can place all the runes in front of you, face down upon the casting cloth, and pass your hand over them,

picking the rune that your hand feels most attracted to. This attraction may manifest itself as a warm, tingling sensation in your hand when it passes over the right rune for you. Once you have chosen a rune, turn it over from left to right and place it in front of you on your casting cloth.

When drawing a rune, it is important that you have a clear intent about the way in which you want the rune to comment. If you wish it to give you a general perspective upon an issue, you need to draw only a single rune. However, you may wish the runes to comment on a number of points relating to a single issue: for example, what has led up to the issue occurring in your life (the past), how you should approach it now (the present) and what the possible outcome could be (the future). In this case, you need to draw three runes, holding one of these aspects clearly in your mind before you draw each rune. In this way you can achieve quite specific guidance which will be of great help to you in coming to a decision about the problem that is concerning you, and more generally on your journey through life.

Interpreting the Runes

The power of interpretation is available to everyone and it improves with practice. There are specific ways to improve your readings and interpretations which will come with patience and a little discipline. Each time you perform a reading with the runes, make a note of the issue on which you are asking the runes to comment, which runes you draw, and what you think they mean. About a month later, go back and look again at the comments you wrote, noting down any new insights that you have gained between the time of the readings and the present. This will help you to evaluate which parts of your original interpretation were accurate, and which were not. In this way, you will be able to improve your skills and understand more clearly what the runes have to say to you, the way that they say it and how you can learn from them.

Drawing a Rune from the Rune Bag

1 Lay out your casting cloth on a table. Concentrate on what you want to ask before you begin to draw the runes. Then pick individual runes out of the bag.

2 Once you have picked a rune out of the bag, turn it over from left to right so that it is face up, and put it down on your casting cloth in front of you.

Picking a Rune from the Casting Cloth

1 Take all the runes out of the bag and place them face down upon the casting cloth. Pass your hand slowly over them to find which runes you are attracted to.

2 When your hand passes over the right rune, it may become warm and tingling. Turn the rune over from left to right and place it in front of you on the casting cloth.

making and caring for your runes

If you want to get to know the runes, it is vital that you create your own rune set, rather than buying one ready-made. This takes time and energy, but it gives you a much more intimate relationship with the runes. The two materials from which runes are commonly made are wood and stone, although other materials, such as crystals, glass beads or clay, can also be used.

Using Wood

The three favoured types of wood for rune-making are ash (the World Tree), yew (the rune Eoh) and birch (the rune Beorc), as they have direct connections to the runes. However, wood from the following trees can also be used for fashioning magical tools and they are listed here with their principal symbology:

Rowan: a protective tree

Willow: a tree very strongly connected with the moon

Oak: symbolic of strength

Hazel: much favoured by diviners

Blackthorn: masculine symbol of spiritual authority

Apple: linked to love

Hawthorn: blackthorn's protective sister tree

Collect 24 stones and paint them with runic inscriptions. Varnish them for protection.

Using Stones

Wherever you go in the world, there are always stones to be found. Some of the best stones for rune-making can be found on beaches and in stream beds, where they have been worn smooth by the water. The Nordic and Celtic people believed that every stone has a spirit within it which needs to be honoured if it is to work well for you, so it is important to leave a small offering at any place where you take something from creation. The traditional offering is sea salt, as it is said to be formed by the fusion of four primal elements – earth, air, fire and water. Alternative offerings include tobacco (which is sacred to the Native Americans), corn (which is sacred throughout the Old World) and coloured ribbon.

Making Runes from Wood

You will need to cut a branch from a living tree to make your rune set. This may be a tree that has special significance to you, perhaps growing in a wood or garden that holds particular memories.

Before cutting any wood from the tree, ask its permission for your act, and leave a small offering in exchange. Select a branch that is about 2–5cm/¾–2in thick. You will need a fairly straight, even length of about 30cm/12in.

1 Ask permission from the tree by placing your hands on its trunk and saying a short prayer.

2 Sprinkle an offering of sea salt at the base of the tree to honour it before cutting off a small branch.

3 Using a handsaw, carefully cut the branch into slices for the 24 runes, about 5mm–1cm/¼–½in thick.

4 Using a poker, a pyrography tool or a soldering iron, carefully burn one runic inscription into each rune.

5 When you have rubbed in a little natural beeswax to protect the wood, your runes are ready to be cleansed.

Cleansing your Runes

When you have finished making your set of runes, it is important to cleanse them spiritually. This can be done in a variety of ways: they can be laid out in the light of a full moon for a night, or you can waft smoking herbs over them (this process is called "smudging"). However, the simplest method of cleansing them is to use naturally flowing water from a well, spring or stream. Do not use tap water as it is full of additional chemicals that are bad for everything, including humans!

As you work with your runes, especially if you do a lot of readings for others, you will need to cleanse them regularly. You may also want to perform an annual re-empowering ceremony. After a while, as you get to know your runes better, they will let you know when they need cleansing: they will start to feel uncomfortable to hold. If this happens, simply re-cleanse them. If your runes have been locked away for any period of time, you will need to re-energize them with the energies of the sun and moon by laying them outside for 24 hours.

Care of your Runes

Runes can be powerful and helpful allies provided that you treat them with the care and respect they deserve. Remember that when you have cleansed and empowered your runes, they will be imbued with your own unique energy and they should never be lent to anyone else for them to use. This does not mean that other people should never touch your runes at all; on the contrary, it is sometimes essential for someone else to touch them, especially if you are giving them a reading and you need them to focus on the runes. But no one else should work with your runes on their own behalf.

To store your runes you will need a bag, which you can make from a piece of natural, unbleached fabric. You can select runes by drawing them one at a time out of the bag. You will also need a piece of natural-coloured fabric to make a casting cloth on which to lay the runes whenever you use them.

Before cleansing your runes, make an offering, then place the runes in a bag and dip them in a stream, for a short while or overnight – let your intuition guide you.

Empowering your Runes

Once you have cleansed your runes, you need to empower them. This can be done in a variety of ways. Some runemasters lay their runes out in the midday summer sun, while others bury them in the earth for nine days. Here, the power of the four elements has been used to empower the runes.

1 Place the runes on a casting cloth and sprinkle them with sea salt to empower the runes with earth.

2 Pass each rune through incense smoke while asking the element of air to empower the runes.

3 Then pass each rune individually through a candle flame to empower the runes with fire.

4 For the final stage, sprinkle a few drops of spring water over the runes to empower them with water.

The Runic Alphabet

The most widely used runic alphabet is the Early Germanic or Elder Futhark, which is used in this book. The word "futhark" refers to the first six runic letters, whose English equivalents are f, u, th, a, r and k. Each runestone depicts one letter from the runic alphabet. The letters of the Elder Futhark are divided into three groups of eight letters, called aetts, as follows:

F U Th A R K G W

H N I J Y P Z S

T B E M L Ng D O

Here is the English alphabet with its equivalent runes (there are no equivalent runes for the letters c, q and v):

A B C D E F G H I J K L M N O P Q R S T U V W X Y Z

interpreting the runes

To become adept at interpreting the runes it is important to train your intuition, the connection to your higher self. This part of you knows your purpose in life and how it can best be achieved. It also knows the purpose of everyone you meet and how best you can guide those people who seek your help. Training the intuition allows you access to that knowledge and the runes can act as catalysts in this process.

Training the Intuition with Meditation

Meditation is a most efficient way of training the intuition because to hear the guiding voice of your higher self, you must have a mind that is in a receptive state to receive those messages. Whenever you pick out a rune to interpret, it is important to meditate with that rune to access your intuition. The following exercise shows you how to do this.

Settle yourself in a place where you feel relaxed; this may be outside if the weather is good, in a place where you feel comfortable and close to nature. If you are planning to consult the runes indoors, sit in a dimly lit room. Make sure that you will not be disturbed by telephones or people. You may wish to light a candle to help you to focus your mind.

Sit down in a comfortable position, hold your rune bag in your hands and close your eyes. Take a few deep breaths to centre yourself and imagine every muscle in your body relaxing. Now you need to empty your mind of all thoughts and to quieten its chatter. Continue to breath steadily and try to focus on your breathing, or picture yourself beside a beautiful lake on a calm, still day. Every time a thought pops into your mind, calmly allow it to leave and refocus upon your breathing or upon the image of the tranquil lake.

Drawing a single rune is a simple way to seek guidance.

Meditating on a Rune

When you feel ready, without opening your eyes, pick a single rune out of the rune bag and hold it in your hand. Keeping your eyes closed, try to tune into its vibration while asking the rune to speak to you. Allow your mind to become open so that different images and thoughts are free to enter it. Remain like this for as long as it feels comfortable. When you feel ready, thank the rune for speaking to you and then open your eyes and look at the rune. Make a note of all the images and messages that came into your mind during your meditation.

Now look up the meaning of the rune and see how this relates to what you felt during your meditation. Note the differences and similarities between the images that you felt during your meditation and the images and lessons given in the book. Now meditate again, asking the rune to show you how all these different images fit together, then note down all your thoughts and impressions.

As you become more experienced at working with the runes, you will be able to review exercises such as the one above and any points that seemed unclear will become clearer as you gain more understanding. The trick is to be patient. The runes reveal different aspects of themselves only when they know you are ready to learn them.

Interpretation of Reversed Runes

Some of the runes reveal a different sign when you view them upside down. These are called reverse runes. If, when you first turn over a rune, you find that you are looking at it upside down, it has a separate meaning to when it is the correct way up. Many people used to regard reversed meanings as negative. For instance, the first rune – Feoh – has an image of wealth and richness, so it was common to regard Feoh reversed as having an image of poverty. This is incorrect.

Each rune has its own lessons to teach. An upright rune has an image that teaches us something. If the rune is reversed, it means that the lessons of the upright rune are what we are lacking and therefore what we need to strive for. Therefore, the image of Feoh reversed does not mean "poverty", but "discovering richness". The difference is subtle but very important. The reversed meanings do not show us problems, but solutions to problems. One should always look at every rune in terms of what it has to teach, rather than looking at the negative aspects of the rune.

divination with the runes
Draw a single rune to act as a guiding rune for the day or before beginning a project, or to gain insight into a problem. It gives an overview of an issue, and is often all the guidance you need. The three-rune spread is particularly useful in giving an overall picture, placing an issue in its context by showing the events that have led up to it, the issue itself and, finally, the most likely future outcome.

THE SINGLE RUNE

Holding your rune bag, focus on the issue upon which you wish the runes to comment. You may say one of the following:

1 "I wish the runes to comment upon the day ahead."
2 "I wish the runes to comment upon (name a future endeavour)."
3 "I wish the runes to comment upon (name an issue or problem)."

Then pick a single rune from the bag or the casting cloth. Meditate while holding that rune, then look up its meaning.

Sample Reading

Tony had just been made redundant from a job that he did not like. Although he was in some ways relieved to be free from it, he was also fearful for his future and was concerned about finding new employment. He asked the runes to comment about this, and drew Rad.

Meaning: The rune Rad means the wheel of life, and signifies that life goes in cycles which will present challenges. Tony learned that he had just come to the end of a cycle in his life. He needed to live in the present and learn its lessons while trusting that the future would provide him only with valuable opportunities to learn more.

After several failed interviews for jobs in the same field as his last one (which anyway he had not enjoyed), he realized that the lesson he should be drawing from his experience was that he needed a different type of job. He decided to look for a job in the open countryside. Here he was much more successful and now thoroughly enjoys his work.

The rune Rad means the wheel of life.

THE THREE-RUNE SPREAD

The three-rune spread is like a signpost at a crossroads. Once you have an issue clearly fixed in your mind, draw your first rune. While focusing on it, think of the events that have led up to the issue or how you have attracted it into your life. Now draw your second rune, and while focusing on it consider the present moment regarding the issue. Finally, draw your third rune, focusing on your wish to be shown where the issue is taking you. Focus on what each rune represents when drawing it. The stronger your focus and intent, the clearer your answers will be.

Sample Reading

Anne had been suffering from ill-health for over six months. She had consulted both medical doctors and alternative health practitioners but to no avail. She did not understand why her illness kept returning, whatever she did to fight it. She drew the following three runes: Geofu, Tyr and Eoh.

Meaning: The rune Geofu means a gift. It showed Anne that her illness was a gift which she was trying to reject instead of accepting. The gift was the lessons the illness had to teach her. Tyr, the warrior god, showed Anne that if she remained true to herself and her beliefs, she would gain victory over her illness. Eoh, the yew tree, stands for transformation, and showed Anne that major change was coming and that by embracing the future while letting go of the past, she would enter a new phase of her life. Anne realized that the cure to her illness lay within her. She dealt with several unresolved issues from the past and was quickly restored to health.

The three-rune spread of Geofu, Tyr and Eoh.

the four-element spread

The runes can be used in many different spreads or patterns to give deep insights to help you on your spiritual path. The spreads are designed to help you understand and learn from the lessons that life is giving you. In the four-element spread, each rune is placed at one of the cardinal points, each of which is associated with one of the four universal elements, Earth, Water, Fire and Air.

The Four Elements

The Nordic tradition views the four elements as the building blocks of the universe, and a different direction and quality are assigned to each element. The north is the place of earth, the west of water, the south of fire, and the east of air. By compiling a spread where the runes are positioned at each point of the compass, each one is imbued with the qualities of its corresponding element.

Sea salt represents Earth, which is grounding and is symbolic of all physical lessons in our lives.

Stream represents Water, which is symbolic of emotional balance and going with the flow through life.

Candle flame represents Fire, which is symbolic of how we express ourselves in our lives and on our spiritual path.

Smoke represents Air, which is symbolic of turning knowledge into wisdom to benefit our future lives.

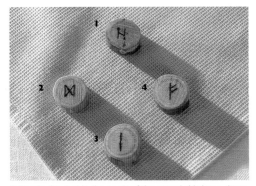

1 Earth: Situated in the north of the spread, this has a downward, grounding pull and represents all your physical lessons.

2 Water: Positioned to the west, this is an upward and buoyant sign and represents all your emotional lessons.

3 Fire: At the south of the spread, fire represents your spiritual lessons and is closely linked to your unfolding destiny.

4 Air: Positioned to the east, air can draw in knowledge and therefore represents the place where you should go to seek wisdom for the future.

Sample Reading

Jenny had just lost her mother. Although it did not come as a shock, she was still having problems dealing with it. She asked the runes for help and guidance and drew the following: Hagall, Daeg, Is and Feoh reversed.

Meaning: Hagall spoke of a challenge on the physical level. Jenny understood this to mean the physical challenge involved in organizing her mother's funeral, and that although times were hard at present, they would not last forever.

Daeg spoke of a light and Jenny realized that she had been emotionally in a very dark place since her mother's death. It also reminded her that her mother was now in the light and this gave her great comfort.

It showed Jenny the need for patience and the importance of allowing the grieving process to unfold, of using this time to look back over her life with her mother and to recognize all the lessons she had learnt from this.

Feoh showed Jenny that she needed to acknowledge the rich gifts of love and teaching that her mother had given her. It reminded her that no one can take her memories away from her. This reading proved a source of great strength and inspiration for Jenny during this difficult time in her life.

the world tree spread

This spread is designed to act as a guide to the next stage of your spiritual journey, giving knowledge about the next lesson you can learn, the next challenge ahead, your guides, allies and omens. It will speed you along your adventurous path towards new enlightenments, teaching you that everything that enters your life offers an opportunity for learning so that you can become a better, stronger and wiser person.

The World Tree

One of the oldest and most universal symbols in the world, images of a sacred tree appear among most earth-based belief systems and in such religions as Christianity and Kabbalism. In the Nordic tradition, Yggdrasil was the sacred ash tree of life and death. The roots of the tree are said to connect to the underworld, which is inhabited by many nature spirits, plant divas and elementals. By descending the tree while in a visionary state, the shaman could seek guidance and wisdom from these beings. The upper branches of the tree are said to ascend to the upper world, which is inhabited by angels, advanced souls and supernatural entities who are again sought out by the shaman on his visionary journeys. Some

Carving of Yggdrasil, the world tree.

representations of the world tree also show the leaves and branches inhabited by discarnate souls on their way either to or from the earthly plane. The world tree is a powerful archetypal image and a source of great wisdom and knowledge.

Using Runes as an Oracle

The spread begins at the earth and rises up the trunk of the tree towards the heavens. It represents a phase of your spiritual journey, and this image should be clearly fixed in your mind when using the spread. You are not coming with a question or a problem, just an open heart, eager to learn how to make sure you progress on your path of learning. In this spread, the runes speak directly to you and for you. Listen to their wisdom.

Sample Reading

The positions have the following meanings:
1 What do you need to learn?
2 What will challenge you?
3 What is your guiding rune?
4 What power will help you?
5 What comes to warn you?
6 What do you need to let go of?
7 What will be the outcome of learning this lesson?

1 **Nied:** You need to learn that the past is just a memory and the future just a dream; the present is all you can influence.
2 **Tyr reversed:** You are challenged to look honestly at your weaknesses and resolve to turn them into strengths.
3 **Peorth:** Your guiding rune tells you to remember that you always have a choice in everything.
4 **Feoh:** The power behind you comes from the fact that you have a spiritual richness that is to be used for the benefit of all.
5 **Hagall:** You are warned that challenges are entering your life and that these are not to be feared, rather embraced.
6 **Elhaz:** You need to let go of fear for you have the power of protection within you.
7 **Jara:** This will lead to a time of reaping rewards for the seeds sown in the past.

runes and their meanings

runes and their meanings

There are many different varieties of runic writing, ranging from the Early or Elder Germanic script of 24 letters, to the Anglo-Saxon script with an original 28 letters rising to 33, and various Nordic, Danish and Swedish runic alphabets varying from 15 to 16 letters. Over 4,000 runic inscriptions and several runic manuscripts are still in existence, the vast majority of which originate from Sweden. Others are mainly found in Norway, Denmark, Britain and Iceland, and some have also been discovered on various islands off the coasts of Britain and Scandinavia, as well as in France, Germany and the former Soviet Union.

In the past, there were two main types of people who worked with the runes: runecutters, who had a limited knowledge of the runes and their protective qualities, and runemasters, both male and female, who had undergone many initiatory experiences to discover the deeper secrets of rune lore. These runemasters were held in the highest esteem. They knew not only how to divine successfully with runes, but also how to use runes to their advantage in magical and healing work.

Since the beginning of the 20th century, runes have been growing in popularity. Many books about runes are now available, and there are even schools teaching runic divination and the finer arts of rune lore. The fact that runes have lasted two whole millennia is an indication that their potential power has been undiminished by the years.

Rune lore is closely linked to the long spiritual history of the Scandinavians and their gods and goddesses, who are described in the ancient sagas. In Norse mythology, the chief god was Odin, the discoverer of the runes and the first runemaster. He was married to Frigg and they had two sons, Balder (the beautiful god) and Thor (the thunder god). Odin's brother, Loki, was the trickster god. Many other gods and goddesses are mentioned in the sagas, including Njord, god of the sea, Freya, goddess of war, love and magic, Idun, goddess of healing and Tyr, the warrior god. The attributes of these deities are reflected in the meanings and magic of the runes.

Odin, the all-father of the Norse gods, experienced a shamanic initiation, during which time the runes appeared to him. Legend tells that he hanged himself upside down on the great ash tree Yggdrasil, the World Tree or Tree of Life. After nine days and nights Odin died on the tree, but was reborn through his unquenchable will, bringing back with him to the world the knowledge and wisdom of the world beyond – and the runes – as a gift to humankind.

feoh ᚠ

Meaning: Cattle

To the Nordic people, cattle were a sign of status and wealth. Like all animals, cattle were sacred but they were also killed and their meat feasted upon at times of celebration, showing that wealth should be used for the benefit of all. While physical wealth is transient, spiritual wealth is permanent and can never be taken away from you, no matter how many times you share your wisdom. If you are unaware of your gifts it does not mean that you have none; on the contrary, it means that you have not yet uncovered them. Each person has many gifts; once they are recognized, they can be used.

Interpretation of Rune

"Wealth should never be hoarded but used for the benefit of all."
Feoh speaks of a spiritual richness that is to be used for the benefit of all. Let your unselfish abundance shine forth to lighten your path and the paths of others. It will never run out but you should not waste it on those who will abuse it.

Interpretation of Reversed Rune

You have great richness within you, but its light is masked by emotional imbalances. Strive for balance in your life and you will discover the rich wealth of gifts and talents that are already yours. Claim your destiny.

FEOH
Corresponding letter: F
Rune: ᚠ
Meaning: Cattle
Divinatory meaning: Spiritual richness

Associations
Tree: Elder
Colour: Light red
Herb: Nettle
Gemstone: Moss agate

---

ur ᚢ

Meaning: Auroch

Aurochs were wild oxen and a powerful totem of Nordic tradition symbolizing strength. Nowadays, many people equate strength with dominance and inflexibility. They also confuse pride with strength, whereas pride is actually a weakness created by the ego. To find your true strength, you must first face your weaknesses. You can then turn them into strengths. This process can be frightening for many people.

Interpretation of Rune

"To find your true strength, you must first face your weaknesses."
You have the strength within you to fulfil all your dreams, but with that strength comes responsibility. It should not be used to exert power over others, but to stop others exerting power over you. Use it to keep you focused on your path. Some people are always negative. Strength comes from not letting them upset you and this in turn comes from mastering the ego.

Interpretation of Reversed Rune

To be strong, you must first know weakness. Look honestly within yourself without fear, knowing that once you recognize those areas of weakness, you will be able to work on them to turn them into strengths.

UR
Corresponding letter: U
Rune: ᚢ
Meaning: Auroch
Divinatory meaning: Strength

Associations
Tree: Birch
Colour: Dark green
Herb: Sphagnum moss
Gemstone: Carbuncle

thorn ▶

Meaning: Thorn

The shamans and magicians of northern Europe have long asso-ciated thorn trees with spiritual authority. Blackthorn was greatly favoured as the material for making staffs and powerful wands. Thorn trees are symbolic of protection and their wood was often used to make talismans to ward off evil. The protection that comes from the thorn tree is the protection of spiritual author-ity, and gives you the power to stand up for the truth when sur-rounded by lies, and to claim the spiritual path that is your birthright. The blackthorn has a sister tree, the hawthorn, which, while being a powerful protective tree like the blackthorn, also has soothing and balancing feminine energies.

Interpretation of Rune

"You have the power to face anything that might cross your path."
Fear nothing, for you have the authority to claim your destiny. Let no one deter you from your search for the truth. Hold fast to your birthright, be a spiritual being, but always remember to keep your feet firmly on the ground. Spiritual authority brings power and it is up to you to use that power in an unselfish and loving way. Power can corrupt if you do not have a true and honest heart. You should never need to tell others of your authority; knowing that you have it should be enough. To utilize the power of this rune fully, you must first master the ego.

THORN

Corresponding letter: Th
Rune: ▶
Meaning: Thorn
Divinatory meaning:
Spiritual authority

Associations

Tree: Thorn/oak
Colour: Bright red
Herb: Houseleek
Gemstone: Sapphire

ansur ᚨ

Meaning: Mouth

In the Nordic tradition, the mouth is symbolic of communication. Messages come in many forms and communication problems arise from an inability to decipher these messages correctly. A word can have completely different meanings to different people. For instance, to someone brought up in northern Europe, the word "seaside" creates a picture of sand, seaweed and cold sea, while to someone brought up in the Caribbean it creates a picture of palm trees, blue water and scorching sun.

Interpretation of Rune

"Everything that comes to you comes to teach you."
The answers to your questions are already here: you have just not heard them yet. Look for signs and confirmations which are all around you. Everything has significance. If you learn this truth, you will understand the messages around you. Check that you are not ignoring the message because you do not like its con-tents. Trust that everything comes to teach you, and that by acknowledging the truth you will grow in wisdom.

Interpretation of Reversed Rune

You have not found answers because you are asking the wrong questions. Seek in a different way; look within and all will be clear.

ANSUR

Corresponding letter: A
Rune: ᚨ
Meaning: Mouth
Divinatory meaning:
Message

Associations

Tree: Ash
Colour: Dark blue
Herb: Fly agaric
Gemstone: Emerald

rad ᚱ

Meaning: Cartwheel

Life is a journey along which we encounter challenges. Everything in life is cyclical. Once you recognize this fact, you can "go with the flow" and let things unfold rather than always resisting. When times are difficult, be assured that they will not go on forever. Once you have learnt the lessons that the hard times are trying to teach you, you will no longer need to suffer them. The faster you learn, the faster you will progress, so embrace everything with pleasure, knowing that there are lessons to be learnt.

Interpretation of Rune

"When times are difficult, be sure that they will not go on forever." Recognize that everything comes in cycles and that by following these cycles, you will be able to progress quickly and efficiently. Align yourself to the seasons by eating seasonal foods and honouring the turning of the year. Embrace hard times in the certainty that the harder it is now, the more beautiful things will be in the future. Everything has its opposite, and challenges bring equal and opposite rewards.

Interpretation of Reversed Rune

Stop trying to resist the inevitable. Your path is set out before you; tread it without fear. Take one step at a time and you will soon find yourself "flowing" once more.

RAD
Corresponding letter: R
Rune: ᚱ
Meaning: Cartwheel
Divinatory meaning:
Wheel of life

Associations
Tree: Oak
Colour: Bright red
Herb: Mugwort
Gemstone: Chrysoprase

---

ken ᚲ

Meaning: Torch

Illumination allows you to see in the dark. Enlightenment is a spiritual illumination. It is coming into a new understanding, like opening your eyes for the first time or like turning on a light. You are not seeing anything new, you are just seeing it for the first time. Enlightenment is a beginning, not an end. This new understanding needs to be utilized and tempered with wisdom before its true worth and power can be known. With knowledge comes responsibility: it is vital that you use your knowledge and power only for what is good and right.

Interpretation of Rune

"Enlightenment needs to be tempered with wisdom before its true worth and power can be known."
You are coming into a new understanding of life and its meaning. New insights await you but this is not a time for complacency. You must use this new understanding or it will be worthless to you. Always look for ways in which you can use your insights for the good of yourself and others. Enlightenment is like a jug of fine wine: it must be poured out before it can be refilled. Do not be fooled into thinking that enlightenment is your goal in life. It is only the starting point of an adventure of learning that will show you great wisdom and understanding.

KEN
Corresponding letter: K
Rune: ᚲ
Meaning: Torch
Divinatory meaning:
Enlightenment

Associations
Tree: Pine
Colour: Light red
Herb: Cowslip
Gemstone: Bloodstone

runs 245

geofu ✕

Meaning: Gift

To receive a gift, you must also be a giver. Likewise, if you give, you must be willing to receive. The cycle of giving and receiving must never be broken. Those who take without giving on a physical or emotional level lose their own spiritual gifts. To tread a spiritual path, you must also be both a giver and a receiver. To be truly balanced you must be able to receive a gift with total humility, knowing that if you abuse a spiritual gift, you will lose it. Compassion is a sharing of the gift of love and understanding. Encouragement is the sharing of the gift of empowerment. Each person has many gifts; once they are recognized, they can be used for the good of all.

Interpretation of Rune

"To tread a spiritual path, you must be both giver and receiver."
A gift is coming to you and this presents you with a choice. You can either accept it or reject it. If you choose to accept it, you must be prepared to give in return. Everything has its price, but with spiritual gifts the cost is always worth it in the end. You must find the balance between giving and receiving and learn the lesson of responsible giving. You must learn when to give and who to give to. It is not appropriate to give to everyone for there are those who do not wish to receive, so giving to them is a waste of energy and an abuse of your own gifts.

GEOFU
Corresponding letter: G
Rune: ✕
Meaning: Gift
Divinatory meaning:
Spiritual gift

Associations
Tree: Ash/elm
Colour: Deep blue
Herb: Heartsease
Gemstone: Opal

wynn ᚹ

Meaning: Happiness

True happiness only comes to those who are balanced. Happiness is found within and is not dependent on any other person or thing. You must be at peace with your place in life. This requires you to eat, think and act in a balanced manner. Healthy eating (fresh, natural, organic, unrefined foods) is fundamental and will naturally lead to healthy thoughts and actions. So seek balance and harmony within, and you will attract peace and happiness for yourself. Happiness comes from seeking and finding the truth, then integrating it into every aspect of your life.

Interpretation of Rune

"To have happiness, you must be at peace with yourself."
Happiness is yours if you are willing to work for it. You must strive for balance and harmony. Always be looking for solutions rather than dwelling upon problems. For happiness to last, it needs to be founded upon truth and honesty. Seek only what is good and right, and good fortune cannot fail to follow.

Interpretation of Reversed Rune

The happiness you seek is already yours, but your attachment to the past is preventing you from seeing it. It is time to let go of the old and embrace the new.

WYNN
Corresponding letter: W
Rune: ᚹ
Meaning: Happiness
Divinatory meaning:
Balance

Associations
Tree: Ash
Colour: Yellow
Herb: Flax
Gemstone: Diamond

hagall ᚺ

Meaning: Hail

Challenges occur to teach you. When you have a vision of how you would like your future to be, you send energy as thought waves out into the universe. These vibrations attract to you all the things that need to be in place before that dream can become reality. You cannot know all the lessons, but if you stay fixed on your dream, be assured that you will be attracting all the lessons you need. When life becomes difficult, it is not a sign to abandon your dream, it is merely a stepping stone to the realization of that dream. It is an opportunity to learn lessons that you will need when your dream becomes reality. Face the challenge – when you have overcome it, you will be stronger and wiser.

Interpretation of Rune

"Never shy away from challenges as they strengthen and teach you throughout your life."

Challenges are occurring in your life. These are not to be feared, but to be embraced. A hailstorm may seem daunting, but if you catch a hailstone you will realize that it is only water. So it is with challenges. Grit your teeth, fire up your determination, and face the challenges head-on in the assurance that they are just stepping stones to the realization of your dream. Every challenge comes to teach. Remember, the greater the challenge, potentially the more wisdom you can acquire.

HAGALL
Corresponding letter: H
Rune: ᚺ
Meaning: Hail
Divinatory meaning:
Challenge

Associations
Tree: Ash/yew
Colour: Light blue
Herb: Lily-of-the-valley
Gemstone: Onyx

nied ᚾ

Meaning: Need

What we want and what we need in our lives are often completely different. If you want to be strong, you will need to examine your weaknesses. This creates a paradox. It is only when you realize that the weaknesses need to be faced and turned to strengths, that you will begin to understand the difference between wants and needs. To be strong, you must first experience weakness; to find your path, you must first lose it; to be beautiful within, you must first face up to your ugly inner side.

Interpretation of Rune

"To achieve your wants, you often need to experience the very opposite of your wants."

You are getting exactly what you need at this moment to allow you to make the best progress on your spiritual path. It may appear to be the very opposite of what you want, but this state is merely a series of lessons that must be learnt so that you can make the transition from negative to positive. You need to have total acceptance of the past, to keep your mind fixed on where you want to be, while trusting that everything in the present is meant to be there and is to be learnt from. The past is just a memory, the future just a dream; the present is the only place where you can have influence.

NIED
Corresponding letter: N
Rune: ᚾ
Meaning: Need
Divinatory meaning:
Need

Associations
Tree: Beech
Colour: Black
Herb: Bistort
Gemstone: Lapis lazuli

is \

Meaning: Ice

Ice can form an impenetrable barrier. The only thing you can do is wait for the thaw. But winter is not a time for idleness. Although nothing appears to be moving, everything must be in place and ready if you are to take full advantage of the coming thaw. Winter is also a time of contemplation, a time to assimilate all the lessons that the past has taught, to look to the future and reaffirm your dreams. Recognize that the time you are in is just another phase of your unfolding path of learning; when this phase is over, a new one will begin. Use this time to rest a while; you will need to focus all your energies for what is to come.

Interpretation of Rune

"When life seems at a standstill, review the past and look ahead."
Things appear to be at a standstill and this is not a time to try to force movement. Patience and wisdom are called for: patience because you will have to wait until things change externally before you can proceed; and wisdom because you need to decide how best to use your waiting time. This is not the time to be abandoning your dreams; on the contrary, this is an opportunity for you to reaffirm them. This is a time for contemplation and preparation, not for depression and regrets. Be assured that things will change as surely as winter changes to spring and spring to summer.

IS
Corresponding letter: I
Rune: \
Meaning: Ice
Divinatory meaning:
Standstill

Associations
Tree: Alder
Colour: Black
Herb: Henbane
Gemstone: Cat's-eye

jara ᛃ

Meaning: Harvest

Harvest is the time of hardest work. The fruits of your labour must be collected and stored if they are not to spoil. If the winter is to be survived, it is imperative that as much grain and produce as possible is stored. Everything must be done correctly. If grains are not stored in the right way, they will rot and spoil long before the winter is over. This is certainly not a time to be resting on your laurels. The harvest feasting takes place only after the harvest is finished. You are at the end of a cycle, but remember that endings only lead to new beginnings.

Interpretation of Rune

"A time of hard work, and of reaping rewards for past efforts."
This is a time of plenty, a time of joy and celebration. But it is also a time of great work with no time for complacency. The harvest does not last forever. The winter of more hard lessons lies ahead and you would do well to make sure that you have stored enough knowledge and wisdom to face your next challenges. This is another turning point in your life, not your goal. There are greater harvests for you to experience in the future, but before any harvest there has to be preparation of the land, sowing of the seed, tending of the seedlings and support of the forming life-giving fruits.

JARA
Corresponding letter: J
Rune: ᛃ
Meaning: Harvest
Divinatory meaning:
Harvest

Associations
Tree: Oak
Colour: Light blue
Herb: Rosemary
Gemstone: Cornelian

eoh ᛇ

Meaning: Yew Tree

The yew tree has a long association with immortality and the cycle of death and rebirth. As a yew tree grows, its central trunk becomes soft and starts to decay. While this occurs, a new sapling begins to grow within the tree. When the tree matures, the same process continues to occur until the tree is made up of many trees growing from the centre outwards. This amazing regeneration is what enables a yew tree to grow to an immense size and age. A yew tree is said to have known many lives and so can help you remember past lives. Because of its longevity, the yew is also an ancient wisdom-keeper.

Interpretation of Rune

"By embracing change, you will make quick progress along your spiritual path."

This is a time of transformation; a time to let go of the old and embrace the new. It is a time of death, the dying of the past, and yet it is also a time of new beginnings, new life and new dreams. The only constant is change, and if you want to make quick and efficient progress on your path, you have to learn to embrace change instead of resisting it. To resist change is to risk stagnation. Do not be afraid; change is scary, but if you remain true to yourself and keep to your path, you will soon find yourself basking in the fresh sun of new enlightenments.

EOH
Corresponding letter: Y
Rune: ᛇ
Meaning: Yew tree
Divinatory meaning:
Transformation

Associations
Tree: Yew
Colour: Dark blue
Herb: Mandrake
Gemstone: Topaz

peorth ᛈ

Meaning: Dice Cup

The dice cup is the source of chance or fate. A die which is not thrown is just a lump of wood with dots on it. It is only when it is thrown that it has significance. It is in the hands of fate. People think of fate as an inevitable tide, but it merely presents you with choices. There is the choice of whether or not to throw the dice and whether to heed what the dice say. Life is full of choices, but many people choose to let the hand of fate guide them instead of taking charge of their own destiny.

Interpretation of Rune

"Make your own choices and take charge of your own destiny."

You always have a choice in everything. No one can upset you, you can only choose to be upset. No one can exert power over you unless you choose to allow them to. Do not allow others to compromise your truth and do not let others prevent you from doing what you need to do. The only danger here is not to make a choice, to leave things to fate.

Interpretation of Reversed Rune

The dice have been rolled and fate has control of your life, but it does not have to be this way. You can regain power. Start to make choices for yourself instead of following the choices of others.

PEORTH
Corresponding letter: P
Rune: ᛈ
Meaning: Dice cup
Divinatory meaning:
Choice

Associations
Tree: Beech
Colour: Black
Herb: Aconite
Gemstone: Aquamarine

elhaz Y

Meaning: Elk

To the Nordic people, the elk was a powerful totemic animal with very strong protective energies. This rune is said to guard the wearer against all attacks and dangers, both physical and psychic. The rune represents the elk when the animal is viewed face on. Its antlers were thought of as psychic receivers which could pick up the subtle vibrations of living things. The protective energies of the elk come not only from its ability to sense danger, but also its speed and the skill with which it flees dangerous situations. Therefore, the Elhaz rune is a powerful ally to help you to find a safe passage through difficult times.

Interpretation of Rune

"Although your path is fraught with danger, you have the power of protection within you."
You will be safe as long as you do not act recklessly. This is a favourable time for risky ventures, although all things must be built on firm foundations. Do not become complacent.

Interpretation of Reversed Rune

Proceed with caution and do not act in haste. In your present situation you are vulnerable to hostile influences and need to concentrate on building your strength physically, emotionally and spiritually before pressing forwards.

ELHAZ
Corresponding letter: Z
Rune: Y
Meaning: Elk
Divinatory meaning:
Protection

Associations
Tree: Yew
Colour: Gold
Herb: Angelica
Gemstone: Amethyst

---

sigel ⚡

Meaning: The Sun

To the Nordic people, the sun was considered the giver of life, for without its rays there would be no food and sustenance. The sun is associated with all that is good, just and right. The light of the sun banishes darkness and rejuvenates the spirit. It is also the "destroyer of ice", as one Icelandic runic poem describes it, and is therefore a powerful rune to counteract the negative aspects of the Is rune, which means ice and is interpreted as being at a standstill. Sigel is also a rune of truth; the power of light illuminates the darkness of deception, giving clarity of thought and vision. It will show you not only deception in others, but within you. It will shine a light upon the path of all who hold it.

Interpretation of Rune

"You have the power to bring things to fruition."
You have the power to bring things to fruition. Good fortune awaits you and there is a positive feel to everything in your life. This is not a time to rest and relax, however, rather it is an ideal time to look within at the darker aspects of your nature. The power of the sun will enable you to face those dark parts of your being squarely without fear and finally to gain power over them. This is a good time to seek solutions to problems as they are all within your grasp.

SIGEL
Corresponding letter: S
Rune: ⚡
Meaning: The sun
Divinatory meaning:
Good fortune

Associations
Tree: Juniper
Colour: White/silver
Herb: Mistletoe
Gemstone: Ruby

tyr ↑

Meaning: Tyr (the Warrior God)

The path of the warrior presents challenges and initiations. He must be of a good and strong heart, with a firm belief in the sacredness of that which he protects. As a companion, one could not wish for a better ally, for the warrior has a natural instinct to protect and survive. He is always resourceful and focuses on solutions rather than problems. The wise warrior knows that mistakes are not failures, but rather lessons to be learnt if one is honest and humble enough to seek. The man who makes no mistakes in his life becomes an old fool.

Interpretation of Rune

"Now is the time to make use of all the skills and wisdom that you have learnt so far."

This rune symbolizes new challenges and initiations into new understandings. There is a need for fearlessness, for your victory is assured if your heart remains true. Protect your faith, as it will be challenged, but the truth will always be victorious in the end.

Interpretation of Reversed Rune

You have all the powers you need for the challenges ahead but you need to unlock your true potential. Look honestly at your weaknesses and resolve to turn them into strengths. The warrior is within you and it is now time to let that energy come forth.

TYR

Corresponding letter: T
Rune: ↑
Meaning: Warrior god
Divinatory meaning: Initiation

Associations

Tree: Oak
Colour: Bright red
Herb: Sage
Gemstone: Coral

---

beorc ᛒ

Meaning: Birch Tree

The birch tree is a pioneer tree. When forest or scrubland is destroyed by fire, the birch is one of the first trees to re-colonize the land. It is symbolic of birth and new beginnings, like the phoenix rising from the ashes. Magically, the birch tree has long been associated with purification. The birch broom was used to sweep negativity from a house, while the punishment of "birching" was said to drive evil from criminals. The old pagan ritual of beating the bounds to mark land boundaries and to cleanse negativity from the soil also utilized birch.

Interpretation of Rune

"This is an exciting time of new beginnings and fresh adventures."

This is a time of great activity and energy. This is a time to sow seeds, but remember that the harvest is still a long way off; do not expect to see immediate rewards for your efforts, as new ideas need nurturing and feeding before they will bear fruit. This is a time to make sure that the past is truly put in its place. If one has learnt all the lessons that the past has had to teach, it need never be revisited. It can be left behind and you can venture forth with boldness to embrace new pastures. This is also a good time to think about a spiritual spring cleaning, clearing away the old to make way for the new.

BEORC

Corresponding letter: B
Rune: ᛒ
Meaning: Birch tree
Divinatory meaning: New beginnings

Associations

Tree: Birch
Colour: Dark green
Herb: Lady's mantle
Gemstone: Moonstone

ehwaz M

Meaning: Horse

The horse was regarded as a sacred animal throughout the old world and is recorded in many myths and legends as a faithful and loyal ally. Its energy is powerful and primal, helping you to avoid obstacles and to make swift progress along your path. The horse is also associated with fire, the element of free expression and unfolding destiny. The energy of the horse can help to clear stagnation and remove blocks. This makes it a valuable ally on the spiritual path because the only constant is change.

Interpretation of Rune

"Always be as loyal to those around you as they are to you."
You have the support to be able to make swift progress along your path, but this is dependent upon you being as loyal and supportive to those around you as they are to you. The horse is a proud animal but it does not let its pride get in the way of its purpose. In the same way, you should always be proud of your achievements while remaining outwardly humble.

Interpretation of Reversed Rune

You need to make new connections. This will draw the energies towards you that will help you overcome all obstacles. Seek out those who share your attitude, knowing that everyone who enters your life has lessons to teach you.

EHWAZ
Corresponding letter: E
Rune: M
Meaning: Horse
Divinatory meaning:
Progress

Associations
Tree: Oak/ash
Colour: White
Herb: Ragwort
Gemstone: Iceland spar

mann M

Meaning: Human Being

Every human being has a destiny and it is their right to fulfil it. Destiny is all about choice. You can choose to take responsibility for your life, to be a spiritual being, or you can choose to drift along with whatever life throws at you. The path of destiny is not easy, for it holds many lessons and challenges along the way, but it is a path of growth and fulfilment. The other path appears easier, but it is filled with ill-health and dissatisfaction.

Interpretation of Rune

"The path of destiny is a path of growth and fulfilment."
Your destiny awaits you, so claim it. For you to be a spiritual being, you must be balanced in body, mind and spirit. Embrace everything – good and bad – with total acceptance and pleasure. By learning each lesson as it presents itself, you will go onwards and upwards.

Interpretation of Reversed Rune

The path of destiny seems hard, but as you tread it, you become wiser and stronger. Have faith – you have the strength and power to deal with all of life's problems and to make choices as long as you are willing to learn. Do not let your own ego, or those of others, fill your mind with misgivings.

MANN
Corresponding letter: M
Rune: M
Meaning: Human being
Divinatory meaning:
Destiny

Associations
Tree: Holly
Colour: Deep red
Herb: Madder
Gemstone: Garnet

lagu ᛚ

Meaning: Water, Sea

Water is a primal power that can never be truly contained or controlled. All water flows where it will, drawn back and forth by the power of the moon. This includes the sea, the fluid within plants and the fluids within you. To be in harmony with creation, you need to attune yourself to the seasons and the moon. Eating and living in harmony with nature around you gives you a new perspective and opens up many possibilities to acquire new and greater knowledge and transform it into wisdom.

Interpretation of Rune

"Being in harmony with creation gives you emotional balance."
It is only by attunement to creation that your life will truly flow as it is meant to. Emotional balance comes from eating in balance with creation around you. Natural foods lead to natural flow, whereas unnatural foods lead to disharmony and stagnation. The sea is always fluid and moving, so it should be a part of your life. Embrace change, for it is the only constant.

Interpretation of Reversed Rune

You need to learn to go with the flow. There is a need to initiate some movement into many areas of your life, otherwise you will start to become stagnant. A few simple changes can bring about great, positive effects.

LAGU
Corresponding letter: L
Rune: ᛚ
Meaning: Water, sea
Divinatory meaning:
Attunement to creation

Associations
Tree: Willow
Colour: Deep green
Herb: Leek
Gemstone: Pearl

ing ◇

Meaning: Ing (the Fertility God)

Ing symbolizes the spark of creation, the power to give life and to make the land fertile. It is the fire within everyone that drives them forwards and keeps them striving towards spiritual fulfilment; it is the power to keep going when things get tough. This fire can lie dormant for many years, but when it is fuelled by the breath of acknowledgement, by its existence being recognized, it is almost impossible to extinguish. Ing teaches that you cannot change the past; the present is the only place where you can truly have influence. Ing helps you to let the past go, and keeps your eyes on your dream for the future, while you live and work in the here and now.

Interpretation of Rune

"The fire of inspiration urges you to strive for spiritual fulfilment."
You are on a spiritual path and although you may feel isolated at times, you can be safe in the knowledge that within you burns the fire of inspiration which urges you ever onwards and upwards. Feed the fire by always striving to learn more, never resting in the illusion of complacency. Seek only answers and never become waylaid with too many questions. Live one day at a time, knowing that the past is just a memory, the future just a dream, and the here and now is what matters.

ING
Corresponding letter: ng
Rune: ◇
Meaning: The fertility god
Divinatory meaning:
Fire within

Associations:
Tree: Apple
Colour: Yellow
Herb: Self-heal
Gemstone: Amber

daeg ᛞ

Meaning: Day (Light)

Daeg is the rune of midday and midsummer. It represents the positive energy of light at its most potent and powerful and is therefore a rune of great protection when painted over doorways and on window shutters. Daeg is positivity at its strongest, signifying success, growth, progress, clarity of vision and protection against harmful influences. It allows you to see the positive within every negative. Daeg also helps you remember that everything in life is given to you. If you do not use these gifts with love and beauty, they will be taken from you. You own nothing; everything is lent to you by the creator, so always use your gifts with respect and wisdom.

Interpretation of Rune

"While you remain true, only good fortune can come your way."
The power of the light shines before you, guiding you clearly upon your path, as long as you remain true. You need have no fear, for you are well protected by the power of the light. The light will give you clear vision so that you may see and avoid dangers before they enter your life. The only warning is against being blinded, although it is not the light that will blind you, but your ego. The ego, if not mastered, will allow your success to blind you, so always remain humble and thankful for all the good things that come to you.

DAEG
Corresponding letter: D
Rune: ᛞ
Meaning: Day (light)
Divinatory meaning:
Light

Associations
Tree: Spruce
Colour: Light blue
Herb: Clary
Gemstone: Diamond

---

othel ᛟ

Meaning: Possession

Othel is the rune into which energies can be concentrated and focused. It has an image of an enclosure of land or of a magical circle. Although Othel means "a possession", it is in the sense of holding rather than owning. We own nothing; all things are merely loaned to us, including our bodies. For the power of Othel to be experienced, you need to be able to concentrate and relax at the same time. Focus on a thought, then wait patiently for other energies to be attracted to it. Never try to force things, but always keep in mind where you want to go.

Interpretation of Rune

"Focus your thoughts to attract the right energies that you need to make your dream reality."
This is a time to re-focus. Concentration is needed if you are to read all the signs that are appearing before you. Do not try to force issues. Your dream is like a dove sitting in your hand. If you try to possess it or to keep hold of it, you risk killing it.

Interpretation of Reversed Rune

If you try to own something, you will risk losing it. Allow everything and everyone to be. If you do not like something, you can only change by initiating change within yourself.

OTHEL
Corresponding letter: O
Rune: ᛟ
Meaning: Possession
Divinatory meaning:
Focus and freedom

Associations
Tree: Hawthorn
Colour: Deep yellow
Herb: Clover
Gemstone: Ruby

Index

Picture Acknowledgments:

The publishers would like to thank the
following libraries for their permission to
reproduce the pictures listed below:

A–Z Botanical Collection Ltd: 27TL; 27TR;
27ML; 27MR. AKG Photo: 13T; 14T; 14B;
15T; 15B; 16T; 16B; 17T; 17B; 18T; 19T;
19B; 91T; 91B; 105T; 119T; 154; 158T.
Ancient Art & Architecture Collection
Ltd: 114B. The Art Archive: 12T; 38T;
41T; 104T; 104B; 155T.
Axiom: 155B.
BBC Natural History Unit: 20T; 46TL;
46TR; 204BL; 204L; 207TR.

Bridgeman Art Library: 6, 149R; 156; 157;
158B; 166.
Bruce Coleman Collection: 204L.
ET Archive: 205
Fine Art Photographic Library Ltd: 22T;
90T; 92B; 119B.
Fortean Picture Library: 154B.
Galaxy Picture Library: 37BM.
Garden & Wildlife Matters Photo Library:
204B; 242TM; 244B; 246B; 247TM;
247BM; 248T; 248TM; 248B; 249BM;
249B; 250BM. 251TM; 251BM; 252BM;
253T; 253TM; 253B.
Garden Picture Library: 26.
Images Colour Library: 6B; 7B; 12B; 21T;
42; 46MR; 93T; 117B; 121T; 123T; 153B;
204TR; 204R; 204C.
Julie Meach: 207BMR
Natural Image: 207BL.
Oxford Scientific Films: 160; 161B; 163T;
163B
Papilio Photographic: 152; 249T; 253BM.
Planet Earth Pictures: 94TR.
Science Photo Library: 159T.
Skyscan: 148T.
Stock Market: 74, 159; 157; 164.
Superstock: 30TL; 36T; 36B; 250T.
Tibet Images: 150 & 157; 151.
Tony Stone Images: 22B; 23; 25T; 34TL;
34TR; 34TML; 34TMR; 34BML; 34BMR;
34BL; 34BR; 35TR; 35TM; 35BM; 35B; 37T;
37BL; 37BR; 39T; 39B; 44BT; 44BR; 44B;
44BC; 46ML; 46BL; 46BR; 47 TL; 47TR;
47ML; 47BL; 47BR; 51T; 55B; 57T; 59TL;
61T; 63T; 65T; 67T; 69T; 71T; 73T; 75;
76T; 78T; 80T; 85B; 87; 95TL; 95B; 105B;
107T; 109T; 114T; 121B; 122BL; 122BR;
203MBL & 207MBL; 204BR; 207TL;
207MTL; 207MTR; 207BR; 242T; 242BM;
244; 246T.
Werner Forman Archive: 165; 239T.
York Archaeological Trust: 248BM.
AGM AGMüller for illustrations from
reproduced from 1JJ Swiss Tarot Cards.
© 1972 AGM AGMüller, CH-8212
Neuhausen, Switzerland.

Illustrations from Gendron, Pierpont
Morgan Visconti-Sforza tarot decks,
reproduced by permission of US Games
System, Inc., Stamford CT. Images from
Tarot of Marseille reproduced by
permission of US Games Systems,
Inc\Carta Mundi. © 1996 US Games
System, Inc/Carta Mundi further
reproduction prohibited. Illustrations
form the ijj Swiss Tarot Cards, Tarot of
the Old Path reproduced by permission
of AGM AGMüller, CH-8212 Neuhausen,
Switzerland © 1972 by AGM
AGMüller, Switzerland.

NOTES

NOTES

NOTES

NOTES

NOTES

NOTES

NOTES

NOTES